The Election of Andrew Jackson

CRITICAL PERIODS OF HISTORY

Robert D. Cross, GENERAL EDITOR

The Election
of
Andrew Jackson

ROBERT V. REMINI
University of Illinois, Chicago Circle

CRITICAL PERIODS OF HISTORY

J.B. Lippincott Company
Philadelphia New York Toronto

PRINTED IN THE UNITED STATES OF AMERICA

ISBN-0-397-47040-1

LIBRARY OF CONGRESS CATALOG CARD NUMBER: 63–17677

13   15   16   14   12

FOR MY SON

R. W. R.

PREFACE

EVER SINCE Andrew Jackson's inauguration, when the roof of the White House was nearly blown off in a popular demonstration of affection for the great "Hero of New Orleans," critics of the democratic process have wagged their heads over the disaster that befell the presidential office in 1828. For them it was the beginning of an unfortunate change from a system that permitted the best men with the finest records of public service to aspire to the executive mansion to one in which the best men were effectively, though not always, kept out. Since 1828 each generation has had its quota of Henry Clays and Daniel Websters whose applications to serve as President the people have turned down in favor of men with less conspicuous records of public achievement.

This book, then, is about the profound changes that took place in American politics during the contest between Andrew Jackson and John Quincy Adams, particularly in the structuring of party organizations to create mass support for the presidential candidates. It presumes to argue that these changes did not happen simply because a period of transition in American history was drawing to an end or because new forces long in the making were struggling to assume a more advantageous position within the democracy—though both these factors were obviously important. It contends that many, if not most, of the changes were made to happen by politicians who hoped their efforts would inaugurate a "political revolution."

In the preparation of this work I am indebted to many people on the staffs of libraries, museums, and historical societies and to a group of graduate students at Fordham and Columbia universities. Most particularly I am under a heavy obligation to Robert D. Cross, the editor of this series, whose expert hand went over the manuscript many times and helped to bring order out of chaos. Lastly, I am grateful to the American Council of Learned Societies for a grant-in-aid to research this period of history.

ROBERT V. REMINI

Brentwood, New York
May, 1963

CONTENTS

1. The Coalition

I

THE PEOPLE who were jammed into the galleries of the House of Representatives that snowy February afternoon in 1825 strained to hear what the Speaker was saying. It was difficult for them to catch every word because the acoustics in the hall were so "vile." Sounds skidded around the walls before ascending and disappearing into the great dome ceiling that rose sixty feet above the floor.

And it was important that they hear each word, for the Representatives of Congress on that ninth day of February were about to select the next President of the United States. A House election had taken place only once before, in 1801; in another hundred and more years it would not occur again.

Addressing the Representatives, the distinguished Speaker, Henry Clay, looked supremely self-confident; but then Clay never looked anything less than self-confident when he appeared in public. Tall, gaunt, with great hollows gouged in both cheeks and a thin, almost invisible line marking the location of his mouth, this fiercely ambitious, hard-drinking, gambling man from Kentucky knew the full measure of his worth. Critics said he was a hail fellow all wet—a rather sarcastic acknowledgment of his many social triumphs—but their judgment was obviously distorted by partisan distemper.

Right up to the last minute prior to Clay's arrival at the Speaker's desk, managers of the several candidates scurried about the hall in a desperate effort to corral stray votes. There were signs that the contest would be close, and the political strategists were taking no chances on losing by default. Each state cast a single ballot, determined by the delegation, and a majority of states was necessary for election.

Above the confusion and noisy excitement Clay was heard calling for order. Then, in a voice that matched the solemnity of the occasion, he directed each delegation to poll its members.[1]*

II

The election of 1824, held the previous fall, had failed to determine President James Monroe's successor because the electoral ballots were split among four candidates, none of whom had a majority. Thus, according to the Twelfth Amendment to the Constitution, the House of Representatives was required to select the chief executive from among the three men with the highest electoral count. In 1824 these three included the Senator from Tennessee, Andrew Jackson, who had 99 votes; the Secretary of State, John Quincy Adams, with 84 votes; and the Secretary of the Treasury, William H. Crawford, who received 41 votes. The fourth candidate, Henry Clay himself, was eliminated since his total floored the list at a meager 37 ballots.

Had the amended Constitution not designated so precisely the number of candidates permitted in the House, Clay might have won the presidency because of his enormous influence over many state delegations. Instead, he held the balance of power, or thought he did. He had a pretty good suspicion that the man to follow Monroe into the executive mansion would be the lucky individual he chose to favor with his support. So for the next few weeks he struggled with his conscience. He examined and re-examined the claims of the three candidates. He was importuned by every manager and political string-puller in Washington, but he resisted the pressures in an effort to render an independent decision, one beneficial to the country and one compatible with the ambitions of Henry Clay.

* Superior figures refer to the section of Notes at the end of the text.

Coming from Kentucky, though born in Virginia, the Speaker might have acknowledged Western aspirations by awarding the prize to Andrew Jackson. The great General of the Battle of New Orleans was unquestionably popular with the electorate—frighteningly popular, worried some—for he was one of the few genuine American heroes still living. On the other hand, his experience in government was negligible. Most of his detractors (which is to say the managers and supporters of the other candidates) wrote him off as a "military chieftain" with no acceptable qualification for the presidency. And, as far as Clay was concerned, the Hero was a rival for Western votes; so in terms of future political advantage, it seemed wiser to exclude him from the contest.

To some commentators Jackson's candidacy was a terrible judgment on the times, in that an uneducated, untrained, uninformed, and inexperienced Indian fighter would presume to challenge tried and tested statesmen for the highest office in the nation. What could he possibly offer the American people except the achievement of the battlefield? And was it not obvious that the framers of the Constitution had endeavored to protect the executive branch from such "adventurers" as well as from popular, democratic control? In providing an electoral college they expected thoughtful and dedicated men from the different states to select the President from a number of possible contenders, each of whom had previously earned a national reputation as a wise and just man, devoted to public service.

Andrew Jackson's career could not remotely measure up to such standards, thought Clay. The Hero had demonstrated a remarkable talent for slaughtering Indians and Englishmen—and sometimes American militiamen when they got out of line or temporarily forgot the rules of military discipline—but that was all. While the populace might thrill to such exploits, responsible citizens understood that the presidency demanded loftier credentials. To be sure, he had served short terms as a member of the House of Representatives, a judge, governor of the Florida Territory, and currently as Senator from Tennessee; nevertheless, these services were singularly undistinguished.

Still, as Clay understood full well, it was not easy to dismiss Andrew Jackson. His electoral count in 1824 was impressive, representing solid backing from the South, Pennsylvania, most of the West, and substantial political pockets in several Middle Atlantic states. Equally impressive was his appearance. Tall and slender, he carried himself with military stiffness. His face was long, accentuated by a sharp lantern jaw, and lighted by clear blue eyes. His gray-white hair bristled with electricity and stood nearly as erect as the General himself. If appearance meant anything, Jackson was the most presidential-looking of the three candidates. There was an air and grace about him that signaled the presence of a leader.

The Hero was born of poor Scotch-Irish parents in the Carolina back country and later moved to Tennessee, where he became a lawyer, small businessman, land speculator, and planter. But he was no crude or simple frontiersman—not Andrew Jackson. By any standard of the time he was a gentleman, and, as a Tennessee planter of moderately good income who owned slaves and resided in a handsome mansion called the "Hermitage," he lived like one. He was naturally warm and affectionate toward his family and close associates; at the same time he could be harshly vindictive toward political adversaries, and vindictive for unreasonably long periods of time. He was stubborn and quick to take offense and, when angry, easily lost his self-control. The canings he administered to a few unfortunate men were marks of his lively temper. It was not a light thing to cross him, but by 1824 Clay was well along toward making a habit of crossing Andrew Jackson.

The Kentuckian's eventual decision to reject the General's presidential pretensions in the House contest came as no surprise, but it probably stemmed more from the Hero's lack of qualifications than personal jealousy. Clay would agree that a military chieftain had value and worth, but not as the President of the United States.[2]

The second candidate was William H. Crawford of Georgia, the Secretary of the Treasury. He and his friends were known as "Old Republicans" or "Radicals" because of their strict adherence to the states' rights philosophy of government. They vigorously opposed a strong central government in Washington and insisted upon a narrow reading of the Constitution when interpreting the powers delegated to Congress and the President; they called for rigid economy in budgeting national expenditures, disapproving in the same breath such issues as protective tariffs and federally sponsored public works; finally, they believed in a tightly organized and well-disciplined political party controlled by a congressional caucus. Sternly doctrinaire and dogmatic, these Radicals saluted themselves as the sole heirs of Thomas Jefferson's political faith; all other Republicans were contemptuously dismissed as apostates.

Their chief, William Harris Crawford, was a "plain *giant* of a man," very affable, talkative, not brilliant in any way yet extremely popular among Congressmen. Politically adroit, he loaded the government bureaus with partisan friends, waiting for the moment when he would marshal them into useful personal service. But his hopes for the presidency were suddenly smashed in the summer of 1823 when he suffered a paralytic stroke. He lost the use of his arms and legs, his sight was dimmed, and his speech was markedly altered. When the illness finally ceased its devastating attack upon his faculties, medical "experts" renewed the assault. At his home in Virginia they bled him twenty-three times, almost "to the verge of death."

Stroke or no stroke, Crawford's friends would not withdraw him from the presidential race. As they repeatedly insisted, there were principles at stake. With any luck they would lift his broken body into the executive chair, thus providing the nation with the blessings of an inactive federal government.

The stroke did not hinder Crawford from winning the electoral votes of his own state, Georgia, those of Virginia (where he was aided by Thomas Ritchie, editor of the Richmond *Enquirer* and chief of a political machine called the "Junto"), and scattered votes in New York, Delaware, and Maryland. While his total was small, he managed to slip into the House contest ahead of Henry Clay. And by 1824, after the medicine men ceased their infernal bleeding, he began to rally from his illness, though he was still physically unable to assume the burdens of the presidency.

Clay scored Crawford on two counts: the Secretary's unfortunate breakdown and his impossible political principles. Clay was a nationalist who advocated an energetic central government actively engaged in assisting the country's economic growth. He preached a doctrine of protective tariffs, internal improvements, stable currency, distribution of federal surpluses to the states, and a sound banking system. He publicized his program in a series of speeches in Congress, the essentials of which were known as the "American System." Radicals, of course, condemned the System as an outrage against the Constitution, and one Southerner later remarked that it was the devil's own plot brewed to enrich the West and Northeast at the expense of the South.

With Jackson and Crawford out of the way, that left the third and last candidate, John Quincy Adams of Massachusetts. Unquestionably, Adams was the best qualified for the presidency, unless political astuteness is a prerequisite of a candidate. Son of the revolutionary patriot and second President, he had been educated at Harvard, served admirably as American Minister to the Russian court, and assisted at Ghent in drawing up the peace treaty that concluded the War of 1812. As Secretary of State under Monroe, he added toughness and brilliance to American foreign policy without making a public display of his virtues. A thoughtful, unworldly, studious man, he frequently retired to his library to find in his books one of the few pleasures worthy of his time. Short, stout, and balding, he looked as dour as the most stereotyped of colonial Puritans. His face masked all signs of emotion, while his politics masked everything but ineptitude. "I am a man of reserved, cold, austere and forbidding manners," he once wrote. "My political adversaries say, a gloomy misanthrope; and my personal enemies an unsocial savage. With a knowledge of the actual defects in my character, I have not the pliability to reform it." Devoted to public service, like most Adamses, and yet incapable of attracting professional politicians to his cause, he was by virtue of intelligence, experience, and education fully seasoned to assume the office of President.

In the election of 1824 Adams drew heavy support from the New England states and New York and a sprinkling of votes from Louisiana, Maryland, and Delaware. Like Clay, he envisaged a national government fostering the intellectual and economic progress of the American people. He was the only one of the three candidates capable of understanding and appreciating the value of the "American System." Were Clay to endorse him now, their coalition in the House of Representatives would unite the Northeast with the Northwest to form a powerful sectional alliance.[3]

III

Henry Clay might have had an easier time with his choice had it been possible to resort to party labels; but all the candidates in 1824 belonged nominally to Thomas Jefferson's Republican party. The old Federalist party of Alexander Hamilton had gradually disappeared from national politics following the Hartford Convention of 1814 (though it hung on for years in several states), and many Federalists had drifted into the Republican party so that men of differing and contradictory principles now belonged to the same political organization. Though rent by its battling inmates, the Jeffersonian party ruled the country unchallenged. National politics dissolved into personality contests, and a two-party system degenerated into factionalism. Such was the so-called "Era of Good Feelings."

For their part, the Radicals were convinced beyond argument that the problems facing the Republican organization could have been resolved in 1824 had President Monroe exercised a modicum of party leadership and either designated his successor or summoned the traditional congressional caucus to make the selection for him. But Monroe had refused to follow either procedure. When he realized that a clutch of candidates were sharpening their knives in a squabble over the nomination, he had characteristically reacted to the unpleasantness by ignoring it. Presumably, what he did not notice would pass away. His refusal to intervene and his apparent indifference to the fate of the Republican party earned him the scorn and contempt of the leading Radicals. "The old gentleman (Mr Monroe)," said one, "is a wavering, undecided, timid, pickle minded man—So I have discovered by a great variety of circumstances."

The paramount reason for Radical anger was the certain knowledge that a congressional caucus, if summoned, would nominate William H. Crawford. Naturally, then, the other prospective candidates repudiated the archaic caucus and justified their action by claiming adherence to more democratic procedures; as an alternative, they accepted nominations from state legislatures. Yet the cries that "King Caucus is dead" or should be "knocked in the head" did not deter the Radicals from organizing a meeting in the traditional manner. They were convened by a relative newcomer to Washington, the junior Senator from New York, Martin Van Buren, known as the "Little Magician" or the "Red Fox" in recognition (however sarcastic) of his surpassing skill as a political manipulator. Short in stature, elegantly dressed but always in good taste, fair-complexioned with light yellowish-red hair and "small brilliant eyes" under a bulging forehead, he possessed the "most facinating manners" imaginable. Never giving or taking offense over political disagreements if he could help it, Van Buren was polite to all, even those who rudely insulted or attacked his private and public life. Among other things he was a broker politician, quick to spot the possibility of compromise in any deadlocked situation. Furthermore, he was an organizer, methodical to a fault, who created a state-wide machine in New York, called the "Albany Regency," to protect his interests at home while he advanced his career in Washington. This Regency was a governing council set up in Albany and consisted of some of the best political talents the state produced, such as William L. Marcy, Silas Wright, Jr., Benjamin F. Butler, Azariah C. Flagg, and Edwin Croswell, editor of the Albany *Argus,* the party's mouthpiece. Into their outstretched hands the Magician placed what had taken him ten years to win: control of the legislature and the patronage. With this control the cronies shrewdly (one might even say wisely) directed the political affairs of the Van Buren faction of the Republican party, called "Bucktails" because the sachems of Tammany Hall had the habit of attending party meetings with a buck's tail stuck in their hats.

As leader of the New York party with considerable local power, Van Buren naturally scouted around for a presidential candidate who would respect the states and the privileges of the men who controlled them. Because New York was building the Erie Canal at her own expense, he also required a candidate who opposed federally sponsored internal improvement. The reasoning behind this argument may have been shaky, but at least it was frankly stated: if New York could finance her own projects, so, too, could all the other states. But aside from such pragmatic considerations, Van Buren regarded himself as a devoted Jeffersonian, intellectually committed to the doctrine of states' rights. He believed that popular control of the government should be tempered by party control to ensure what he called that "sober second thought" of the people which can never be wrong.

The presidential qualifications delineated by Van Buren, and those who thought as he did, were amply filled by William Crawford. The congressional caucus they convened in his favor was an expression of their faith in his dedication to their brand of Republicanism. Yet only a small fraction of Congressmen acknowledged the caucus summons, so the meeting proved very disappointing. Crawford went on to receive his nomination from this rump—placing him for the moment in the tradition of Jefferson, Madison, and Monroe—but he gained little benefit from it; indeed, many felt that it damaged his candidacy by linking his name with a nominating procedure that was outmoded and undemocratic. The Radicals blamed the high percentage of absentees on the selfishness of the other candidates, whose stubborn refusal to submit their ambitions to the "impartial" decision of the caucus was certain to perpetuate the deep fissures within the party. Many, if not most, of the Radicals were professionals in the political game and played by the rules, particularly those rules specifically drawn to inculcate discipline among party members. Hence, they regarded the action of the caucus-absentees as a kind of treachery to the Jeffersonian system. But as strong as their language was in condemning the other candidates, it paled before the abuse they reserved for "that fool," Monroe. Among other things, they accused him of deliberately destroying the Republican organization.

Such sweeping criticism was inaccurate and unfair. The organization had been disintegrating since the presidency of James Madison, and there was probably little that Monroe could have done to arrest it, even if he had been inclined to make the effort. By 1824 all semblance of unity, vigor, and discipline within the party had vanished. And if Republicans found it impossible to agree on one presidential candidate, they found it equally impossible to agree upon a single course of governmental action, since opinions on issues varied from one extreme to another, some of which were Jeffersonian and some Hamiltonian.

Nor were conditions any better within the states. Factionalism or, more exactly, party cannibalism flourished in the wreckage of national politics. In New York, the hunting ground for cannibals with gourmet tastes, a Republican might belong to the Van Buren faction or the De Witt Clinton faction or the People's party. Sometimes, these groups, or cliques within the groups, functioned under other names (to the mystification of the electorate), calling themselves Martling Men, Quids, or Bucktails.

The quarrels between rival factions, sections, and states were caught up to a degree in the presidential election of 1824. Allegedly, Adams was the candidate of the East, Crawford the South, and Clay and Jackson the West. When the contest ended, nothing had been settled, not even the selection of the President. Now that the task belonged to the House of Representatives, it was earnestly hoped that a choice could be made without disgracing the nation or the Congress that acted in its name.[4]

IV

After many consultations with his friends, Clay finally made up his mind. On January 8, 1825, in spite of official instructions from the Kentucky legislature to back Jackson, he tapped John Quincy Adams as the man privileged to receive his support. Two weeks later his decision was announced to the public. He invited other Congressmen to imitate his example and deployed agents among the delegations to start the band wagon rolling.

A few Crawford men, like Thomas Hart Benton, Senator from Missouri, went over to Jackson. Benton was a large, heavily framed man, with black curly hair and side whiskers and a long nose that wandered crookedly down his face. His shift to Jackson surprised many, since he and the General were old enemies and had let off excess energy in a barroom brawl back in 1813. Although his decision meant damaging his relations with the strong Clay party at home, Benton elected to follow the popular Hero because he knew that Crawford's chances were nil and he could not abide the granite-faced Adams. Van Buren, meanwhile, spent the last weeks of the canvass trying desperately to hold up the invalid Crawford, unheedful of the frantic appeals from all sides to abandon the shattered hulk. Francis Johnson of Kentucky approached him one day with arguments for deserting to Adams. He claimed that union between the business interests of the East (represented by the New Englander) and the rising capitalists of the West (represented by Clay) would form an unbeatable coalition, one pregnant with enough political possibilities to satisfy even a New York politician. While Johnson argued his case, the Magician smiled and said nothing. Always courteous, Van Buren heard him out before flatly refusing to join the new alliance. Annoyed at having wasted his time, Johnson departed hastily, remarking as he went out the door that they would elect Adams with or without Van Buren's help. "I think that very possible," the New Yorker called after him, "but . . . if you do so you sign Mr. Clay's political death warrant."

Van Buren did not know it but Mr. Clay had already signed his own death warrant several weeks before during a conversation with Mr. Adams. There had been one of those obliquely worded agreements between the two men as they sat in Adams' library, talking about the future and indicating that they understood their duty to the nation and were about to act upon it. Nothing improper was said or suggested; nothing improper was even remotely contemplated. But no sooner did Clay announce his support of Adams than rumors started flying around Washington that the two men had clandestinely arranged a "deal" to settle the presidential question. An unsigned letter appeared in the Philadelphia *Columbia Observer* on January 28, 1825, accusing Clay of promising sufficient votes in the House to elect the New Englander in exchange for the post of Secretary of State. The Speaker properly denied the charge, denounced the anonymous slanderer as a "dastard and liar," and called upon him to reveal his identity and give satisfaction. To the amusement of many, the "dastard and liar" turned out to be one George Kremer, a Representative from Pennsylvania who was known for his sometimes startling eccentricities. The thought of Clay challenging this crackpot over a point of honor was as ridiculous as Kremer himself.

A few days later Congressman Chauncey Forward of Pennsylvania confronted Kremer with the accusation. "Why Mr Kremer," he bawled, "you surely do not mean to charge any corruption or dishonorable conduct to Mr Clay, do you?"

"No indeed," stammered Kremer, "I had no such idea, and I am willing to say so in the House."

Before Forward could steer Kremer back to the House to make good his offer, James Buchanan, another Representative from Pennsylvania, intervened. "Mr Forward," commanded Buchanan, "you had better let Mr Kremer alone; he is in the hands of his friends and *they* will take care of him." With that, Buchanan took his colleague by the arm and led him away.

A congressional investigation subsequently looked into Kremer's "unintended" charge of corruption but failed to turn up incriminating evidence. No effort was made by the partisans of Jackson to press the matter before the election for fear of possible injury to their own candidate. Still, the rumors persisted and the atmosphere in Washington during the winter of 1825 was charged with suspicion touching each of the candidates. According to one story, General Jackson himself had visited Crawford with an offer of "any terms . . . as the price of his cooperation & support." According to another tale, the wily Van Buren dropped in on Adams to find out if any patronage in the State Department had suddenly become negotiable. At first he detected signs of encouragement but later was told to return *after* the election. For a fleeting moment Van Buren thought Adams had at last arrived as a politician.

One rumor in particular worried the Clay men. They allegedly heard that Jackson, if elected, would "punish" the Speaker and exclude him and his friends from the Cabinet. Through several intermediaries they relayed their fears to Buchanan, assuring him that they would "end the presidential election within the hour" if the General would first declare his intention of dismissing Adams from the State Department. Buchanan, a born busybody, could not resist the opportunity to stick his nose into presidential politics. Besides, he disliked Adams and hoped to eliminate him from the contest. So he cranked up his courage and presented his information to John H. Eaton, the Hero's friend and colleague in the Senate, and afterward to Jackson himself. As he stood before the stormy General, narrating what he had heard, he could not control the nervous affliction that troubled one eye. He kept winking at Jackson as he spoke. And what he said was so confused and made so little sense that Old Hickory had trouble understanding the details.[5]

So it went. According to the rumor-mongers there were deals, bargains, and attempted bribery. Sometimes it was all very subtle, as subtle as a winking eye, or two men sitting in a library discussing what their friends thought the future held in store for them; sometimes it was more blatant. Right up to the day of the election, managers of the several candidates cajoled, implored, pleaded, and argued with the Representatives, urging them to pledge their vote and save the Republic from disaster.

On the sidelines, watching all this cajoling and pleading, was still another faction, this one grouped around the dark-eyed and bushy-haired Secretary of War, John C. Calhoun. Originally Calhoun was the fifth candidate for the presidency, with support ranging from his own state of South Carolina northward to Pennsylvania and New Jersey. To obtain additional strength from the Middle Atlantic states he tried to undermine Radical influence in New York but ran afoul of Van Buren. When Pennsylvania later deserted his standard in favor of Jackson and nominated him for the vice-presidency, he reluctantly withdrew from the important contest and consented to run for second place. In the November election he encountered no substantial opposition; the Jackson and Adams electors awarded him a total of 182 votes, while his nearest rival, Nathan Sanford of New York, polled 30.

When the presidential contest ended in a standoff, Calhoun could not make up his mind whether to grab the coattails of Adams or Jackson. Consequently he did nothing. Yet to most observers he appeared to be allied with the Hero, which irritated the Radicals, because they were inclined to switch to Jackson but balked at having to associate with Calhoun. They could not stomach the South Carolinian. They abominated his policies as War Secretary, especially his exorbitant expenditures to improve the military establishment, and his support of the Tariff of 1816. Moreover, Calhoun quarreled with Crawford each time the Secretary of the Treasury dared to question the amount of money he proposed to spend for his Department. Van Buren explained him away as a Republican with Federalist leanings—this despite the fact that several of the Magician's Radical colleagues were former

Federalists themselves. But their opinion of Calhoun was best summed up by Dr. Thomas Cooper, a flaming South Carolinian who was not above preaching the dismemberment of the Union whenever he thought Southern interests were being auctioned off in Washington. "Calhoun is the author of all the measures we condemn," Cooper wrote. "He was the adviser of that fool Monroe; he is a national—internal-improvements man; he is fortification mad; he spends the money of the South to buy up influence in the north, or at least he proposed doing so. He is active, shewy, fluent, superficial & conceited."

That was Calhoun, agreed the Radicals: showy, superficial, and conceited, but mostly ambitious—the kind of ambition that annihilates any thing, any principle, or anyone who gets in its way. So the Radicals as a group "held out" against Jackson, although a few, like Benton, defected. Their strategy in the House election —a strategy devised by Van Buren—was predicated on delay, for if they could prevent Adams or Jackson from winning on the first few ballots, then, after successive ballots and repeated failures to elect the President, the delegations might be persuaded to turn to Crawford to break the deadlock. In this way the once speechless, sightless, paralyzed Secretary of the Treasury would become the President of the United States.

On the day of the election, as the Speaker ordered the states to poll their members, Senators and guests sat in the galleries and watched the proceedings. The audience hushed at Clay's command. The "long agony" was about to end.[6]

V

Van Buren's strategy failed. And it failed on the very first ballot when 13 states went to Adams, 7 to Jackson, and 4 to Crawford. By a bare majority, John Quincy Adams was elected the sixth President. Of the eleven states that had voted for Jackson in the electoral college, four—Louisiana, Maryland, Illinois, and North Carolina—deserted him in the House election. Crawford's three states—Virginia, Georgia, and Delaware—stood fast, and he picked up the additional state of North Carolina. Adams' majority included the six New England states, Maryland, Louisiana, Illinois, Ohio, Missouri, Kentucky, and—to Van Buren's chagrin—New York.

Poor Jackson. He had had a plurality of electoral votes and was seemingly the choice of the country, yet he was denied the prize he felt was his right. At first he took his defeat with gentlemanly good grace. At a reception given by James Monroe on the night of the election he exchanged pleasantries with the President-elect.

"How do you do, Mr. Adams," said the Hero. "I hope you are well, sir."

"Very well, sir," replied Adams. "I hope General Jackson is well!"

As this civilized conversation clearly indicates, the mood in Washington immediately following the contest was one of quiet acquiescence to the will of the Congress. The Speaker reported correctly that the election, in every way, "was creditable to our institutions and to our country."

Then came the explosion. Adams announced his intention of appointing Henry Clay as his Secretary of State. It was foolish of him to offer the post, but it was political suicide for Clay to accept it. Howling their indignation, the Jacksonians set up a cry that a "corrupt bargain" had been struck between the two men just prior to the election, that the will of the people, expressed in November, had been criminally subverted by Washington politicians. "So you see," wrote Old Hickory in an impassioned outburst, "the *Judas* of the West has closed the contract and will receive the thirty pieces of silver." To cynical voters around the country who were prone to believe that politics was a dirty business at best and that "deals" were normal in the operation of government, the accusation required no proof so long as it was repeated at regular intervals; others wondered whether the spirit of the Constitution had not been violated by arrogant men who presumed to tell the people what was best for them.

The first political effect of the President's announcement was to send the Calhoun men rushing headlong into the Jackson camp. The Adams-Clay Coalition blocked the road to the presidency for possibly sixteen years, and the impatient Calhoun could not wait that long for his own turn to come round. Friends of the new Vice

President had advised Adams "that if Clay should be appointed Secretary of State, a determined opposition to the Administration will be organized from the outset. The opposition will use the name of General Jackson as its head." Since the flinty Adams had obviously disregarded their threat, they had no alternative but to join the Hero.

Yet it was clear to anyone studying the Washington scene that even before the inauguration was held, something extraordinary was going on between Jackson and Calhoun. Senator Rufus King of New York noted that "a Party is forming itself here to oppose Mr. Adams' administration. South Carolina is headquarters, and I understand that a Dinner takes place today [at] the Quarters of this Delegation, when Gen'l Jackson, Mr. Calhoun . . . and others are to be guests. . . . This first step may serve to combine the malcontents."

In view of the rumors and suspicions that followed their informal interview early in January and the certain opposition that would form if the appointment were conferred, the question arises why Adams and Clay deliberately stuck their necks into this political noose. Characteristically, the President answered the question squarely: "I consider it due to his [Clay's] talents and services, and to the Western section of the Union . . . and to the confidence in me manifested by their delegations." No one could seriously deny the Speaker's talents and services, and under ordinary circumstances the appointment would have been applauded as wise and beneficial to the country. But these were not ordinary circumstances, and if Adams was indifferent to the political consequences of his action, surely Clay had more sense.

The Speaker quite naturally consulted with his friends before replying to the President's invitation. He knew that the situation was steaming with possible "embarrassment," but he also knew that the office of Secretary of State was the fastest way to get to the White House. So, in order to bring the presidency closer, Clay gambled on a long shot. Later, he justified his move by declaring it inexcusable to support Adams in the House election and then refuse to serve under him. Acceptance of the State Department would renew his endorsement of the President, he contended, and provide an opportunity to formulate the policies of the new Administration.

Still, with all his reasons and excuses and explanations, Clay had blundered badly. He let the gambler in him take over; what is more, he handed the Jacksonians a rallying cry with which to form an opposition.

On March 7 the President sent his Cabinet nominations to the Senate, most of which were carry-overs from the Monroe Administration. In typical Adams fashion, he even invited Crawford to remain as Secretary of the Treasury. The ailing Georgian refused the generous offer and the post was subsequently given to Richard Rush of Pennsylvania. Samuel L. Southard of New Jersey, William Wirt of Maryland, and John McLean of Ohio agreed to stay on as Secretary of the Navy, Attorney General, and Postmaster General, respectively, while Senator James Barbour of Virginia was selected to replace Vice President Calhoun in the War Department. These nominations were quickly confirmed, although the Senate was first obliged to sit through several hours of bitter laments by the Jackson men.

The Radicals, for the most part, calmly accepted the announcement of Clay's reward, even to the extent of voting for confirmation. As seasoned politicians with no particular ax to grind by objecting to the appointment, they understood Adams' position and would have been surprised had the President acted differently. Furthermore, the Radicals might have been persuaded to go along with the Administration for a session or two if only the President had used just a little common sense. But no; from the first moment he assumed office, Adams served notice that he would go his own way even if it meant distressing the political sensibilities of every man in Congress. In his inaugural address he dared to advocate federally sponsored public works. "To the topic of internal improvements," he said, ". . . I recur with particular satisfaction. It is that from which I am convinced that the unborn millions of our posterity . . . will derive their most fervent gratitude to the founders of the Union." To compound his mistake, Adams expressed the hope that any constitutional objection inherent in the issue would be overcome and the "speculative scruple" resolved "by a practical public blessing."

That last remark about the "speculative scruple" floored the Radicals. Had Adams wished to provoke them into joining the Jacksonians—and join them without wasting time about it—he chose the quickest way to do it. Only a few days before his inauguration they had generally decided to remain neutral and watch the course of events. "All things here," said Silas Wright of the Albany Regency, "and all parties I may say here too, are waiting to determine whether they are to support or oppose the national administration." Now they knew. The message, recalled Thomas Hart Benton at a later time, "furnished a topic against Mr. Adams, and went to the reconstruction of parties on the old line of strict . . . construction of the constitution."

And so it happened—though few understood how it could happen so fast—that within three days of his inauguration, John Quincy Adams had performed the stupendous feat of creating an opposition bent on destroying his Administration and denying him, like his father, a second term in office.[7]

VI

When the congressional session ended, the disappointed Hero of New Orleans headed for his home in Tennessee by way of West Alexandria, Pennsylvania. As he reached the little town, an old comrade by the name of Edward McLaughlin came up to him and offered his sympathy over the results of the House election. "Well, general," he said, "we did all we could for you here, but the rascals at Washington cheated you out of it."

"Indeed, my old friend," rumbled the Hero, "there was *cheating*, and *corruption*, and *bribery* too."

With each mile that took him closer to home, Jackson's anger mounted. Over and over he recalled the scene when James Buchanan stood before him, winking at him, beckoning him to betray the people's trust. He remembered Buchanan's words, something the Clay men had said about ending the election in an hour if he would expel Adams from the Cabinet. Suddenly it struck him. That "Judas," Henry Clay, had authorized an "arrangement" and sent Buchanan as the emissary, and when there was no response the deal was made with Adams.

In Brownsville, Jackson repeated his tale of skulduggery in Washington, only this time he added several embellishments. To all who would listen—and there were many—he accused Henry Clay personally of attempted bribery.

Almost as swiftly as Jackson's anger turned to fury, his indictment of the Coalition spread to neighboring towns. When he reached his next stop the citizenry surrounded his carriage and asked if Clay had truly dared to corrupt America's great hero. "Yes, sir," stormed the General, "such a proposition was made. I said to the bearer—Go tell Mr. Clay, tell Mr. Adams, that if I go into that chair, I go with clear hands and a pure heart, and that I'd rather see them together with myself, engulphed to the earth's centre, than to compass it by such means."

In Frankfort, Kentucky, Jackson re-enacted his outrage, but his words had been sharpened in the meantime to a finer political point. *"The people* [have] *been cheated,"* he bellowed. *". . . Corruptions and intrigues at Washington . . . defeated the will of the people."*

So what started as suspicion in Jackson's mind ended as conviction: that he had been betrayed, abused, and cheated by a wicked Coalition. Not himself alone but the people, too.

By the time he reached his home in Tennessee, a well-marked trail of political propaganda reached back to Washington right into the halls of Congress. Jackson had placed the Adams-Clay Coalition on notice. The campaign for the presidency in 1828 had already begun.[8]

2. Transition

I

A TIRED and disappointed Vice President left Washington for South Carolina shortly after the adjournment of Congress to seek the peace and quiet of home. The strange events of the past winter had depressed the lonely man, for it seemed, he said, that when unscrupulous politicians put their heads together for individual profit, constitutional principles could be violated with impunity and the power of the people set at naught. He regarded the mode of Adams' election and the subsequent payoff to Clay as the most dangerous blow that the liberty of the country had yet sustained, one so frightening in its implications as to require a constitutional amendment to prevent a recurrence in the future.

There was no possibility of Calhoun finding rest and quiet at home, not while he continued to suffer from an advanced case of Potomac fever and not while friends kept reminding him that he was expected one day to occupy the White House. So much talent and ability fused into one man could not be wasted forever on inferior offices; he owed it to himself and to the country at large to win the presidency, even if it meant allying himself with the military chieftain, General Andrew Jackson. Once home, Calhoun quickly disposed of his family by dumping them for the summer at his mother-in-law's estate. That accomplished, he commenced a long tour of South Carolina, seeing his planter constituents, talking with them, gauging their reactions to recent events, and listening to their advice. As he no doubt anticipated, much of what he heard conflicted with those nationalistic concepts he had been preaching for the past dozen years. For one thing, Southerners complained that the price of cotton had started on a long, steady decline following the passage of the Tariff of 1824 and that unless it was halted they faced inevitable financial ruin. To their minds the tariff was a government subsidy paid to Northern manufacturers out of the pockets of Southern planters and farmers. What the Congress had done in effect, they argued, was to create an illegal and immoral system that penalized (and perhaps in time would pauperize) one section of the country for the economic benefit of the other.

From the beginning of his legislative career Calhoun had advocated a broad national program. That program included higher tariff rates, internal improvements (especially fortifications, roads, and highways to strengthen the country's defenses), and the recharter of the United States Bank. Now he heard and saw how injurious some of those ideas were to the people he represented and how dangerous to his future political career. Suddenly, like the price of cotton, Calhoun's opinion of the tariff fell sharply. Soon his other youthful ideals about nationalism and fortifications and improvements were in decline until by 1826 he was no longer an ardent nationalist but rather the stout defender of states' rights.

The Radicals should have been overjoyed with Calhoun's conversion to their philosophy, once they became aware of it; and perhaps some of them genuinely were, since he would bring to their school a towering intellectual force possessed by no other active politician. But many more had long memories and were not so quick to forgive him his past "abominations." More important, they could not forget his mistreatment of Crawford in Monroe's Cabinet. A few of them patiently nurtured their grudge and waited for the day when they could deal him a crippling blow, thereby terminating his presidential availability once and for all. If only Pennsylvania would drop him, wished one Radical, "then he goes down. I do not much regret it, d–mn him."[1]

II

"Black Dan" they had called him in college, this distinguished Representative from Massachusetts. "Black Dan." At a tavern in Concord one day, General Stark peered at the young man and then with all the candor of age fortified by several stiff drinks said, "Daniel, your face is pretty black, but it isn't so black as your father's was with gunpowder at the Bennington fight."

True, Daniel Webster was quite dark, so swarthy in fact that some people kiddingly told him he looked like an Indian. But when he opened his mouth and started to speak, he made sounds such as no Indian or white man or anyone else in the country could imitate. It was a huge voice, powered by a barrel chest and pro-·jected out of a cavernous mouth. Though rich-sounding, it was pitched higher than most people expected to hear. And whether he spoke indoors or out, Webster could hurtle it to the last row without effort or strain and seemingly at about the same volume that he plopped it into the first row. His control of the instrument was faultless. It never broke or cracked even when he raised it as high as it would go to embellish a climax or emphasize a point. Occasionally he suffered a momentary vocal paralysis as he started to speak—one of those strange phenomena speakers are sometimes afflicted with—but after his throat had been properly lubricated the paralysis miraculously disappeared.

When Webster first moved from New Hampshire, where he was born, to Massachusetts, he used this uncommon gift to argue the reverse of nationalism, the side of shippers and merchants who were states' righters and anti-tariff. Later, he discovered that many of his wealthier constituents were switching their investments from shipping to industry. Now they expected him to defend protection, along with the other features of the American System. Since he was a practical man and a sound politician, Webster heeded the gentle command and promptly demonstrated the sincerity of his conversion by personally investing his own money in textiles. Before long, his good sense resembled nothing so much as pure statesmanship to his devoted constituents; by that time he was the nation's ablest exponent of American capitalism.

But it was not capitalism specifically that Webster was expected to extol at his first important address after the adjournment of Congress. That address was scheduled for June 17, 1825, when the cornerstone of the Bunker Hill Monument was to be laid at ceremonies commemorating the fiftieth anniversary of the famous battle. A great crowd, including General Lafayette, who was currently touring the United States, turned out to hear the godlike Daniel. As Webster stepped forward to swallow away his paralysis and begin his speech there was a period of confusion when some of the seats, temporarily arranged around the hillside, gave way. People started shouting and crying. There were momentary fears that a panic might ensue.

"It is impossible, sir, to restore order," said one official to the speaker.

"Nothing is impossible, sir," replied the indomitable Webster; "let it be done."

And somehow or other whatever needed doing was done, just as the godlike commanded.

When order was restored, Webster resumed his speech. He reviewed for the crowd the many changes that had taken place during the last half-century, how the country had prospered and how the people had advanced under a free government. Finally he turned to the small knot of surviving veterans of the Bunker Hill Battle and addressed himself directly to them. "Venerable Men," he began. Then he stopped and looked at the few old men seated in the place of honor. "But, alas! you are not all here," he said softly. "Time and the sword have thinned your ranks."

It was a magnificent speech, one completely worthy of Webster and the heroes he honored. And while he stood there speaking, putting his audience through an emotional wringer, piling one massively constructed, gorgeously worded sentence on top of another, in New York another politician was talking to his people—but in a different way. Martin Van Buren did not use the language of the orator when he toured the grass roots. He spoke plainly and quietly. Every year, after the adjournment of Congress, he visited some part of the state. This year it was the western counties; and this year he labored with "holy zeal" to revive among the people an affection for his Bucktail party after the thorough thrashing they had given him in the last election. Yet much of the talk he heard in the West that summer centered around the Erie Canal, which was scheduled to open on November 2, 1825. Built at a cost of 7,500,000 dollars and stretching 363 miles from Troy to Buffalo, the canal was officially opened when Governor De Witt Clinton, accompanied by a group of leading citizens, boarded a boat at Buffalo and ten days later arrived in New York City, where he poured a barrel of water taken from Lake Erie into the Atlantic Ocean. This symbolic marriage of the waters, as the newspapers called it, presaged the coming birth of New York's economic and political pre-eminence among the other states in the Union.

Van Buren did not join in the ceremonies and celebrations marking the opening. The honor and praise all belonged to Clinton. However, he did attend one public dinner given at Albany to commemorate the occasion, and his companion during the feast was John W. Taylor, soon to be elected the Administration's Speaker of the House of Representatives. Naturally, Taylor could not resist needling the little man about Clinton's accomplishment; and half smiling all during the meal, though not amused, Van Buren just listened. He and Clinton had been fighting for control of the Republican party in New York for nearly a dozen years, and their feelings for one another reflected the many and bruising battles they had fought. When the Magician could stand Taylor's barbs no longer, he turned to his tormentor and flatly predicted that he would win the next election. It was no idle boast. Van Buren had not been touring the state without purpose, and the reports he had received from leaders in the several counties all concurred that the next election belonged to him.[2]

III

The new Congress under President Adams began its session in December 1825. Generally speaking, it contained three major political groups: the Coalitionists or Administration forces; the Jacksonians with their allies the Calhoun men; and the Radicals, now led by Van Buren after William Crawford's retirement from public life.

The first order of business in the House was the selection of a suitable Speaker. Directed by Daniel Webster, the Coalitionists succeeded in electing John W. Taylor to the office, and while the margin of victory was small, it nevertheless demonstrated that, if careful, they could control the House. Over in the Senate, Vice President Calhoun avoided open partisanship at first, yet he and his friends frequently consulted with the Jacksonians to plot the derailment of the President's program. "Hints" were passed along to the Radicals that, should they care to express an opinion on any of the issues likely to come before the Senate, their views would receive respectful attention.

The formation of a congressional opposition to the new Administration was accelerated by President Adams' own "misuse" of his presidential powers. His appointments were weak, as a rule nonpartisan, and sometimes politically brainless. For example, he renominated James R. Pringle, collector of the Charleston port in South Carolina, although he knew that Pringle belonged to the opposition. Again, despite the objections of wiser heads, Adams offered the post of Minister to Great Britain to De Witt Clinton who was, in addition to everything else, an active and vocal Jacksonian. The offer was promptly rejected. While it failed to swing the Clintonians over to the Administration (presuming for the moment that Adams was really capable of so blatantly political an intention), it succeeded admirably in infuriating the Van Buren faction. "The administration are intent upon sustaining themselves," snorted the Magician, "& it appears to be immaterial whether they derive their aid from Jew or Gentile or whoever else can help." As he promised in the days before his election, Adams dispensed the executive patronage upon former Federalists, Republicans, and any other person he believed worthy of office, irrespective of party. "I determined to renominate every person against whom there was no complaint," he announced happily. But later he admitted that he was "importuned to serve my friends and reproached for neglecting them, because I will not dismiss, or drop from Executive offices, able and faithful political opponents to provide for my own partisans."

The President's relations with Congress were equally unfortunate.

He did little to consolidate his strength in either House, though his friends needed all the help they could get to check the rampaging Jacksonians. In the House of Representatives, Daniel Webster carried the Administration almost singlehandedly, but Adams distrusted him and withheld any expression of confidence or favor. The situation was worse in the Senate, where the Coalitionists were distinctly outclassed. There was no one to match the intellectualism of Calhoun, the organizational skill of Van Buren, or the speaking talents of Benton and John Randolph. Jackson was gone from the Senate, having resigned his seat the previous fall, but Hugh Lawson White more than filled his place. Significantly, White established residence in Washington with two of Calhoun's closest associates from South Carolina: Senator Robert Y. Hayne and Representative James Hamilton, Jr. Through White and John H. Eaton, the General was kept informed of developments, and information and instructions were constantly transmitted between the Hermitage and Capitol Hill.[3]

The circle of opposition already formed around the President was drawn tighter on December 6, 1825, when the first annual message was sent down to Congress. In a bold assertion of the government's responsibility to hasten the material well-being of its citizens, Adams proposed a program of public works and improvements that revealed in each word his own intense nationalism and his personal commitment to Henry Clay's American System. After first reviewing the nation's friendly intercourse with foreign powers, Adams announced that a congress of the newly independent states of Latin America would assemble shortly at Panama to discuss problems of mutual concern, that the United States had been invited to attend, and that the invitation had been accepted. Within a few weeks, he declared, ministers would be named. Next, he asked Congress to consider a uniform bankruptcy law and the necessity of reorganizing the militia. He referred to the flourishing state of the nation's finances, Indian affairs, and the needs of the army and the navy. Then he returned to a politically explosive theme: "The great object of the institution of civil government," Adams averred, "is the improvement of the condition of those who are parties to the social compact, and no government, in whatever form constituted, can accomplish the lawful ends of its institution but in proportion as it improves the condition of those over whom it is established." Accordingly, roads and canals ought to be built at government expense. A national university should be established, since knowledge was the first instrument for the betterment of man. Along with the university, an astronomical observatory might be erected to observe the phenomena of the heavens. In Europe there were upward of 130 such "light-houses of the skies," he lectured, while in America there was not one.

Pursuing this vein, Adams called for the exploration of both the western territories and the entire northeastern coastline. He proposed the establishment of a naval academy similar to West Point, a more effective patent law to protect inventors, and a uniform standard of weights and measures. "The spirit of improvement is abroad upon the earth," he proclaimed. "It stimulates the hearts and sharpens the faculties not of our fellow-citizens alone, but of the nations of Europe and of their rulers." But why all this improvement at fantastic expense? Why such a prodigious program? "Liberty is power," said Adams; the United States, possessing the greatest measure of liberty, must be the most powerful nation upon the earth. And how was all this power to be achieved when a substantial body of Republicans claimed that the Constitution sharply limited the scope of governmental authority? The President denied any such limitation. There was more than sufficient authority to encompass his program, he said, and a failure to exercise it in the interest of agriculture, commerce, manufactures, the mechanical arts, literature, and science would be "treachery of the most sacred of trust."

Then Adams unwittingly demonstrated what a political dimwit he was, why so many people believed he hated the democracy. In urging passage of internal improvements he told the Congress not to give the rest of the world the impression "that we are palsied by the will of our constituents." An unfortunate expression, and one that the opposition would later use to convince the electorate that John Quincy Adams was an enemy of the people.

Despite this monumental slip, the message was one of the greatest presidential papers sent to any Congress. The language was stilted in places, the manner pedantic, and the politics grotesque;

yet the challenge to advance the nation's intellectual and material strength never had a more courageous advocate.

As the clerk ended his reading of the message, the Radicals sat back in their seats utterly stunned by the incredible interpretation given the Constitution. It was filled with "well-wrought encomiums [and] . . . plausible definitions" of the federal power, wrote Van Buren at a later time, "yet not one of the followers of the old Republican faith . . . could fail to see in them the most ultra latitudinarian doctrines." Thomas Ritchie, editor of the Richmond *Enquirer*, pretended to doubt that the message was a presidential document. "Are we really reading a state paper," he asked, "or a school boy's Thesis?" Both Thomas Jefferson and William Crawford agreed that the message was replete with unconstitutional claptrap. Even a few Administration men were skeptical, and Representative Albert Tracy of New York said it was a "commonplaced [*sic*] production."

The Jacksonians ridiculed the "light-houses of the skies" expression, gasped over the invitation to disregard "the will of our constituents," and cited the specific recommendations as the sort of unconstitutional proposals the country might expect from a corrupt and venal Coalition. The Hero himself—never forgetting to allude to his defeat—thought the message "was well calculated to swell to indignation the dissatisfaction which the mode of his election had already created." Until he read the President's words, said Jackson, he honestly believed Adams possessed "a tolerable share of common sense" and would avoid the asperities of 1800 that eventually wrecked the Federalist party. Now he realized that Adams had nothing but "a hypocritical veneration for the great principles of republicanism."

Almost as soon as the message was published, a strong contingent of Radicals were prepared to end their supposed neutrality and go over to the opposition. Perhaps they had always intended to join the Jacksonians once they found an acceptable excuse. Perhaps their case against Adams, based on his alleged violation of Jeffersonian principles, was a simple pretense to justify what they already intended to do. They knew, of course, that the presidential election of 1828 would be limited to Adams and Jackson. Sooner or later they had to make a choice; yet what choice did they really have? The Coalition was scarred by scandal—or the suspicion of scandal, which was just as bad. Furthermore, the President was a political flyweight, too stern to compromise, too proper to mingle with professional politicians, too antiseptic to dirty himself with grubby politics. Unlike Jackson, Adams was devoid of popular appeal and seemingly indifferent to his public image. Moreover, his proposed measures did violence to Radical doctrine.

These were all good and substantial reasons to justify an immediate movement into the ranks of the Jacksonians, yet the cautious Van Buren urged his followers to delay any declaration of future intentions. "*You* must hold yourself uncommitted," he told a North Carolina Representative, "until you see how measures are to be conducted here—so that our late party may again act in concert." To join the Jacksonians without some prior understanding or agreement would destroy their identity and their importance in the realignment of political forces. On the other hand, if they waited until Jackson or his advisers granted concessions—a statement of adherence to Jeffersonian principles would indicate a proper respect for Radical sensibilities—then they could again act as a group, "in concert," and ally themselves with the Hero to form a new political combination. Said Van Buren: "If Gen Jackson & his friends will put his election on old party grounds, preserve the old systems, avoid if not condemn the practices of the last campaign we can by adding his personal popularity to the yet remaining force of old party feeling, not only succeed in electing him but our success when achieved will be worth something. We shall see what they are willing to do."[4]

Still, it was one thing for the Radicals to postpone a direct assault upon the Administration or join the opposition, and quite another to suffer the President's incredible message. They had no problem with his legislative proposals, since they could kill them in committee; but the Panama Congress, to which Adams had already committed the nation, necessitated more drastic action. Imbued as they were with the "no entangling alliances" doctrine of Washington and Jefferson, they plotted to scuttle the conference.

As a preliminary step, Van Buren went to see the Vice President at his home in Georgetown to sound him out about the mission. He was hardly surprised to learn from Calhoun that the Jacksonians agreed not only that the conference departed from established foreign policy but that they owed it to the country to block executive action in sending ministers to Panama. Van Buren hastened to admit his own opposition, after which he assured Calhoun that Radical assistance could be counted on to defeat the mission. Nothing was said about a permanent alliance, although, as Van Buren later wrote, their "concurrence in opinion" to oppose "so prominent a measure of the Administration could not fail to lead to an ultimate union of efforts for its overthrow."

The Panama Mission was formally proposed by Adams on December 26, 1825, when he nominated Richard C. Anderson of Kentucky and John Sergeant of Pennsylvania as ministers and William B. Rochester of New York as secretary. A special message accompanied their names to the Senate. In discoursing upon the conference's possible advantages for the United States, Adams underscored the importance of promoting "liberal commercial intercourse" with Latin American countries. The doctrine that free ships make free goods and the rule of reason upon the extent of blockades, he said, might be established by general consent. Likewise, "an agreement between all the parties . . . that each will guard by its own means against the establishment of any future European colony within its borders may be found advisable." Lastly, Adams concluded, the mission would demonstrate to South American countries "the interest that we take in their welfare" and would lay the "foundation of our future intercourse with them in the broadest principles of reciprocity and the most cordial feelings of fraternal friendship."

The reciprocity and friendship between the northern and southern continents envisaged by the President and his Secretary of State was premature by a century. Like the proposed national university and observatory, the Panama Congress staked out the distance separating Adams and Clay from most of their contemporaries. And try as the President might, he could not close the gap.

In the Senate, John Branch of North Carolina immediately challenged Adams' position that he could act without the prior consent of the Congress. A resolution was submitted to this effect, coupled with a request for an opinion from the Committee on Foreign Relations. Since a majority of the committee members were Radicals and Jacksonians, the opinion as eventually given was perfectly bipartisan: only the President's views were omitted. The report condemned the acceptance of the invitation without first consulting the Congress, questioned the objectives of the conference, and predicted disastrous consequences should the United States participate.

Far from clarifying the issue, the report touched off the first important battle between the Administration and its opposition. And with the commencement of that battle, the size, the composition, and the character of the opposition became clear. Its leaders included Benton of Missouri, Eaton and White of Tennessee, Macon and Branch of North Carolina, Tazewell and Randolph of Virginia, Levi Woodbury of New Hampshire, and Martin Van Buren. A good half of these men were Radicals. Also arguing against the mission were John Berrien and Thomas Cobb of Georgia, John Chandler of Maine, Mahlon Dickerson of New Jersey, Thomas H. Williams of Mississippi, John Rowan of Kentucky, and Robert Y. Hayne.

As part of the over-all plan to kill the mission, the Senate arranged its sessions to consume as much time as possible. Since delay is one of the most effective legislative killers in Congress, the Jacksonians conducted an interminable harangue against the conference. At one point in the debate Robert Y. Hayne reminded his Southern colleagues that the Negro-controlled island of Haiti would be represented at the conference. Would the Senators, he asked, care to hazard "the peace and safety of a large portion of our Union" by an indirect acknowledgment of Haitian independence? The delegates at Panama would probably discuss the suppression of the slave trade, he ventured. "With nothing connected with slavery can we consent to treat with other nations," he thundered.

Berrien, Benton, Holmes, and Van Buren delivered speeches of stupefying length on the constitutionality of the mission. Manifestly, they chorused, without the direct consent of the Senate the United States was prohibited from participating in a conference that might bind her to some future action. And it seemed to these men that the Panama delegates planned to involve all the participants in a general agreement or alliance that would supersede the powers of the American Congress and destroy the authority of the United States Senate. In effect, the nation was asked to join an armed confederacy to change the political condition of the world.

But it remained for John Randolph of Roanoke, Senator from Virginia, to bring the debate to a boiling climax. This wildly Radical aristocrat, eccentric to the point of lunacy, fired off a speech of astounding personal spite against Adams and Clay. Of the President, he asked: "Who made him a judge of this body. . . . Above all, who made him the searcher of hearts, and gave him the right, by an innuendo black as hell, to blacken our motives." After likening the Coalition to that of "Blifil and Black George," the "puritan and the black-leg," he lifted his hands high in the air and swore "to God & country" to wage an unrelenting war against an Administration brought to power through "stinking" corruption and bargain. In passing, he pronounced the Panama mission "a Kentucky Cuccoos Egg laid in South America."

The thin-skinned Clay, sensitive to the mere mention of the word "bargain," chose to regard Randolph's language as insulting and improper. Forthwith he challenged the Senator to a duel, and on April 6, 1826, they exchanged several shots at a place near Little Falls Bridge on the southern shore of the Potomac River. Neither combatant was injured, but Randolph left the field with a bullet hole in his coat. According to Van Buren, the Virginian had magnanimously decided beforehand to spare Clay's life because the Secretary was "a husband & father of a numerous family." Ever the doctrinaire Radical, Randolph said he would "never make a widow & orphans. It is agt. my principles." But ever the good politician, he compromised his principles when he learned that Clay would take "deliberate aim at him." Instead, he fired his first shot at the Secretary's legs in order to disable him. He missed, and during the second exchange he discharged his pistol into the air. After that display of bravado, the two men were prevailed upon to cease their murderous quarrel. Clay agreed that his honor had been satisfied and the contest terminated.

But the ridiculous duel silenced neither Randolph nor the Jacksonians. Clay, they said, hatched a nest of "Cuccoos" eggs, one of which contained a conspiracy to thwart the will of the people and produced the weirdest "cuccoo" bird of all, President John Quincy Adams.[5]

IV

On March 14, the first round in the contest over the Panama mission ended in the Senate with a decisive victory for the Administration. A resolution submitted by Van Buren declaring the conference inexpedient and a departure from the traditional foreign policy of the United States was defeated, twenty-four to nineteen. Shortly thereafter, the Senators confirmed the nominations of the ministers and the secretary.

In the final analysis, the Jackson-Calhoun combination could not at this time defeat the Adams-Clay Coalition, even with Radical assistance. Thanks to the efforts of the Secretary of State, a sufficient number of Senators from New England and the Northwest lined up behind the Administration to form a majority. This majority increased slightly during the debate because of the delaying tactics employed by the Jacksonians. Too many Senators regarded their obstructionism as a political gambit—or, as Benton said, a easy way "of turning the tide . . . against Mr. Adams and Mr. Clay" —and not a sincere disapproval of the mission itself. As long as such tactics were used, the Jacksonians courted defeat.

In the House, the opponents of the conference tried to block the appropriations bill despite a favorable report from the Foreign Affairs Committee. All during the session the Representatives had engaged in a furious debate over the bargain charge on the pretext of amending the Constitution to prevent future presidential elections from ending up in the lower House of Congress. Led by the nervous, easily excited George McDuffie of South Carolina, the anti-Administration men staged a gross performance of partisan ill feeling, going so far as to accuse the President of "seducing" Henry Clay to win the election. With graphic detail, McDuffie described the lurid scene. "Clothed in the opposing garb of patriotism in dark and secret conclave," he ranted, "perhaps in the dead hour of the night when there is no eye to behold and no hand to deliver it, he . . . unfolds his fascinating allurements with such artful casuistry, that the unconscious victim does not know the Circean draught he is drinking until he finds himself converted into a swine."

Henry Clay a swine! Thomas Metcalfe of Kentucky bolted to his feet and demanded immediate satisfaction in the name of his friend. So another duel was arranged, and everything was proceeding splendidly until Metcalfe insisted on rifles to settle the dispute. Such an unsportsmanlike demand was unthinkable and James Hamilton, Jr., who served as second for both McDuffie and Randolph, refused to stretch the rules of the game to include these weapons, despite their effectiveness in blasting both antagonists into permanent silence. The duel was therefore canceled.

Meanwhile, the Administration attempted to push the Panama appropriations bill through the House. James K. Polk of Tennessee protested that the members had a duty to examine the expediency of foreign missions before allocating the money, and most Jacksonians were prepared to duplicate the Senate debates, argument for argument, in their own chamber. More time was wasted; but when the vote was finally called, the bill passed overwhelmingly, 134 to 60, and went up to the Senate. There the Jacksonians consumed additional time by subjecting the measure to another round of amendments. Patiently the Adams men rejected each one, and on May 3 the appropriations passed by the same tally that confirmed the nominations of the ministers.

The Administration's victory was short-lived, however. One of the envoys, Anderson, died while en route to the conference, and the second minister, Sergeant, did not arrive in Panama until after the congress had adjourned. Moreover, the conference achieved few positive results, to the intense disappointment of its sponsors. As for the Jacksonians, they were delighted with the results. They dubbed the conference "the Panama Abortion," which was always good for a few laughs. The country had been spared the evil of an "entangling alliance" (so they said), some rather lusty remarks about the corrupt bargain had been deftly inserted into the public record and could be used again in the campaign, and a congressional opposition had been organized which drew sympathetic support from the Radicals.

V

Although the President was outwardly indifferent to the effort
of the Jacksonians to realign political factions in Congress, Clay
was disturbed by what was happening. At first he tried to break up
the combination against the Administration with patronage offers
to the Crawford men. The Post Office Department should have been
Clay's best source of job supply to carry out his project, but the
Postmaster General, John McLean of Ohio, stubbornly refused to
initiate the removals suggested to him. Since McLean had shown
signs of leaning dangerously close to the Jacksonians—slipping
them small tokens of his favor on occasion—his own removal became a matter of practical necessity. Yet his popularity in certain
parts of the West and among Methodists generally dictated removal
through promotion. So it was decided to get him out of the way
by elevating him to the Supreme Court of the United States, where
he would cease to bother the Administration. The method chosen
to execute the scheme was through an increase in the membership
of the Court and an addition of new circuits to the Western states.
A bill authorizing these changes went to the Senate Judiciary Committee, over which Van Buren presided. After sitting on the measure
during the Panama debate, the committee finally reported it out
on April 7; but in the interim the Little Magician had inserted two
significant amendments: one combined the circuit court of Ohio
with that of Kentucky (rather than Indiana or Illinois), and the
other required judges to be residents of their respective circuits.
Under the conditions imposed by these amendments, McLean was
automatically excluded from appointment to the high bench, since
a Kentucky judge already sat on the Supreme Court. Because he
had punctured Clay's removal scheme, Van Buren gave his bill
little chance of success. But he was sure of his main object, which
was to keep McLean in the Post Office Department where he could
continue to embarrass the Administration.

During the debate on Van Buren's amended measure the Radicals
chose this opportunity to monopolize the floor and preach first
principles. To the infinite annoyance of everyone else, they argued

the rights of the states, condemned John Marshall's broad definition of the Constitution and his readiness to strike down state legislation, and explored the possibility of requiring unanimous consent by the Supreme Court before a federal or state law could be invalidated. Not until they decided that the Jacksonians had been sufficiently instructed about Radical terms for any future alliance did they finally permit a vote on the emasculated court bill. The Senate approved it, but the House refused to accede to Van Buren's amendments, and the measure was lost.

At this juncture Senator Thomas Hart Benton submitted a preposterous report on the President's alleged misuse of the appointing power. The substance of the speech may have been flimsy, but the manner in which it was delivered was robust and persuasive. In carefully measured cadences Benton's stentorian voice rose and fell as he accused Adams of attempting to bribe the Congress with patronage in order to build up a personal party for himself. In time, Benton predicted, votes and patronage will be interchangeable. *"I will VOTE as he wishes, and he will GIVE me the office I wish for."* This "new abuse" by the Coalition begged for congressional correction. Accordingly, the Missourian had prepared six bills to limit executive authority, all of them in the interest of better, more democratic government. One bill regulated the publication of laws and public advertisements; another reduced the President's control in appointing postmasters, cadets, and midshipmen; while a third blocked the executive privilege to dismiss army and navy personnel. The bills stumbled along the legislative path and were finally tabled, but they were useful to the opposition in publicizing what Senator Nathaniel Macon called the "monstrous influence" exercised by Adams. Andrew Jackson was deeply impressed by Benton's report, since it substantiated his darkest suspicions about the Coalition. If they could steal the presidency, he reasoned, there was no limit to their villainy. The Hero vowed that as chief executive he would eradicate the abuse from the federal government!

Senator Benton also challenged the validity of the Administration's public land policy. Like Alexander Hamilton, he said, Adams and Clay improperly sought to use the land for purposes of revenue, instead of encouraging its speedy occupation by settlers. He therefore proposed a reduction in the price of land in order to stimulate sales. With increased migration and sale, he asserted, the national debt would be lowered, after which the tariff could be adjusted to the advantage of consumers in the agricultural West and South.

Another controversy with the Administration centered around the perennial problem of internal improvements. No sooner was the subject broached in Congress than a flurry of amendments to the Constitution were tossed into the legislative hopper. All were subsequently blocked, but they did impede the Administration's maneuvers to press forward a program of public works. A few bills squeezed by, however. Funds to keep the Cumberland Road in repair and to extend it westward from Wheeling, Virginia, to Zanesville, Ohio, were appropriated. In addition, the Congress made land grants to or purchased stock from various canal companies such as the Dismal Swamp Canal Company, the Louisville and Portland Canal Company, and the Chesapeake and Ohio Canal Company. But these were token measures, and Adams' mighty program of internal improvements was mostly forgotten.[6]

VI

When this Nineteenth Congress reached the end of its first session in the spring of 1826, the Administration and its opposition were still engaged in a slashing verbal duel, now and then transferred to and continued in the city's newspapers. Watching the slashing and enjoying every moment of it were the uncommitted Radicals, still maintaining their neutrality but still leaning away from the Coalition and voting with the Jacksonians. However, their professed neutrality was proving costly, and defections from the party were increasing at an alarming rate. One North Carolinian reported that his delegation "will . . . be divided on the subject of politics in the future," with one contingent joining Adams and another merging with the opposition. As the leader of the Radicals, Martin Van Buren was strongly inclined to go over to Jackson without delay; but several considerations slowed his forward motion.

The first and most important consideration was the lack of any assurance from the General or his friends that the political principles of the Old Republicans would be respected or incorporated into the new party. As one Radical said: "Nothing can be gained therefore in principle by turning out Adams and electing Jackson." Because he was a realistic politician, sensitive to the needs of his own state and yet anxious to gain national distinction, Van Buren was not averse to compromising certain issues. The tariff and road-building appropriations, for example, might be adjusted to satisfy different sections; but on the general question of states' rights and its complement, the extent of the authority of the national government, there had to be an understanding. Such an understanding would prove Jacksonian willingness to accord the Radicals a respected place within their ranks. That was all they wanted—plus a "little" patronage, which was the outward sign of respect.

The second consideration was more personal. His rival in New York, Governor De Witt Clinton, had long supported Jackson, and for Van Buren to engineer a truce with the governor at this time might weaken the Senator's control of his own state party. Certainly it would "convulse" the members of Tammany Hall, whose hatred for the governor was an abiding, unchanging factor in New York politics. Van Buren confessed that it would take much "care, management, and time" to bring Tammany around, although he never for the moment doubted the persuasive powers of his Regency. Unfortunately, Clinton died in February 1828 before final arrangements for the truce could be completed; but prior to his death there was general gossip that something extraordinary was going on in Republican circles. "The coquetry between Van Buren and Clinton begins to assume the appearance of open prostitution," one New Yorker jokingly told Clay. It was not known who made the first advance, he laughed, but "we are quite confident of the fornication between them—and very indignant at this infringement of the decalogue."

Another difficulty for the New York Senator was continued Radical opposition to John C. Calhoun, despite the Vice President's recent conversion and the obvious fact that he was fast becoming the intellectual leader of the states' rights school. Van Buren himself wasted no love on Calhoun and recalled a period in 1824 when the Vice President schemed to challenge his control of New York.

Furthermore, it was blindingly clear that Calhoun expected to take the presidency after Jackson, and Van Buren was ambitious for the office himself. Neither man had enough patience and grace to wait his turn. For the moment, however, Calhoun served as a useful link between the several factions opposed to the Administration, and whether the Radicals liked him or not, he was essential to the Jackson cause.[7]

Before the end of the congressional session Van Buren paid Calhoun another quick visit; this time he had a friendly suggestion to offer, one that insinuated his willingness to work out an agreement between the factions they represented. Would it not be wise, he asked, to establish a newspaper in Washington that could speak with authority for all the anti-Administration parties? Van Buren had great faith in the value of a newspaper as a unifying political force. With it, he once wrote, "we can endure a thousand convulsions. Without it, we might as well hang our harps on the willows."

Calhoun probably regarded the suggestion as impertinent since a national newspaper had been established just a short time before. The old Washington *Gazette* had been bought out and its name changed to the *United States Telegraph*. True, the Jacksonians had experienced difficulty getting it started; but after Duff Green, the former editor of the St. Louis *Enquirer*, took over, their problems ceased. Green's writing was so vigorous and hard-hitting that other newspapermen began calling him "Rough" Green.

Still, Van Buren wanted to replace him. He thought Editor Thomas Ritchie of the Richmond *Enquirer* a better choice, one who could help ease the eventual transition of the Crawford men into the Jackson camp. As an outsider, he did not know that party money subsidized the *Telegraph*, that a 3,000-dollar loan to Green had been endorsed by Senator John Eaton, and that portions of the note were backed by James Hamilton, Jr., James K. Polk, Samuel D. Ingham, John Branch, George Kremer, and others. As Calhoun patiently and correctly explained to Van Buren: "A paper is already in existence, and it does seem to me that two on the same side must distract and excite jealousy. Each will have its partisans."

Van Buren persisted nonetheless. During the summer and fall of 1826 he badgered Calhoun about another newspaper. He spoke of a great national organ to spell out the party line for all; he emphasized its importance for the Radicals and enclosed several letters from different politicians to bolster his arguments. In reply, Calhoun diplomatically rejected the arguments, implying that the neutral New Yorker was hardly in a position to dictate policy until he was ready to come over to the Jacksonians unreservedly. But whatever their slight differences of opinion about the newspaper, he wanted the little man to know how close they were in matters of party principle. "I entirely concur with you as to our course," he cooed, "Our liberty and happiness depend on maintaining with inflexible firmness, but with moderation and temper, republican grounds and republican principles."

If Van Buren needed assurances, Calhoun would gladly provide them.[8]

3.

Structuring a National Party

I

THE POLITICAL TURMOIL of this Era of Good Feelings developed just at the time when an industrial revolution was spreading across the land, when the entire nation was shifting into a new era of territorial expansion and economic thrust. People were moving, clearing, planting, exploring the avenues toward a more prosperous life. Within twenty-five years they encompassed a continent and began to erect what Thomas Jefferson had earlier dreamed of: "an Empire for Liberty . . ."

The signs of these changes were not difficult to find. They were posted in towns and shops and along the rivers and routes that led into the forest. They were posted on wood-burning steamboats as they paddled upstream in defiance of wind and tide; on canals such as the Erie in New York, which sliced across the state and linked itself to the Great Lakes; on the hundreds of miles of roads, highways, and turnpikes that stretched from city to city; and on the general economy, now galvanized by foreign and domestic investments and ready to exploit a large and hungry market.

Democracy, too, made strides, though the pace varied from section to section. Property qualifications for voting by white adult males lingered in some places, but new states entered the Union without them, while the older ones were well along toward removing them from their constitutions. By 1824, popular selection of presidential electors was permitted in all but six states. And within the next few years four of those six joined the majority, leaving South Carolina and Delaware to continue the outmoded custom of legislative selection.

In this rapidly changing and expanding society it did not take political genius to recognize that the party system, through which the government normally functions, was in complete disarray, that it badly needed repair if it was to continue to serve the needs of a dynamic and heterogeneous society. Not a few times in the conversations of political men the insistence upon change was bluntly expressed. In Richmond, Congressman John Floyd, soon to be governor of Virginia, hopefully predicted at a public dinner given in his honor that a "revolution" would accompany Jackson's election to the presidency. Martin Van Buren would never use such a violent word to convey his opinion, so he settled on "substantial reorganization" to express what he thought the political system required. As dissatisfaction mounted and as the urgency for reform became more palpable, the shrewdest politicians sensed a need to bring the people closer to the government, to root the party not simply in alliances between states or sections or representatives of certain economic interests, but in the great mass of the American electorate. During the next few years several such politicians labored to inaugurate this change. Through fervent appeals to the fears and aspirations of the ordinary citizen, they sought to build a party with a mass following. Their motives for doing so were almost entirely pragmatic; but, whatever their motives, by their actions they advanced the cause of democracy throughout the country. In the process they recast the style and tone of American politics.

The organization of this new party, which later became known as the Democratic party, began with the election of 1828. It proceeded upon two distinct but related levels: the national level, in which alliances were formed between the factions in Congress opposed to the Coalition, campaign funds were raised, a "chain" of newspapers was established and subsidized, and some rather halting and imperfect attempts were made to convene a national convention to nominate the Democratic ticket; and the state level, in which local, county, and state committees were organized to bind the people to the party, and state conventions were summoned to choose a slate of electors and designate the officials responsible for directing the campaign. All of these activities were coordinated by a driving corps of politicians and newspapermen who mobilized a popular majority and fashioned a single, united party.

But a political party is more than an organization of men seeking office and power through the manipulation of the electorate. It should advocate a particular course of governmental action, implemented by a specific program or platform, which it can offer the American people for their approval. Because the Jacksonians were intent upon creating popular support for their candidates, using any technique to accomplish that end and inventing and improvising techniques as they went along, some politicians deliberately fuzzed their position on national issues for the sake of party harmony. But that is not to say they were without a basic concept of government. Several of the most important leaders of the party earnestly sought a reaffirmation of the Jeffersonian principles of states' rights as the fundamental philosophy of the Democratic party. It would take many long years and several more elections before the confusion was completely dispelled (if it ever was) and the organization fully established throughout the country. Nevertheless, in 1828, the essential ingredients of party were inherent in the Democratic organization. However embryonic, they were there. And they endured.

Jacksonians - fuzzed on issues, just wanted to get AS elected.

II

The initial formation of the congressional alliances, out of which the Democratic party eventually emerged, occurred sometime in the winter of 1826-27. The key man in the anticipated realignment of factions was Martin Van Buren, and upon his return to Congress in December he was prepared to "go over" to Jackson—although not openly, not until he was re-elected in February and not until he had the guarantees he wanted. He wrote the Regency reiterating his insistence on a clear understanding with the Jackson men before committing himself. "My language here to our friends," he declared on December 22, 1826, "is that we will support no man who does not come forward on the principles & in the form in which Jefferson & Madison were brought forward & this they will in the end all assent."

Principles and form! In the many letters and papers Van Buren left behind after his death there is not a single document to prove he received the assurances he required. Several suggest that he did and that he received them from Calhoun. However, his words and actions during the campaign, particularly when he stumped the South for Jackson, strongly imply receipted guarantees. "When I had the pleasure of seeing you in Richmond," Thomas Ritchie wrote him a short time later, "I was struck by your views of the benefits which we might promise ourselves from Gen. J's election," benefits like ending the feuds between sections, safeguarding "the rights of States from encroachment" by the central authority, yet securing "to the General Govt all energies needed" to function effectively. On another occasion during this same Southern tour Van Buren told a crowd of Old Republicans in Virginia that the matter of "form" no longer divided the members of Congress, that the "leaders intend to make a nomination in the good old way, by Caucus or Convention, for the next Presidency." Moving along to North Carolina, he assured a vocally appreciative audience that he was unyieldingly committed to "that great political principle . . . a desire to confirm the action of the Federal Government within the limits designed by the framers of the Constitution." Finally, at Charleston, Van Buren toasted the "speedy extinguishment of Sectional and State jealousies—the best and most appropriate sacrifice that can be made upon the altar of State Rights."

The man who actually claimed that Jackson had declared himself a "politician of the Richmond School" was the tall, lean, and energetic editor of the *Enquirer*, Thomas Ritchie. He conceded that the General was not as rigid on "Roads and Tariffs" as the Radicals might like. Nevertheless, the Hero had been thumped on both sides and pronounced politically sound—first, because of his support of the "true literal meaning" of the Constitution and his rejection of "the dangerous doctrine of implication," next, his opposition to "foreign alliances," then his advocacy of "economy in the public disbursements," and finally, his opposition to any "system of [federal] loans."

It is extremely unlikely that Ritchie received anything like a formal or complete declaration of political faith from the Hero. Probably he was given a few general comments by Senator Eaton which he could interpret as he pleased; still, throughout the campaign, he spoke and wrote as though Jackson had bound himself hand and foot to Radical principles. In several letters to the General's closest advisers in Nashville, particularly Major William B. Lewis, Ritchie defined the election as one that must produce "necessary reforms—cleanse the Augean stable—circumscribe the sweep of the Genl. Government within its constitutional limits, and in fact restore the good old Republican era of the Jeffersonian School."

Without being doctrinaire like Ritchie and the other Radicals, Jackson did indeed support the states in all their privileges and prerogatives, just as long as they acknowledged their bond within an indestructible Union. But let them threaten the Union and he would teach them the meaning of treason, rights or no rights. So he did not hesitate to assure Ritchie that he was a Jeffersonian; yet in the next breath he warned the editor against publicly interpreting his words as hostile to "domestic manufactures or internal works." Rather cleverly—and wisely—he welcomed the Radicals into his political house without slamming the door to nationalists or protectionists or Federalists or anyone else who could assist his campaign.

Although Jackson was a great double-talker, basic Jeffersonianism did undergird the Democratic party, at least as far as he, Van Buren, Calhoun, and several of the other major leaders were concerned. Not one of them approved a powerful central government nor advocated an increase of responsibility in Washington at the direct expense of the states. As George Bibb, a party organizer in Kentucky, declared to Representative Felix Grundy, "It is time for every lover of free government to be on the watch, & contribute his might to bring back the Govt. to the plain republican tack. To do this, it is important that the friends of limited constitutional power should unite upon Genl. Jackson as the next Prest."[1]

Van Buren was a lover of free government as well as an advocate

Van Buren

of limited constitutional power. He was also a carefully calculating politician. Hence, when he finally decided that the time had arrived to climb down from his fence and declare openly for the Hero, he arranged a conference late in December 1826 with Vice President Calhoun at the home of William H. Fitzhugh of Virginia. Seated before the Vice President, one leg thrown over the other, his tiny foot swinging aimlessly back and forth, Van Buren offered Radical support to the Jackson-Calhoun factions. He was confident that he could command a high percentage of New York's electoral votes and could influence those of Virginia and Georgia for a total of 59 to 69 electoral ballots. Adding this to the Jackson-Calhoun strength in Tennessee, Pennsylvania, the Carolinas, Alabama, and Mississippi, the total would be raised to 132 or 142, a fraction more than the necessary majority. Furthermore, in order to create this new "Combination" (as the opposition newspapers later called it), Van Buren also promised to swing over the Richmond Junto through Thomas Ritchie and later, after his own re-election to the Senate, to "go to work" and tour the South, seeing all the political "lions" and converting the last remaining Radical holdouts. Possibly in return Van Buren received the assurances that he told his Regency he would demand as the price of his support, though he never said so directly.

Only on one point did the Vice President differ with Van Buren during their conversation. Principles of the Radical variety no longer troubled Calhoun, but he objected to the form which the New York Senator suggested they adopt to nominate the ticket. He disapproved the idea of convening another congressional caucus, proposing instead that they sponsor the first national nominating convention. Although Van Buren preferred the "good old way" used by Jefferson, Madison, and Monroe, he did not argue the matter. The caucus had been thoroughly repudiated in 1824, and only a stubborn politician would insist upon reactivating it. He was "not tenacious," he wrote, "whether we have a congressional caucus or a general convention, so that we have either." A meeting, in whatever form, would unite the several factions, he said, eliminate "personal preference," and "draw anew the old Party lines."

When the conference between Van Buren and Calhoun ended, the Magician promised to write to Thomas Ritchie and bring him into the alliance. First, however, he would show the letter to both the Vice President and Representative Samuel D. Ingham, "the pamphleteer and the manager-general of the Jackson party in Pennsylvania," and incorporate any suggestions they cared to offer. This said, Van Buren took his leave. Calhoun rose, extended his hand, and the two men "united heart and hand" to defeat John Quincy Adams.

A few weeks later Van Buren presented his letter to the two men for their inspection and approval. In it he urged Ritchie and his Junto to join him, not simply to defeat Adams but to achieve "what is of still greater importance, the substantial reorganization of the old Republican party." Were the General, he said, to succeed on account of his military reputation alone, without reference to principle or party, his victory would be in vain. But his election "as the result of a combined and concerted effort of a political party, holding in the main to certain tenets & opposed to certain prevailing principles, might be another and far different thing." The New York Senator argued for a revival of the two-party system based upon the old divisions between Republicans and Federalists. He called for a renewal of Jefferson's alliance between New York and Virginia, between the North and the South, between what he termed the "planters of the South and plain Republicans of the North." The country once flourished under such a system, he said, "& may again."

According to Van Buren's sectional interpretation, the new Jackson party would rest upon a North-South coalition. (And he did not hesitate to remind Ritchie that such a coalition would help quiet "the clamour against Southern Influence and African slavery" when it arose in the North.) Other Jacksonians, notably Calhoun and Thomas Hart Benton, were more inclined to a South-West alliance, but as it subsequently developed, the Radical group proved the strongest, most loyal, and most stable segment of the Jackson organization. Their principles, therefore, tended to become the basic doctrine of the emerging Democratic party.[2]

Like any politician of the day who expected to retain his influence in national politics, Ritchie was forced to take sides. Apart from the cogency of Van Buren's arguments and the implication that the new combination would reassert "certain tenets," what finally jolted the Virginian into accepting Jackson as his candidate in 1828 was John Randolph's defeat for re-election to the Senate by the more sober-sided John Tyler. Tyler's victory was cheered by the Administration as a "signal triumph," but it threw "Ritchie into hystericks." In the spring of 1827 his "hystericks" spilled into the columns of the *Enquirer* when he formally declared his support of Jackson. "An opposition is now organized," he trumpeted, "upon the high grounds of the Constitution, and the interest of the country, which is destined to dash the Coalition to pieces." He summoned the Radical party in Virginia and the rest of the South to unite with him behind the Hero of New Orleans.

The decision of Ritchie and Van Buren sent a horde of New York and Virginia Radicals trooping into the Jackson army. Not only did they swell the ranks of their new party but they brought with them their special skills, their professionalism as politicians, and their grasping ambition. "Between the Regency at Albany and the junto at Richmond," observed Calhoun just a few years earlier, "there is a vital connection. They give and receive hope from each other, and confidently expect to govern this nation." But to govern this nation in 1828, that "vital connection" now had to be extended to include still another junto, this one located in Nashville, Tennessee, and consisting of Jackson's closest personal advisers. First among those advisers was Judge John Overton, a bank president, planter, and lawyer and once reputed to be the wealthiest man in the state; Major William B. Lewis came next, a tall, powerful-looking man, who was known as Jackson's "home confederate"; then Senator John H. Eaton, the General's "traveling confederate," amanuensis, and general handy man around the political plantation; also Felix Grundy, a stocky, beetle-browed, rough-and-tumble Congressman, who composed or revised many of Jackson's public communications when Eaton was off on tour; and Sam Houston, one of Jackson's most promising protégés.

No sooner did Van Buren declare for Jackson than word of it was transmitted to the Nashville Junto by several observers. The Senator's conversion was "in all good faith," Houston wrote the Hero. ". . . Your friends who know him best are satisfied as to his course, and pleased with it." Although Van Buren was on fairly friendly terms with Eaton and Grundy and would soon attempt to cultivate

Houston's friendship, his best contact with the Nashville crowd came through Alfred Balch, a Tennessee lawyer and former Radical, who used his growing influence with Jackson to advance Van Buren's reputation and prestige. Several years later Balch admitted that he made "no terms with mortal man when the interests of Van Buren are brought in question. For ten years—even whilst the old Crawfordites lay in the ditch totally overthrown, I have laboured for him incessantly night & day 'in season and out of season' as the apostle saith."

To strengthen the Albany-Nashville connection beyond what Balch could accomplish, Van Buren immediately began a correspondence with Major Lewis. Six months later he was in direct communication with Jackson himself. Leaving no avenue unexplored, he also dispatched one of his friends, James A. Hamilton, the son of Alexander Hamilton, to Nashville with instructions to improve relations between the two organizations, to keep him informed of developments in Tennessee as they occurred, and to assure the Hero of his patriotism, good will, and personal loyalty.[3]

Meanwhile the Richmond politicians became better acquainted with their new friends in Nashville. John Eaton and Felix Grundy were the first men to be contacted. "I wish you would communicate my views to Eaton," David Campbell advised James Campbell in November 1827, "and such others as you think proper." Ritchie, of course, immediately got in touch with Major Lewis, while other members of the Richmond clique corresponded with Sam Houston and one or two lesser advisers in Jackson's council, such as Tom Claiborne.

Apart from encouraging more cordial relations between the Albany, Richmond, and Nashville managers, Van Buren also tried to persuade the entire corps of Southern Radicals to follow him into Jackson's camp. His best contacts with North Carolina politicians came through Senator Nathaniel Macon and Representative Romulus Saunders. Through Saunders he gained access to Bartlett Yancey and Governor Hutchins G. Burton, both important operators in North Carolina. "Rest assured," Saunders informed Yancey, "that [Jackson] is the man that alone can be run with success. . . . I have had several free conversations with Van Buren."

In these conversations—not only with Saunders but later during

his tour with Yancey and Burton—the New Yorker artfully dispelled
their fears and doubts about the General and what he stood for.
More than that, he reminded them that if they did not take Jackson
they would be stuck with Adams. "The old Republicans are in a
state of betweenity," sighed Governor Burton, "but I expect will
have to holler for 'Old Hickory' however much against the grain."
Most of the Southern Radicals, under the prodding of Van Buren,
Ritchie, and others, eventually swung around to the Hero, for as
Saunders told Yancey, the period of neutrality had ended.

To hurry the Radicals along, Van Buren began a grand tour of
the South in March 1827. Along the route he conferred with all the
"lions" of Savannah, Charleston, Raleigh, and Richmond. In Georgia, he wheedled William Crawford into accepting the alliance
despite the presence of Calhoun; in South Carolina, he flattered
Thomas Cooper into thinking that his imprecations against the
tariff would be heeded; in North Carolina, he nudged Governor
Burton further away from his state of "betweenity"; and in Virginia, he renewed his earlier promises with Ritchie about the
"benefits" they would receive from the Hero's victory. Everywhere
he went he was met with courtesy and good will. ". . . As soon as we
can get out of the hospital [sic] hands of our friend Burton," he
wrote ahead to Littleton W. Tazewell of Virginia, "[we will] make
the rest of our way homeward. By Sunday we confidently expect
to be at Richmond & sincerely hope to have the pleasure of meeting you there."

In creating—or, more properly, revitalizing—this North-South
combination, Van Buren had help from other politicians, most
notably John C. Calhoun. While the New Yorker paraded through
Georgia, charming Southerners with his manners and Republican
orthodoxy, the Vice President made several quick trips to North
Carolina, one of them to participate in a public dinner given in
honor of Romulus Saunders. Shortly thereafter, Saunders declared
for the Hero. At another dinner—a more private affair—Calhoun
zeroed in on Willie P. Mangum, the Radical Senator from North
Carolina. "Mangum, Mangum," said the surprisingly effusive Calhoun as he seized the startled Senator's hand and hung on, "do—do
sir, call and see me frequently and spend some of your evenings
with us—without ceremony—come sir. We shall always be glad to
see you, and bring any friend with you."

By the time Calhoun, Van Buren, Saunders, Ritchie, and others completed their self-imposed assignments, four Southern states—the Carolinas, Georgia, and Virginia—were reasonably safe for Jackson and would award him fifty-nine electoral votes.

It was a solid beginning. Yet not everyone was impressed. "Is Martin progressing in his grand Plan of a General resurrection of the dry bones of democracy," asked one Coalitionist half in jest, "or is this a Scheme to which he has consulted his inclination without measuring his Powers?"[4]

The answer came in 1828.

III

The work of Calhoun, Ritchie, and Van Buren was essential to the creation of a new national party, but without the name, reputation, popularity, leadership, and political wisdom of Andrew Jackson, they were all wasting their time. From the very beginning of the attempts to organize an opposition, the Hero was the head of the party—without question and without doubt.

At his home in Tennessee the General carefully watched the events occurring in Washington through the information supplied him by a corps of devoted Congressmen. The "various communications from Eaton White and Houston," he wrote, "with a great run of company has occupied all my time." Although he had voluntarily relinquished his Senate seat and presumably had retired from public life, Jackson was a busy man, attending to his voluminous correspondence, meeting the delegations of politicians who called upon him regularly, and generally keeping himself in the public eye as the innocent victim of the corrupt bargain. He was the first presidential candidate to engage actively and publicly in his own campaign, violating what many regarded as a near-sacred tradition among presidential aspirants to remain silent during the canvass. "I regretted," he wrote to one friend, "that . . . so much of my time was taken up by the calls of my friends abroad, and here, for documents and statements." As he became more active and more vocal in directing the campaign, several party leaders, including Van Buren and Eaton, urged him to be "still," implying that his conduct was most unseemly. "Candidates for the Presidency," pontificated one Radical, ". . . ought not to say one word on the subject of the election. Washington, Jefferson, & Madison were as silent as the grave when they were before the American people for this office."

But Jackson had special problems in seeking the presidency. It was difficult for him as a man without office to engage public interest in his candidacy without violating that tradition. Despite his popularity as a great national hero, he knew from his experience in 1824 that popularity alone was not enough to capture the White House, at least not while sinister men lurked in the corridors of the Congress. Aside from that, when his wife was viciously slandered in the newspapers, "it was more than my mind could bear to hear it, and not redress it", he argued, "with that punishment it deserved."

During 1827 and 1828 hardly a month passed without the newspapers printing a long letter by the General answering some charge brought against his public and private life. Many of these letters, it is true, were written by others. Since Jackson had a rare talent for mangling the English language, he had to exercise extreme caution in releasing statements for publication lest they prove the Coalition's contention that his "illiteracy" disqualified him for the presidency. Nevertheless, most of these letters were written under his supervision or were the corrected versions of his own compositions. Writing, he admitted, was "laborious," but like the fiercely determined man he was he kept working at it, asking his many friends for editorial assistance. Painfully, he struggled to improve his communications with the public, and in the end he succeeded admirably. Adams, on the other hand, was dismayingly inarticulate, despite a Harvard degree.[5]

Like all sensible politicians, Jackson sought the widest possible audience for his opinions and public statements. By the last year of the campaign he had become expert in reaching every quarter of the Union where his ideas could be used to advantage. For example, in March 1828 he instructed Major William Lewis to send "one hundred extras [of a newspaper containing an important pronouncement] to every printer & Jackson Committee [in] Ohio, Indiana, Illinois, Mississippi, Louisiana, and Alabama—and to the north Pennsylvania, Virginia, Maryland, New Jersey, New York and New Hampshire. Those you may send me I shall distribute in Virginia and Kentucky," he added.

In seeking this publicity the General operated directly through correspondence committees in the states, newspaper editors, congressional leaders, and—most important of all—his own Central Committee in Nashville. This Committee, called the "White-washing Committee" by the friends of the Administration, was set up in the spring of 1827 for the avowed purpose of detecting and arresting "falsehoods and calumny, by the publication of truth, and by furnishing either to the public or to individuals, whether alone or associated, full and correct information upon any matter or subject within their knowledge or power, properly connected with the fitness or qualification of Andrew Jackson to fill the office of President of the United States." Major Lewis put it more succinctly. The Central Committee was formed, he told the Ohio party, "for the purpose of corresponding with other Jackson committees in the different sections of the union."

The announcement of the Committee's formation sent the Administration newspapers bawling their indignation. "When its organization was first announced," raged the Washington *National Journal* on May 22, "it struck us as a matter of surprise, that any man, presenting himself to the nation as a candidate for the chief magistry, should think it necessary to form so extraordinary an association for the purpose of promoting his views." But for an astute politician like Jackson there was nothing extraordinary about it at all. Aside from "promoting his views," it also helped to unite the state organizations, after they formed, into something resembling a national party.

Of the eighteen members comprising the Central Committee, Overton, Lewis, Balch, George W. Campbell, Tom Claiborne, John Catron, Robert Whyte, John McNairy, William L. Brown, and Robert C. Foster, who sometimes acted as the "chairman pro tem.", were the most important. In letters introducing these men to the Central Committees of the other states, Lewis described Overton as "an old & intimate friend" of the General; Campbell, he ventured, "is well known to the nation"; Foster, in March 1827, was the speaker of the Tennessee senate; Whyte and Catron were two judges of the state supreme court; Brown was a former judge and "now at the head of the Bar"; while McNairy was the federal district judge for western Tennessee. The activities of this Committee, though normally directed by Overton and Lewis, were carefully superintended by Jackson himself. "I should have been down this week to have seen you," he wrote Lewis early in May 1827, "but . . . I do not wish to be seen mingling with the members of the Committee, *now*." Shortly thereafter he was in full command of their operations. For example, when he was accused of participation in the Burr Conspiracy, he snapped his friends to attention. "If the Committee are not ready to come out (if they do intend)," he said, "the great necessity that some notice should be taken in todays Republican [newspaper]. . . . This will give time for me to make an address to the public, but the Committee under all circumstances ought to say something on the subject first."

Along with directing the Central Committee and the Junto, Jackson frequently assigned specific tasks to his friends in Congress. On one occasion, when a partisan informed him that an Ohio newspaperman named Charles Hammond had been to Kentucky to see Henry Clay to gather materials for a low-swinging broadside, the General asked Eaton in Washington to check into it. Eaton confronted the scowling Clay with a demand for an explanation, but the Secretary had no idea what the Senator was talking about. Clay frankly admitted seeing Hammond in Lexington but denied giving the editor any documentary information. However, when Hammond later published an article charging Mrs. Jackson with adultery, the General was certain that Clay was responsible. At another time Jackson asked Sam Houston, on his return to Congress, to question a Dr. Wallace and a Colonel Grey about a statement made by the Secretary of the Navy, Samuel Southard, at a dinner in Fredericksburg, Virginia. Houston was to obtain the statement in writing, retain the original, and forward a copy to Nashville. This done, Houston was told to present himself to Southard, hand the Secretary a note from Jackson, and wait for a reply. Do this quickly, commanded the Hero, for the Department heads had been "secretely [*sic*] intimating slanderous things of me. This I mean to expose, and put down, one after the other, as I can obtain the positive proof."

Jackson also had a small band of men traveling through the country eagerly campaigning for him. They conferred with state leaders, kept tabs on organizational developments, and reported their findings directly to the General or to the Central Committee. "In N. York I saw many of your friends in various parts of the State," wrote John Eaton, the Hero's chief roving ambassador. "I was in Ohio some time . . . and in Indiana." Major Henry Lee was another "circulating medium" who scouted the Middle Atlantic and New England states and submitted comprehensive reports on party operations in Connecticut and New York. Occasionally the work of the "mediums" was supplemented by local leaders. Caleb Atwater of Ohio, for example, took a carefully planned excursion through the Eastern and Northeastern states, following a long and confidential meeting with Jackson at the Hermitage. "I have visited our friends every where," he told the Hero. Later, Duff Green, Calhoun, Clinton, Edward Livingston, Thomas Ritchie, Samuel D. Ingham, and others stumped various sections of the country, each submitting statements of their success to Lewis, Overton, Jackson, or the Central Committee.[6]

In directing all these varied activities, the General committed only one serious blunder. He still remembered James Buchanan's confused story about a bargain, the details of which he sent to Duff Green, editor of the *Telegraph*, with instructions to investigate. Green contacted Buchanan and asked if he had been authorized by Clay to approach Jackson with an offer. Buchanan replied that he had had no such authorization, and requested that the unfortunate incident be forgotten. He said he was making excellent progress in organizing the Jackson party in Pennsylvania and did not wish to be "provoked into a public statement." Green accepted the disclaimer and agreed to let the thing alone. But not Jackson. Every politician who visited him at the Hermitage he chilled with a dramatic account of the dark deed. According to the General, a "congressman of high respectability" came to him in the dead of night with an offer from Clay's friends. Like the pure-of-heart he was, he "indignantly" rejected the offer. So he was cheated of the presidency.

One of the men who heard Jackson's tale of corruption in high places was a Virginian named Carter Beverley who later published the story in the Fayetteville *Observer* in North Carolina. Demands for confirmation followed, and the General, always ready to remind the people of his and their betrayal, replied in a letter to Beverley dated June 5, 1827, in which he confirmed the essential points of the story. Henry Clay answered this with a "direct, unqualified, and indignant denial" of the charges, swearing that no friend of his had been authorized to approach Jackson on any matter.

As the furor mounted, there were calls for the name of the "congressman of high respectability." Never one to duck a challenge, Jackson named James Buchanan and claimed that Buchanan told him—and also told Eaton and Kremer—that the Adams men had definitely offered Clay the State Department in exchange for House votes.

Now it was up to Buchanan to confirm or deny Jackson's words. Now he must pay the price for his stupid meddling. On August 8, 1827, he addressed a letter to the editor of the Lancaster *Journal*, reconciling, as far as he was able, the points of conflict between what actually happened and what Jackson reported. But no matter how he tried to shield the Hero behind a flimsy veil of words, the gist of his letter was his reasonably clear denial that emissaries from Clay ever came to him with an offer. Earlier, he told Green he had no authority from Clay or Clay's friends to go to Jackson on any matter. Yet the impression he left with the General—an impression no one could have missed, insisted the Hero—was that he represented the Kentuckian.

Jackson was livid with rage over the letter. The blinking, sniveling, little busybody had dared to trifle with him. "The outrageous statement of Mr. Buchanan will require my attention," he threatened. Meanwhile the unhappy meddler, who really meant no harm, apologized profusely to the Hero. "I regret beyond expression," he wrote, "that you believed me to be an emissary from Mr. Clay. Since some time . . . I have been your ardent, decided, & perhaps without vanity I may say, your efficient friend." Indeed, he was an efficient friend and too important to the Pennsylvania party to be reprimanded or (as some demanded) expelled from Jackson's ranks. So the Hero calmed down and the Nashville Junto agreed to "touch" Buchanan's statement with "tenderness" in order to "preserve his friendship and needful influence." The task of applying the tender touch was turned over to Eaton, who, in a letter to the public dated September 12, 1827, contradicted nothing Buchanan had written except the time of the interview.

The unfortunate outcome of this incident in no way lessened Jackson's enthusiasm to charge into the public prints whenever he could lash the Coalition with the sharp words of one of his assistants. Besides initiating, supervising, or approving public letters, pamphlets, and handbills and studying the findings of his "travelling corpsmen," the General personally kept up a vast correspondence with state leaders and Congressmen. He was the natural center of the party organizations just beginning to emerge in each community to block Adams' re-election. "I have given you the annexed list," wrote one of his correspondents, "for the purpose of enabling you, if you should think proper, to write to certain men in this state, and at the same time, to give you the best data now at command, from which to estimate your present strength in Kentucky." If the Hero did not himself write to these "certain men," most assuredly someone on the Committee did so in his behalf.[7]

At first, few of Jackson's contemporaries recognized what a superb politician he really was, a politician straight to the bone whose natural instincts for the game were probably refined by his many years in the army. Even historians have failed to credit him sufficiently for his political astuteness. Not only do they downgrade his importance in conducting this election, but during his administration, later on, they tend to overemphasize Van Buren's role in shaping public policy, especially in the Bank War and in the decision to read John C. Calhoun out of the party. Actually Jackson's control of his own administration was unshared with any other public officer.

Very early in this campaign—even before he was formally renominated by the Tennessee legislature—the Hero made it clear that he regarded himself as the candidate of the people, as the man "taken up" by the electorate to defend justice and virtue, as a popular champion sent against an entrenched elite who viewed the government as a private operation restricted to certified gentlemen. There was nothing hypocritical or cynical in this pose. He sincerely believed what he said. Probably most really good politicians think this way, whether true or not, and in Jackson's case there was more than an element of truth in what he said.

There was also a touch of craft and guile in the old General. No sooner did Calhoun and Van Buren draw close to him than Jackson began repeating that he was much too old and ill to serve *two* terms as President. (He was sixty in 1827, the same age as John Quincy Adams.) Four years as chief executive was all he wanted; then he would turn the reins of government over to younger men. His protestations of feebleness had Calhoun quivering with anticipation, to say nothing of Martin Van Buren. Perhaps the Hero meant what he said; but whether he did or not, his words were perfectly calculated to swell the loyalties of several important and ambitious men in Washington.

Jackson always insisted that he would not electioneer for the presidency, but every letter he wrote, every delegation of visitors he entertained at the Hermitage, every politician he sent off on an assignment in different sections of the nation, was part of a careful campaign to wrest the presidency from John Quincy Adams. His trip to New Orleans in January 1828 to celebrate his victory over the British was electioneering in the grand manner. Ostensibly nonpartisan, the celebration happily combined national pride in a great historical event with the political ambitions of the man who was responsible for that event.

Around this popular and politically wise old gentleman other men were now constructing a new national party; yet as long as he lived Andrew Jackson remained its head and vital force.

IV

As Van Buren had promised earlier, once re-elected to the Senate in February 1827 he really got down to the work of forging a "new political combination." Characteristically, he began his task by calling a series of conferences among Jacksonian Congressmen, where, according to one opposition report, "schemes [were] devised, questions debated & the minority was ruled by the majority." It was said that the conferees agreed to commence their "labors" to elect

Jackson on July 4, 1827, "in every part of the Union at once." There may have been no such agreement as reported, but conferences were held and the formal canvass did begin on the assigned date. "Little squads in the North and East, West and South," in recognition of Independence Day, "made toasts of egregious length" to the election of Old Hickory and to the restoration of liberty.

Present at Van Buren's conferences were representatives from most of the large states, including Calhoun; Senators Benton, Eaton, Dickerson of New Jersey, Johnson of Kentucky, and McLane of Delaware; and Representatives Buchanan, Moore, Ingham, and Houston. Reportedly, they met several times a week, although that sounds a bit excessive even for such a caucus-minded politician as Van Buren. Whatever the frequency, the meetings were extremely fruitful in initiating plans for the "substantial reorganization of the old Republican party."

As soon as the congressional conferences were under way, new lines of communication were opened between Washington and the Nashville Central Committee, principally through the good offices of Alfred Balch. The letters that Balch received from Van Buren, Benton, and others kept the Central Committee abreast of breaking developments on Capitol Hill. Not a few times a select group of Jacksonians held private conversations in Washington to improve campaign strategy, the essentials of which were forwarded to Nashville through Balch. "I have talked with V. B. & others," read one of Benton's communiqués, "[and] they think as I do" about the Central Committee's issuing policy statements. If a "friend," he hypothesized, should ask the Committee about Jackson's views on internal improvements, that "friend" should be made to realize that "there is no necessity for any public answer." If an "enemy" should ask, and do so in such a "respectable" way as to make an answer "indispensable, we think it ought to be given rather by a *general* reference to the votes given by J——— in the Senate than by a *particular* confession of faith." Of course, Benton, Van Buren, and the other Congressmen admitted that the public had a right to know the "political sentiments of a public man," but the "delicacy" of "declaring those sentiments on the eve of an election might be stated," advised Benton. In any event, put them off by referring them to Jackson's record in the Senate; and never forget, he con-

cluded, that newspaper questions deserve only "newspaper answers."[8]

In addition to these congressional conferences and caucus ses-
sions, a Central Committee of twenty-four men was formed in
Washington early in the campaign as a clearinghouse for much of
the propaganda emanating from the House and the Senate. The
Committee's meetings were usually held at Williamson's or Carusi's
Assembly Rooms, with only eight men necessary for a quorum.
The chairman was the president of the Bank of the Metropolis in
Washington, General John P. Van Ness. Van Ness originally came
from Van Buren's home town of Kinderhook, New York; his brother
had been one of the Magician's law tutors as well as Aaron Burr's
second in the duel with Alexander Hamilton; and he himself had
contributed financially to Van Buren's legal training. His own family always regarded Van Ness as something of a ne'er-do-well
destined for a tragic end; but he fooled them: he married a Washington fortune and returned to Kinderhook in high feather. Later,
he settled in the District, built a magnificent house designed by
Benjamin Latrobe, and helped in the organization of the Jackson
party by backing the 3,000-dollar note for the *Telegraph* signed by
Senator Eaton. However, the most important member of this Committee was not Van Ness but General Duff Green, that rough-
writing editor who stomped and bit and abused the President so
fiercely. Green was ordinarily a jovial sort, a capital storyteller
and a pleasant host; but, despite his many "noble qualities," especially as an editor and party organizer, he was overly vain and
opinionated and later (after the election) liked to give the impression "that he is the ruler of the nation." Other members of the
Committee included Thomas Corcoran, a dry-goods merchant and
former mayor of Georgetown; Dr. Thomas Sim, the Committee's
secretary; Richard Mason; General Steward; and Colonel Ashton.
On the whole, these men performed yeoman service in keeping the
state organizations stocked with propaganda pamphlets published in
the capital; but their real day of glory came later, when they organized a tradition-shattering demonstration of popular enthusiasm
for Jackson at the Hero's inauguration.

While Green, Van Ness, and company at times looked and acted
as though they comprised a National Committee, it was really the

Jacksonian Congressmen in caucus who served that function. Not only did these Congressmen work closely with the Nashville managers, but they also raised money, founded and subsidized newspapers, and distributed campaign literature under their personal frank. Most important of all, however, they forged the essential political "combinations for electing Gen. Jackson"—so said Representative John Floyd of Virginia, who participated in the forging. And, by the spring of 1827, he advised his Virginia cronies that those "combinations" were "nearly complete."

Partly by design and partly by accident, Floyd's words leaked to the Administration newspapers, and a horrendous cry went up about the "unnatural alliances" being concluded in Washington "under the standard of a new cabalistic party organization." "Combinations—and among whom?" they asked. "The People? No—but the Members of Congress." Despite the leak, Floyd neither denied nor retracted the statement attributed to him. Instead, he boasted of it. At a public dinner given in his honor at Richmond a few weeks later, he proclaimed "a great political revolution in progress" which would be consummated in the election of Andrew Jackson.

Floyd's use of the word "combination" gave the Administration newspapers a needed name for the Jackson-Calhoun-Van Buren alliance. The Adams press used it extensively during the campaign in the hope it would connote something sinister or undemocratic, but they were not too successful in this and the name never really caught on. Most often the factions allied against the Coalition were called simply "Jacksonians" or the "Opposition." Once in a while there were references to the "Democratic" Republican party as distinct from the Adams-Clay "National" Republican party. However, not until two or three years later did the designation "Democratic party" acquire universal usage. By that time it referred to the triumphant organization structured around President Andrew Jackson.

V

Now that the Adams newspapers were privy to the so-called "combinations," they demanded to know on what terms the agreement had been arranged, apparently without realizing that the sole condition required by some men was certainty over Jackson's ability to win the election. These editors jumped to the conclusion, of course, that Van Buren was the only politician slick enough to unite so many disparate groups. "The masterspirit with his magic wand," they said, "cast a spell over the heterogeneous mass, and the wolves and kids mingled together in peace and love!" But how long would this love-spell last? Can Senator Dickerson, the advocate of protection, cooperate with his Southern colleagues, asked the *National Journal?* Can John Randolph and Littleton W. Tazewell unite with the men whose opinions on improvements collide with their own? "Can the Tennessee and Kentucky and Virginia Hotspurs long coalesce with their new allies who desire to oust the present Administration because of alleged hostility to federal men and federal measures?" Surely such excellent men as McLane, Ingham, Buchanan, Houston, Drayton, and Macon, continued these editors, owed it to the public to "announce the terms and conditions of the agreement that has been made."

There were indeed many differences of opinion dividing the Jackson men, both in and out of Congress. The problem of settling on terms and conditions was complicated by the necessity of creating a national voting majority out of a patchwork of conflicting interest groups, classes, and factions. These groups ranged from farmers and mechanics to planters, businessmen, and bankers. They included Republicans and Federalists, nationalists and states' righters, conservatives and liberals. Some Jacksonians in Pennsylvania, New York, Ohio, Indiana, and Kentucky called for a protective tariff, a system of national roads and improvements, and the continued support of the Second National Bank; others, often from the same states, objected to these proposals and urged a freer capitalistic system, unhampered by governmental controls.

Undoubtedly, if these Congressmen had attempted a settlement on national issues, the alliances would have been stillborn. Because they represented a wide range of diverse interests among coalescing Jacksonians, no basic statement of purpose and direction seemed wise or feasible. Their first objective was to win the election, nothing more. What the Administration editors by their questions were really trying to do, therefore, was prove to the public that the Democrats were irresponsible opportunists bound together by little else than a will to oust Adams, even if that meant supporting an incompetent and illiterate military chieftain.

The problem of the Jacksonian Congressmen was, to a degree, solved by the General himself. When asked specifically about certain issues, he responded by following one of several alternatives: either he took Benton's advice and referred to his voting record in the Senate, or he refused a direct answer on the ground that it might be interpreted as electioneering (and no gentleman would ever electioneer for the presidency), or he wrote long, highly ambiguous replies that could be interpreted several ways, or he ignored the question and simply struck a pose as the Hero of New Orleans cheated of the presidency in 1825.

A) ambiguous on issues

Yet for all his double talk and concern for his public image, Jackson did subscribe to a national program, one he vaguely alluded to during the campaign (very vaguely) but one he later outlined in detail to Amos Kendall, editor of the Kentucky _Argus of the West_. As he subsequently defined. it, his program was neo-Jeffersonian and conservative, leaning toward states' rights and the economics of laissez-faire, but so bland and inoffensive that those previously disposed to follow him could not seriously object to a single point.

In the first place, Jackson told Kendall, he intended to reduce the patronage of the federal government. (By interpreting his words as loosely as the rules of language allow, this could mean a policy of economy, though the General did not say so specifically.) The Hero believed that Adams had used the patronage to pay off the men responsible for "stealing" the presidency in 1825, a belief documented to his entire satisfaction by the report on executive appointments submitted to the Senate by Thomas Hart Benton. Hence, Jackson saw as his first duty the wholesale removal of these Coalitionists, along with anyone else who campaigned for Adams' re-election. "All men in office," he assured Kendall, "who are known to have interferred in the election as committee men, electioneers or otherwise . . . will be unceremoniously removed. So also will all men who have been appointed from political considerations or against the will of the people, and all who are incompetent." Throughout the campaign this issue became a favorite theme with Jacksonian editors and politicians, who assured the people that the removals were necessary in order to "purify the Departments" and "reform the Government." "Let the cry be JACKSON and RE-FORM," they thundered. But obviously the word "reform" was hardly more than a euphemism for political head-chopping.

Next, Jackson informed Kendall that he favored a "middle and just course" with respect to the tariff question. As he had stated several years before in a letter to Littleton H. Coleman, he thought the rates of protection should be "judicious," a remark that prompted Henry Clay to declare his preference for an "*injudicious*" tariff. In an Albany speech Martin Van Buren seconded Jackson's position by calling for a tariff that would be "wise" and "just" and "salutary." One man in the audience cheered the speech and then turned to his neighbor and asked: "On which side of the Tariff question was it?"[9]

Jackson may have preferred the "middle course"—wherever that was—but his friends frequently reshaped his preference to conform to local prejudice. In "protection-mad" Pennsylvania, Samuel D. Ingham assured his people that Old Hickory would "raise the tariff everytime he touched it." Yet in the South the Richmond *Enquirer* and the Raleigh *Register*, among others, expressed amazement that anyone could claim Jackson as a friend of protection. He favored a tariff, they wrote, only as a source of revenue and a means of strengthening the national defense and liquidating the national debt. Any other interpretation was unjustified. To clarify the matter the Indiana legislature pressed Jackson during the campaign for a more precise declaration, but the General refused to be drawn out. "Not, sir, that I would wish to conceal my opinions from the people upon any political, or national subject," the foxy Hero replied, "but as they were in various ways promulgated in 1824, I am apprehensive that my appearance before the public, at this time, may be attributed, as has been the case, to improper motives." The Hoosiers were delighted with his clarification and expressed their complete satisfaction with it. One report insisted that it even converted three Adams committees within the state!

The General did not double-talk all the issues, however. Regarding federally sponsored public works, he straightforwardly admitted his opposition. Then he modified his statement slightly by proposing to distribute surplus revenues to the states to permit them to undertake their own improvements. After all, the issue was important to the people of Kentucky, Ohio, Indiana, and Illinois, and it was necessary to relieve their minds about his intentions without antagonizing, at the same time, the people of New York and Virginia. Once again his attitude about the question was reshaped to accord with varying sectional opinions. In Pennsylvania, Jackson's partisans went so far as to declare that "His triumph will give expansion to the 'American System.'"

The final point in his program was the most startling of all. He actually told Kendall he was looking for "plain, business men" to assist him in running his administration. Presumably, these hardheaded realists would help restore the government to fiscal and ethical soundness. No Cabinet officer, he concluded, could be a candidate for President, and all members must concur in his "policies."

One additional policy might be added to this list, though Jackson did not include it himself. It concerned the Indians and their removal to the West, an issue that developed when Georgia renewed her efforts to despoil the Creek Nation. When President Adams negotiated a treaty with the Creeks by which the Indians were to cede their land in Georgia except for a strip west of the Chattahoochee River, Governor George M. Throup of Georgia objected. He wanted all the land. Defying both the President and the Secretary of War, he threatened to use his militia if they attempted to carry out the terms of the treaty. Adams responded to the verbal cannonade by vowing to employ "all means under his control to maintain the faith of the nation."

Jackson, whose affection for the Indian about equaled his affection for Henry Clay, unreservedly endorsed the policy of total removal. "Say to them [the Indians]," he once wrote, "their Father, the President will lay off a country of equal extent, transport them to it . . . and give them a free [sic] simple title to the land." But, as the General's friends in Georgia understood only too well, it was less important to tell the Indians anything than it was to assure the electorate of the Hero's commitment to removal.

Meanwhile the Jacksonian-controlled Senate appointed a committee, headed by Thomas Hart Benton, to investigate the Administration's trouble with Governor Throup. As expected, Benton's final report faulted the government for its unwarranted interference in the internal affairs of Georgia and justified everything the governor had been "compelled" to do to protect the interests of his state. But long before Benton's report was published, Adams was "politically dead" in Georgia, and the stench arising from the corpse permeated the entire Southwest. In the Georgia 1828 race, both sets of electors pledged themselves to Jackson.

These policies, as Jackson liked to call them, revealed his excellence as a politician of compromise and accommodation; they explain in part why so many discordant groups could unite behind him in his campaign for the presidency, why the wolves and kids could mingle together in peace and love. For some people, of course, the issues had nothing to do with their decision to join the General's party. Far more important than a meaningless program was the energy, leadership, and exciting personality they felt Jackson could bring to the presidency—qualities that make history, not simply wait upon it. Others had an even more basic reason for supporting the Hero. He "is the man," commented one politician, "that alone can be run with success."[10]

VI

Perhaps the single most important accomplishment of the Democrats in Congress and in the states was the creation of a vast, nation-wide newspaper system. The initiative and drive for this enterprise came from Congressmen, but the work was aided by governors, state legislators, county leaders, and politicians of every rank. Together, they strove to paper the country with enough propaganda to wrap the Coalitionists in defeat.

In one of their earliest sessions, Democratic Congressmen in caucus reportedly agreed to establish "a chain of newspaper posts, from the New England States to Louisiana, and branching off through Lexington to the Western States." While the report was exaggerated, if not invented, it is nonetheless true that an enormous number of new journals did appear in virtually every state—certainly in every section. North Carolina politicians, for instance, started nine new Jackson sheets by the summer of 1827, and in Ohio eighteen were added to the five that existed in 1824. During a single six-month period three papers were founded in Indiana and several were organized in Pennsylvania, Massachusetts, New Jersey, and Illinois. Even Mississippi came up with another organ, only to have it slip out of existence within a few weeks despite the pleas for financial help mailed to other states under the frank of Jacksonian Congressmen.

"We have at considerable expense," boasted Senator Levi Woodbury, "established another newspaper in the northern part of the state of New Hampshire. We have organized our fences in every quarter and have begun & shall continue without ceasing to pour into every doubtful region all kinds of useful information." Several other Congressmen either powered new publications into life or sustained those in danger of faltering. A Virginia Representative, for example, circulated a prospectus to party organizers in eastern Tennessee asking them to obtain subscribers for a journal in Lynchburg; at the same time Senator John Eaton poured 1,500 dollars into the tottering *Columbia Observer* in Philadelphia to keep it yapping at the President's heels. Most other Democratic Congressmen contributed or solicited funds, wrote articles under a favorite disguise, or supplied news and information to help the newspapers mount a driving campaign.

Snapping with irritation, established prints complained of the "mushroom rapidity" with which these new journals suddenly popped up, and the choking cost of maintaining them. By 1828 there were an estimated 600 newspapers in the United States, 50 of them dailies, 150 semi-weeklies, and 400 weeklies. The cost of publication for all these papers, approximating 1,000 copies of each, was placed at a half-million dollars per annum. Still they poured out. Each month a raft of publications flooded the reading market in all forms: newspapers, books, pamphlets, addresses, biographies,

½ million$ worth of campaign literature.

and throwaways. "I had a meeting of 12 or 15 friends . . . at my house last night," bragged one politician to a crony in Congress, "& arrangements were made to publish and distribute extensively some of the best things that have appeared against the administration and in favour of Genl. Jackson."[11]

The willingness of the Jacksonians to assist in the creation and distribution of these newspapers—especially the assistance they gave to journals outside their districts and states—was persuasive evidence of their concern for the national character of their party. When Duff Green admitted printing 40,000 weekly copies of the *Telegraph* (including the "Extra" that started publication on March 1, 1828), he said he relied "upon the Committees of Vigilance and Correspondence, appointed to promote the election of General Jackson . . . to obtain subscribers." Isaac Hill, the short, lame, and cadaverous-looking editor of the New Hampshire *Patriot,* sent his brother into Vermont with instructions to establish a hard-hitting newspaper around which the Jackson party could rally. Impressed by the technique, John C. Calhoun asked North Carolinians for their assistance when the first Southern magazine was established in Charleston. "It would be gratifying," he wrote, ". . . to see it receive a due share of its patronage from your state, both in circulation of its contents and the contribution of its pages."

The task of filling the columns of this enormous press taxed the energies of all Jacksonians. Without the willing cooperation of party men from every section of the nation, the publication problems would have been insurmountable. In New England, for example, one Massachusetts politician sent down materials to New York with the comment, "You have the same authority with this, as with the others—change—expunge, add or withhold entirely at your discretion. I need not repeat that as to political writings I have none of the vanity of an author, and consult only the good of the cause and the party." In North Carolina a worker reported that the "Central Jackson Committee have in *press* a publication of 'Military Documents' accompanied with a pretty *spicey* introduction of 15 or 16 pages." And in Kentucky, Congressman T. P. Moore requested his colleagues from Virginia, Pennsylvania, North Carolina, and New York to keep him supplied with publishable materials. "I *beg* you to let me hear from you weekly throughout the summer," he added.[12]

While this "mushroom" growth of the Jackson press was the work of an army of party organizers, a few nationally prominent men rendered outstanding service. In the *Telegraph,* Samuel D. Ingham contributed some of the most delectable slanders to appear in print against the President. Thomas Hart Benton was another powerful writer. His style was simple and direct and usually laced with invective. John C. Calhoun proposed valuable techniques for raising money to pay for all these newspapers, and Van Buren bought out journals and solicited articles from several gifted writers. On the Senate floor the New Yorker chided the government printers (they were editors of Administration newspapers) for their "improper" reporting of the proceedings of Congress. Manifestly, his only objective in making the complaint was the removal of the Adams men as printers and their replacement by Jacksonians. The *National Intelligencer* returned the fire by accusing him of maneuvering the presidential election "within the control of a Central Junto in Washington" and of establishing "machinery" to regulate "the popular election by means of organized clubs in the States, and organized presses everywhere." One of the purposes of his Southern tour, the editors charged, was "buying up or crushing all refractory newspapers which will not join the cry against the coalition."

As though to prove this accusation, two newspaper publishers in Delaware issued a sworn statement that Van Buren and his henchmen had attempted to blackmail them. They said that they were advised to turn over editorial control of the "American Watchman Newspaper Establishment" to the Democrats, or else suffer economic boycott. When they refused to be intimidated, 300 subscriptions were promptly canceled at a net loss of 1,200 dollars a year.

In the long "chain" of newspapers extending from New England to the South and "branching" off through Lexington to the West, several were authoritative and influenced wide areas of public opinion. These included: Green's *Telegraph* (unquestionably the most important), Ritchie's *Enquirer,* Edwin Croswell's Albany *Argus,* Hill's *Patriot,* Amos Kendall's *Argus of the West,* Nathaniel Greene's Boston *Statesman,* the New York *Courier, Inquirer,* and *Evening Post,* the Nashville *Republican,* the Baltimore *Republican,* the Philadelphia *Palladium,* and the Charleston *Mercury.* Besides turning out daily or weekly propaganda, these editors often exercised a more direct form of political power. Ritchie and Croswell operated through the Junto and Regency respectively; Duff Green belonged to Jackson's team of political strategists and had much to say in congressional circles; Isaac Hill, another former Radical, ran a well-oiled machine in New Hampshire, where it was said "he is determined to revolutionize the state by the next Presidential election." Finally there was Amos Kendall who was without doubt the biggest political noise heard in Kentucky since the arrival of Henry Clay.

As this newspaper "conspiracy" spread across the country, propagandizing the people about Jackson and his party and instructing the masses on the proper use of their franchise, the Adams editors groaned their fears for the safety of the Republic. "Why are *affiliated* presses erected throughout the Union, created by a common fund from the contributions of the opposition leaders, and maintained by their aid?" asked one. There was a hidden "identity of purpose" to subvert the democratic institutions of the nation, pontificated Joseph Gales, co-editor of the Washington *National Intelligencer*. Nonsense, snapped the Albany *Argus* in reply. "Professing a common political faith—members of the same great national party —and mutually seeking to promote its welfare, such 'an identity of purpose' was not only natural, but, we are free to say for ourselves, desirable."

The final word, however, came from Duff Green. "Mr. Gales knows," he wrote, "that an attempt is now making to organize new parties in the country."[13]

VII

The establishment of this enormous press was one of the first important results of the alliances concluded in Washington among the Jacksonian Congressmen. Yet equally important was their attempt to raise money to subsidize this press, along with all the other costs with which presidential elections are encumbered. Setting an example for party members in future elections, the Democrats pleaded poverty right up to the day of the inauguration. "We are poor devils in purse," wailed Senator Levi Woodbury, "our opponents are . . . wealthy and cunning." Still, with all their difficulties, it was truly amazing how much hard cash they managed to raise.

At an early Democratic caucus, Vice President Calhoun offered a possible solution to their money problem by suggesting that the Senators and Representatives assume financial responsibility for the "Extra" *Telegraphs* to be sent into their counties and districts. They would then be at liberty to devise the best means of distributing this cost among the local leaders. Calhoun also proposed that they advance money to their poorer colleagues and accept a promise of future repayment. Apparently the suggestions were adopted, for Representative T. P. Moore of Kentucky later acknowledged a debt for the "money due Green for Extras sent to Indiana &c &c," but he complained of his difficulty in obtaining reimbursement. "Mr Calhoun originated the idea," he wrote, "[and] I have cheerfully paid my portion, & performed all the labor & recd all the abuse. If the amt cannot be raised—be it so, I must & will pay it." And this was for "Extras" sent outside his own state!

It is also likely that Calhoun asked the Jackson Congressmen to accept responsibility for copies of the regular *Telegraph* sent to nonsubscribers, though Green repeatedly denied support from "secret service money" and insisted that his costs were met by public subscriptions. (For a subscriber the daily *Telegraph* cost ten dollars a year, while the weekly cost four dollars.) The editor was finally obliged to go to Boston in the summer of 1828 and secure additional loans. Still denying assistance from a contingent fund, he nevertheless accepted 11,000 dollars from the Massachusetts Jacksonians. Later he billed individual Congressmen for the papers sent into their districts, prompting one Westerner to complain of a ghastly misunderstanding when the bill came to several hundred dollars.

One of the most interesting and persistent rumors in the campaign was the report that the Democratic Congressmen created a special fund for the purpose of establishing "presses in the several states." It was also reported that the money amounted to 30,000 or 50,000 dollars and that Van Buren administered it. Furthermore, it was claimed that the fund was tapped for 25,000 dollars to underwrite the publication of the *Telegraph* and permit its distribution to every voting ward in the country.

Despite these rumors it is most unlikely that Van Buren controlled a 50,000-dollar bankroll. But he was a party treasurer of sorts. Amos Kendall, for instance, was sent to him with a letter of introduction from Senator Richard M. Johnson of Kentucky requesting a loan of 2,000 or 3,000 dollars. Kendall needed the money to repay a debt owed to Henry Clay, and he assured Van Buren that, should the money be advanced, "you will confer on me a favor which will never be forgotten." The editor was once the tutor of Clay's children but resigned to enter the newspaper business. Clay helped him: he loaned him 1,500 dollars and later offered him a job as a clerk in the State Department at a salary of 1,000 dollars. Kendall asked for 1,500 dollars, and evidently this financial haggle irritated Clay, who wrote back that he had no position to offer at that salary. When the arrangement fell through, Clay demanded repayment of the loan. Financially desperate, Kendall asked for and received an extension of time—at the usual rate of interest. When the editor again defaulted at the end of the grace period, Clay began legal proceedings. At this point Van Buren was invited to settle the difficulty with a loan, and the Democratic party bought itself a first-rate editor and politician.[14]

The money given to Kendall by Van Buren, along with other sums disbursed by the Magician during the campaign, was probably raised in the New York-Philadelphia area—and raised under the Senator's own supervision. His Regency controlled the Mechanics and Farmers Bank in Albany, which in turn controlled most of the banks in the western counties of the state. The president of the Mechanics and Farmers, Benjamin F. Knower; the cashier, Thomas W. Olcott; and several members of the board of directors, such as Benjamin F. Butler (Van Buren's former law partner), Charles Dudley, and William L. Marcy (Knower's son-in-law), were all Regency lieutenants. The Magician repeatedly hounded them to step up their activity in obtaining campaign contributions. Nor did he forget the splendid resources in New York City. "Let me entreat you to give your undivided attention to the subject of funds," he wrote one crony. "You must absolutely do more in New York than you promised."

Most of the money Van Buren obtained was spent on newspapers (there were approximately fifty Bucktail newspapers in his own state which had first claim on his treasury) and other forms of propaganda. In addition, he established several new journals in other states, one of them as far west as Illinois; and, to hear the Coalition tell it, he bribed a small army of publishers. According to one report he also accepted campaign contributions from "foreign interests." Documents discovered in 1828 (possibly forged) indicated money received from "*English* merchants in New York and some from Montreal." Presumably, the funds were given to influence the tariff question and to hold down duties on those manufactured goods that would compete with British and Canadian products. If New York Jacksonians did accept such money (and there is no proof of this), they obviously did not consider it a bribe but rather legitimate support for their continuing fight to lower the tariff.

As in most elections, the regular costs incurred in this campaign were absorbed by local organizations in the states. Large contributions, the lifeblood of the party, were again solicited; but because the creation of popular majorities proved fantastically expensive, new techniques were introduced to procure additional revenue. In many states, delegates to a convention or a county meeting were taxed a fixed amount to pay for the publication and distribution of their address to the people. One of the most efficient organizations in the nation, Hamilton County, Ohio, requested each ward to "appoint a fund committee . . . for the purpose of receiving . . . contributions . . . and that the same be paid over to the treasurer of the general committee of the county." Elsewhere, public dinners and banquets at an individual cost of five dollars were sponsored to fill the party's coffers; or an admission of fifty cents was charged at local meetings. Since the party now belonged to the masses, leaders in towns and school districts were instructed to go among their people and collect whatever they could get. They accepted any amount and from any source. Even the notorious Aaron Burr supposedly contributed to the Jackson organization in Virginia. In a detailed financial statement to Senator Levi Woodbury, Isaac Hill complained that his costs in printing New Hampshire's convention proceedings, five important pamphlets, his biography of Andrew Jackson, the Fourth of July orations, and various addresses greatly exceeded the amount of money received from party members. Since the state convention had "authorized" him to take necessary steps to obtain remuneration, he asked Woodbury for a "contribution for the purpose," along with a loan of 2,000 dollars.[15]

While it is impossible to give anything like a complete accounting of costs for this election, it appears certain that the largest single expense, running into the hundreds of thousands, was ingeniously shifted to the United States Government through the franking privilege. Hezekiah Niles estimated that over 2,250,000 dollars a year were involved in the privilege, but this figure sounds exaggerated; nevertheless, the amount of money did run quite high. The delivery of franked newspapers alone cost the federal government 40,000 dollars each year in allowance to postmasters. Except when Congress was not in session, hundreds of newspapers circulated freely throughout the country. Representatives and Senators were hounded by confederates at home to mail every scrap of campaign literature that crossed their desks. Thomas Ritchie happily noted that many enterprising Jacksonians were also franking wrapping paper, which they then turned over to local committees in their states to be used as needed. One Kentucky Representative sent pamphlets, books, letters, handbills, and other educational materials to a *single* post office at a cost of 150 dollars to the government. Even buttons, banners, and insignias went through the mails under the frank. Something close to the entire bill for delivering campaign propaganda was ultimately borne by the American taxpayer. And, in this regard, the usually fastidious Radicals found nothing in their dogma to forbid government participation in party affairs.

The Democrats, in other words, tried to shift the main burden of their campaigning costs to the federal government. There were several ways to do this. Besides the frank, there was money to be had from printing the laws of the United States. Duff Green received several thousand dollars as initial compensation when he was appointed printer for the United States Senate in 1827. Other editors, not elected by Congress, held their lucrative printing posts at the pleasure of the executive, but if they became too conspicuously Jacksonian they ran the risk of removal by Henry Clay. Isaac Hill lost his printing stipend in just this manner, whereupon his colleagues along the newspaper "chain" set up a howl that his dismissal was the "first movement of the same spirit which produced the *alien and sedition laws* and brought in the reign of terror in 1798."

Next, there was the state government on which to saddle election expenses. Wherever the Democrats controlled the legislature and executive branches of a particular state, they awarded the position of state printer to the editor of their official organs. To provide additional revenue, editors were sometimes given minor offices that did not consume much time or interfere with their primary responsibility of running a newspaper. The editor of the *Inquirer,* however, made the astounding request that he be appointed sheriff of New York City, assuring the Regency that the "avails . . . goes in fact into the pockets of the party." It could be done, he told Van Buren, with just a few words to three or four persons "who will press the question upon the Committee & no doubt with success."

In time, the procedures employed by the national leaders to raise money in the campaign developed into a system, although it took many more elections to perfect all the techniques. To begin with, Jacksonians tapped the national and state governments for every penny they could shake loose. Then they obligated themselves for additional costs that were repayable by party treasurers of their state or county committees. In turn, these committees drew upon local fund-raising groups. Obviously, such efficiency was not manifested in all areas, and Congressmen were frequently obliged to petition their colleagues and others for assistance. Sometimes they made private arrangements, since their own elections were at stake; sometimes they went to bank-supported leaders like Van Buren; and sometimes they made public appeals. It cost a great deal of money to enter politics, even in 1828, depending on the level at which a man wished to enter. For example, to be elected from a Western state to a disputed seat in the House of Representatives cost about 3,000 dollars (exclusive of mailing expenses), two-thirds of which was spent on the publication of pamphlets, handbills, and newspapers. In the South the figure was much reduced, while in the Middle Atlantic states, particularly Pennsylvania and New York, it was higher by a thousand dollars or so.

Beginning with the election of 1828, the cost of presidential contests soared. Estimating roughly, and including the franking expenses in the estimate, it cost approximately 1,000,000 dollars to elect General Andrew Jackson the President of the United States.[16]

AJ- set prescident for expensive campaigns

VIII

The stunning success of the Democrats in concluding their alliances, establishing "newspaper posts" from Maine to Louisiana, and raising the money to pay for the election were essential but merely preliminary steps to the real work of party building. As many Jacksonians suspected only too well, their "new national party" would never survive on regional or factional alliances alone, not when the people were voting directly for presidential electors. The effectiveness of the "combinations" formed in Washington depended on the ability of the participants to go back into their districts and build organizations based upon popular majorities—or, as one Representative phrased it, for Congressmen to "take their predilections home and extend them through their States." Everything the Jacksonians said, everything they did during the campaign, re-emphasized their understanding of this need. "Our true object," insisted Duff Green, "is to . . . induce all aspirants for office to look to the people . . . for support."

Green's formula for the campaign was heartily approved by Western politicians. "Contending as we are against wealth & power," wrote William T. Barry of Kentucky to the Nashville Central Committee, "we look for success in numbers." "Leave all to us," Caleb Atwater advised Jackson. "Can we do more? I promise you that every friend you have in Ohio, who can get to the polls, shall go there, and vote for you. In the meantime all shall be done, that can be, for you." Atwater did not renege on his promise. Like other hard-bitten politicians, he adopted "extraordinary means and exertions" to build a popular following and create his majority. "I therefore originated," explained one politician, "and with the cooperation of about half a dozen, intelligent and zealous friends, carryed into full and successful operation last year, a plan, or System of Committees, from a Principle or Central

Committee . . . down to Sub-Committees into every ward of the Town, and Captains Company in the Country."

Such was the system by which the party was linked to the people. And such was the Jacksonian Revolution in its initial phase. The same restless energy with which Americans altered and expanded their economic and social environment was visible among politicians as they set about adjusting the political process. But as the Adams editors frequently pointed out, the revolution did not emanate from the people despite the powerful groundswell of popular enthusiasm for Jackson. The real revolution came from the politicians; it moved in one direction only—from the top down.

At first the Jackson campaign wallowed in disorder; nominations, electoral tickets, and high-sounding resolutions came whistling out of unauthorized and independent groups. But after the congressional caucuses, the Democrats settled down to a more orderly and systematic approach to the election. By the closing months of 1827 virtually every county, city, and town of importance in the United States had a functioning "Jackson Committee" of one type or another, sponsoring "Jackson meetings" as part of a coordinated drive to expel John Quincy Adams from the White House. Even the voteless District of Columbia had a committee, and the President confided to his diary that political meetings were being held each night in Washington by one of the two contending parties. He surmised that similar meetings were going on in all the other parts of the nation. Indeed they were. ". . . Governors and Judges of the state," rumbled the disapproving Nathaniel Macon, "forgetting their stations, turn electioneers, probably a word not be found in a dictionary." As early as 1826, Philadelphia had a "Democratic Committee of Vigilance and Superintendence," formed, according to its circular, "to accomplish through the agency of corresponding committees a perfect understanding among the friends of ANDREW JACKSON in all the States" for his election. James Buchanan gleefully recorded that this spirit of "active exertion" for the Hero was already manifest in many counties of Pennsylvania. "Hickory Clubs" had been set up in dozens of communities, and militia companies were undergoing rapid conversion into "electioneering clubs." Further South, the Richmond Junto was pleased to inform the Nashville Central Committee that "we are making a prodigious fuss" in organizing a state convention. "To manage men," said David Campbell, "is as much a science as to manage armies."[17]

In New England, despite its strong and probably unshakable preference for Adams, an engine was under contruction in each of the six states to run over the crusty President. "A party regularly organized and publicly operating under the Jackson standard, is now at work in Connecticut," wrote one of the General's traveling corpsmen, "which though not likely to influence the vote of that state is sure to make a powerful declination from the unanimity claimed for Mr. Adams in the land of steady habits." The Massachusetts and New Hampshire men were well advanced in erecting the party apparatus, and Senator Levi Woodbury detected encouraging progress in parts of Maine. "Nothing will be left undone," he confidently informed the New York committee, to capture New Hampshire and the rest of New England.

Out West, the task of shaping a new party proceeded at breakneck speed. Thomas Hart Benton in Missouri reunited the Republican factions after a split had developed over the congressional election. His "well drilled" party *warriors* drove the dissidents back into line and then prepared for a rousing convention at Jefferson City. In Indiana, the structure of the state organization was so startling in its novelty and efficiency that Eastern newspaper editors advised local politicians to take a hard look and then copy some of the details. In Henry Clay's own bailiwick, Kentucky, the Jacksonians had an elaborate committee system functioning early in 1827. "The organization of this Committee plan, so as to embrace the whole state," the General was advised, "has already been commenced by your friends, as it is expected to be in full and successful operation, before the next August elections, with a view not only to your elevation, but likewise the resuscitation and success, of our local Republican cause."

In building their organizations, politicians followed no set pattern, except in their extensive use of committees. There were committees to raise money, committees to arrange the "Jackson Democratic Festivals," committees to write propaganda "to enlighten the public mind," committees to discipline, committees to supervise, committees to correspond with other committees both in and

each factions had many committees.

out of the state, committees on top of committees, on and on, seemingly without end. Yet all these committees functioned at one of three levels: local, county, or state.

At the local level, the simply named Jackson Committees (occasionally called Hickory Clubs) were established in the election districts. These committees, directed by an executive group appointed by state leaders, arranged the rallies, town meetings, barbecues, parades, hickory pole raisings, street demonstrations, and other forms of entertainment that the public demanded as the price of their interest and cooperation. Invariably, the rallies and meetings were scheduled for a court day or a militia muster day, because a crowd of people was certain to be present. "Get up a meeting," read one order to a local Jacksonian, "on some court day, mount Edward on a rostrum . . . [and have] the ablest men set about to make the necessary arrangements."

This, then, was where the canvass began, and since these rallies and meetings provided a powerful lever to public opinion, they were scheduled wherever and whenever the electorate could be found. "Meetings will now take place all over the state," one Southerner assured another "—perhaps in every county."

At the next level were the county committees; and as important as the local "Hickory Clubs" were in identifying Jackson and the organization with the people, "county gatherings of freeholders" were cardinal to party strength and discipline—at least that was the opinion of the most experienced politicians. It was from the county organization that the activities of the local clubs were supervised and controlled; it was from the county organization that local and state functions were coordinated; and it was from the county organization that representatives were sent to the state convention, which selected the presidential ticket and nominated the slate of candidates for state offices. In addition to these activities, the county groups named vigilance, correspondence, and fund-raising committees, passed a set of resolutions condemning the Administration and urging the election of Jackson, issued a call for a state convention, and prepared an official "Address to the Public."

Frequently, the membership of the county committees came from the local clubs. For example, a group of citizens in Cincinnati,

Ohio, organized a Jackson Committee of twenty men in the summer of 1826, empowering them to add to their number, "appoint subcommittees," and correspond with other Jackson committees throughout the Union. These men subsequently met with similar groups from neighboring communities and formed a county committee. By the beginning of 1827 there were ten county committees in Ohio, each with correspondence and vigilance committees for the separate townships. These "earnestly requested" the remaining counties to follow their example, establish a functioning organization, publish their proceedings, and send copies to the *National Republican* and the Cincinnati *Advertiser*. Ohio was so well organized by 1828 that in a few counties the party extended down to the school districts, each one represented by a vigilance committee.[18]

In some states the initial method of organizing was considerably different from the Ohio example. Samuel D. Ingham, for instance, commenced his work by calling a private meeting of a dozen friends at his home to arrange for the formation of local committees and the distribution of campaign literature. In Kentucky, a Central Committee was first established in Louisville, then "sub-committees" were named in the wards and "captains companies." According to a report sent to Alfred Balch in Nashville, Kentucky also had a "Control committee" in Frankfort which agreed on a "system of conduct" to "inspirit the friends of reform throughout the state." Over in Missouri, a state central committee, a committee of correspondence for each county, and a district committee for each district were appointed at the state convention. In Indiana, the party was organized from township assessors all the way up to a body known as the State Committee of General Superintendence. An easy control was exercised over the Indiana electorate because the party apparatus took pains to direct the listing of voters and influence the appointment of town, county, and militia officers.

To instill spirit, loyalty, and discipline among party members, the county committee frequently sponsored a county convention. At first the membership of this convention was limited to three men from each town, but the disadvantages of such a procedure were immediately apparent and both parties were soon issuing orders to leave each town "free to choose as many on their delegations as they please and for the central committee to request the attendence [sic] of as many (whether delegates or not) as may find it convenient to be present." The purpose of a county convention, after all, was to generate enthusiasm for the party ticket, and that could best be done at a meeting filled to capacity with shouting and applauding delegates.

At the top of the organizational pyramid were the state committees, created usually at the general state conventions. Early in 1827 someone or some group suggested holding all state conventions on January 8, 1828, the anniversary of Jackson's victory over the British at New Orleans. The Indiana and Ohio parties indicated that the idea came from within the Pennsylvania congressional delegation, which, if true, may mean it ultimately originated with Vice President Calhoun. In any event, by selecting this date for their conventions, politicians could squeeze additional political capital out of national pride in a great military victory. As it turned out, many states fell in with the scheme and held their conventions on January 8. Even those states which chose a different date to nominate their tickets celebrated the anniversary in some appropriate manner. Several also sent delegations to New Orleans to honor the General.

In arranging the membership of these conventions, states either appointed or elected delegates according to population or congressional representation, or they convened the Democratic state legislators and authorized special elections for delegates from districts that were unrepresented in the legislature by Jackson men, as they did in Virginia. But once the convention met, the procedures were nearly uniform. A chairman or president and a secretary were selected; resolutions were adopted in favor of Jackson's election; and a Central Committee was formed. This Committee was directed to write an address to the people, communicate with similar committees in other states, and supervise the activities of the county committees. Then an electoral ticket was chosen and the electors pledged to Jackson. If any elector repudiated his pledge later on, the Central Committee was authorized to replace him. Finally, candidates for state officers were designated.

When the "Address to the Public" was returned by the Central Committee, its publication was normally authorized in the amount of 5,000 to 20,000 copies. (In Pennsylvania 15,000 copies were issued, one-third of them in German.) Copies were distributed to newspapers throughout the state, the Nashville Central Committee usually received copies, and Duff Green invariably carried the "Address" and the adopted resolutions in his *Telegraph*.[19]

To sustain the unity of the state convention, the Central Committees kept active throughout the remainder of the campaign, meeting no less than twice a month in most states. Normally they exercised such absolute power over the county committees that they could remove individuals who jeopardized party success; but this was a power to be used with caution, since the county groups were too important in shaping mass support to be treated with anything less than deference and respect. The Central Committees from state to state also maintained close contact with each other, requesting assistance, providing aid and encouragement, and suggesting improved methods with which to attract a popular following.

In extending the party structure throughout the state, some conventions appointed a whole battery of committees—general committee, state committee, superintendence committee, etc.—each with distinct duties and responsibilities. In the assignment of membership to these groups, the first rule required that "each county have some individuals on the various committees . . ." Next, it was essential that responsible and resourceful men be chosen to fill the assignments, for, as one politician wrote, only "the best men . . . by speeches and reports [can] enlighten public opinion." The size of all these committees, whether state, county, or local, varied from 5, 7, or 10 men to 30, 50, or 75. In Franklin County, Ohio, one correspondence committee numbered 103.

This was the first presidential election in which a majority of states held conventions to endorse a national candidate. While the procedure was thought to provide a closer union between the people and the operation of government—and no doubt it did to some extent—its great efficiency lay in generating party discipline and loyalty. Conventions fashioned the apparatus that locked the state parties together to form a national organization. They were "buoys," commented one, "to show in what channel the [public] feeling . . . [should] be steered."

States with pre-existing organizations, such as New York with its Albany Regency, did not bother with a convention. There was no need. The party was already unified through a system of circuit judges, town clerks, and justices of the peace hooked into the central Regency at Albany. Van Buren preferred the "old fashioned form" of legislative caucus, so he simply turned over his machine to the Jackson cause and instructed his lieutenants to "drill" the caucus members in their duty. These legislators—all 110 of them —received their orders and returned to their communities, where they summoned local meetings to endorse the caucus decision and form committees. Circuit judges checked them. Later, Van Buren toured the state to inspect their activities and encourage them to greater efforts. When this machine finally got up a full head of steam, it functioned so smoothly that one of Jackson's roving ambassadors stared at it in wonder and disbelief. "In Albany, in this city [New York] and indeed throughout the state," he declared to Old Hickory, "our party is happily organized, and ardently industrious. Sub committees in every county correspond each fortnight with the general committee here, and the strength of the enemy, and our own strength, is accurately reported twice a month from every neighborhood. So that any adverse impression is instantly counteracted and every favourable one seasonally improved by the general committee."

In many Eastern and Western states the entire party apparatus operated so well that in 1829 one politician suggested that the leaders continue the basic "plan of last year, except that the managers in the Congressional Districts may be dispensed with and the county Superintendents correspond directly with the centre." Of course, he reminded his friends, the initial step in any organizational plan should be a "private meeting" of members of the legislature with "all the good and true men" in the state plus the appointment of a Central Committee and the designation of "trusty agents in every county." And, in selecting these trusty agents, he advised, "you may hold out to them the hope, that if they are active in organizing and training the party, they will probably receive the appointment to take in the census, and efficient means must be taken to reserve it to them, thus proving that fidelity to the cause shall not go without its reward."

Although in some places the organization fell short of what has been described here, the start in all the sections of the nation was remarkably good—and clearly visible. As the party slowly emerged, the Coalition editors watched it, fussed at it, and chronicled its steady progress. First, a "factious opposition" was formed in Congress, they reported, through a series of "unholy" alliances. Then a press had been established and subsidized. Next, the combination "induced meetings of the people in every part of the Union where the Administration could be denounced and their idol set up for worship." From these meetings came "manifestos of defamation" against Adams and Clay with "such modifications as the change of place made necessary." Finally, these documents of hate were "ushered to the world as the *voice of the people*."

"Say what you will," sighed one of Clay's friends, "these Jacksonians are excellent politicians."[20]

IX

The excellence of the Jacksonians as practical politicians was nowhere more evident than in their readiness to reach across state and sectional lines to cooperate with one another in order to ensure the General's victory at the polls. As Duff Green reiterated in each issue of his "Extra" *Telegraph*, "union and concert of action are necessary to success." Although the committee system, which was built into the structure of the party, accounted for most of the cooperation and coordination, it was supplemented, from time to time, by other methods, some personal and some institutional. For example, the tightly knit operation in Indiana and the more loosely constructed apparatus in Ohio "were counterparts to each other, each supplying those elements which the other lacked." The Woodbury-Hill group in New Hampshire constantly relied on the New York party for assistance in swinging their people away from the President. "I know," wrote Woodbury, "that the assurances of a majority in New York encourage us more than the best news from States more remote." The assurances that Woodbury requested were promptly returned, and Hill not only published them in

states cooperated to insure AJ's election w/ other states

New Hampshire but hurried them over to his brother in Vermont, where they reportedly had a "very great effect." Then, to reciprocate, the editor instructed Duff Green to inform "our friends in the west and south that New Hampshire is safe."

Major Lewis sent repeated letters to state committees reminding them to look to Nashville whenever they needed assistance. "We want the Cincinnati Jackson Committee," he wrote, "to call on our committee at this place, for such information as they may have it in their power to furnish." And if the Nashville Committee could not help, then the Washington Central Committee was summoned through Duff Green. The editor himself traveled extensively in the Middle Atlantic and New England states to encourage greater cooperation between the two sections, and he attended at least one state convention where he prepared the "Address" to the people. Elsewhere, political leaders consulted among themselves, with the Nashville crowd, and with the members of Congress. "If [Caleb Atwater of Ohio] is to be believed," said one, "he corresponds with every great man in the nation." Another Westerner urged his Eastern Democratic cronies to "get some of our friends to address a letter to the Jackson delegation in Congress from N York Pa Virginia & N Carolina requesting their opinion of the probable vote in the states above mentioned & forward the answers to me. . . . We have many who desire to be with the strongest party." Shortly after touring the North, Thomas Ritchie made a similar request of William C. Rives, asking him to approach Representatives Buchanan, Ingham, Stevenson, and Baldwin of the Pennsylvania delegation for the latest political information from their state. Letters would help, he said, preferably "letters from members of the Legislature or the Jackson Convention. . . . For myself it is unnecessary; but it may be useful to others."

One of the most striking examples of cooperation between state organizations occurred when the Coalition made a "powerful effort" against the Hero in Virginia through the publication of a story in which Jackson had, many years before, reputedly threatened to fight his way to the floor of the United States Senate and "cut the ears off" Senator John W. Eppes, the son-in-law of Thomas Jefferson. Commodore Stephen Decatur, who overheard the threat, flung himself across the Hero's path, and dramatically declared that the only way the General would reach the floor was "over my dead body."

As soon as this "juicy story" broke into print, John Campbell, a member of the Virginia state committee, summoned the Nashville Central Committee for assistance. "I want documentary testimony," he said. "I wish you . . . to have a conversation with Genl Jackson and give me his account *in detail.*" However, before mailing his letter, Campbell showed it to Thomas Ritchie. The editor not only approved it and said he was "extremely anxious to obtain the information" himself, but he asked Campbell to add a postscript and request details about other stories and rumors. For one thing, he wanted to know if Clay had invited Jackson to travel through Kentucky on his way to Washington just prior to the House election of 1825. An affirmative reply would furnish additional evidence that Clay had hoped to bribe the General. Also, Ritchie asked if Clay had congratulated the Hero on "his great vote from the people."

Campbell incorporated these inquiries into a postscript, but instead of forwarding one letter, he sent several. He chose those members of the Nashville Junto, he said, who had "*tact* & judgment," such as Felix Grundy. Had he written to Sam Houston or Tom Claiborne, "there would have been some flourish about the matter that would have spoil'd the whole affair." When the Central Committee returned its reply, complete with the "documentary testimony," Campbell took it to Ritchie, who published it in his newspaper. At the same time, additional copies were distributed by the Central Committee to the newspaper "chain."[21]

Toward the close of the campaign, several highly placed members of the Nashville Junto urged Jackson to write a long address to the people answering a number of charges brought against his public and private life. Considering everything that had been done to date, the Hero was reluctant to go along with the suggestion; but rather than jeopardize the election by inaction, he finally instructed Major Lewis to ascertain the opinions of "our safest and most prominent friends in other states." Straightaway the letters went out, with Lewis asking for an immediate reply. "If the course contemplated should be thought advisable," he said, "the address ought to be prepared and ready for the press by the middle of next month—giving just time enough for it to circulate generally thro the Union before the election." He frankly confessed to the leaders that Jackson was against making the appeal, "as it will seem to have the appearance of electioneering . . . but if his friends think it advisable probably he may be prevailed on to do it." Enough of the General's "safest" friends agreed with him about the risk, however, so the idea was abandoned.

On another occasion a group of Richmond politicians thought that Jackson owed it to the country to explain his mind on the Constitution and internal improvements. No sooner was this cheeky idea proposed than one of the Virginia Campbells alerted Dr. McCall, who relayed the alarm to James K. Polk. The Tennessee Representative forthwith notified the General in order "that you may not be taken unapprised." Presumably, Jackson was saved in the nick of time from having to comment on the Constitution without prior consideration. This habit of his of ducking away from issues worried a few state organizations. The Indiana and Ohio Central Committees finally asked the Pennsylvania Committee for assurances that the Hero's statements on the tariff and public works were acceptable. Apparently if Pennsylvania could stomach his ambiguities, they would swallow them too. Needless to add, the reply from Pennsylvania was completely favorable.

Indeed, much of the success of the Jacksonians in resolving differences of opinion was due to the readiness of state leaders to assure each other that the Hero was "safe" on this or that question. Senator Eaton, the "party's circulating medium," had a bag full of assurances, which he blithely distributed as he toured the several states. John C. Calhoun, too, took an active hand in promoting party harmony, and his influence was beneficially felt in Massachusetts, Maryland, and Pennsylvania.

However, New Yorkers were the most aggressive Jacksonians when it came to advancing "union & cooperation" on a national scale. At first there was De Witt Clinton, who in 1827 made an extensive "tour of the West and of the East" and privately circulated letters among "improvements men" in the Ohio Valley in time, it was reported, to sway the fall state elections. After Clinton's death his work was continued by the Albany Regency with all the energy and vigor that characterized their political operations. They labored furiously to manage Kentucky, Ohio, and Missouri through a propaganda campaign of newspapers, letters, personal persuasion, and money. The Little Magician, meanwhile, worked his magic on Senator Elias K. Kane to induce him to "Vanbeurenize" Illinois. Together with the lieutenant governor of that state, Kane was coaxed into contributing a "sum of money for the purchase and support of a Jackson Press." Nor did Van Buren forget his Southern friends. Periodically, he reminded Edwin Croswell to "say some civil things" about them in the *Argus*. "It is gratifying to meet Republicans of the South," he declared. "They may always expect to find union & cooperation from the Democrats of the North."

As this union and cooperation steadily improved throughout the campaign, state leaders happily noticed its exhilarating effect in re-energizing Jefferson's old Republican party. "What a pleasure it is to see," noted William C. Bradley of Vermont, "that party almost unbroken rising in almost every part of the union to put down the men who would have corrupted and betrayed it." Coalitionists also observed what was happening. "My belief," wrote James Clark to John W. Taylor, "is that the success of our opponents is mainly attributable to their concert and better organization."[22]

X

Yet certain deficiencies were apparent. Most serious was the uneven development of the party from state to state and section to section. It was strongest in Missouri, Louisiana, Kentucky, Illinois, Indiana, Ohio, New York, Pennsylvania, New Hampshire, Maryland, Virginia, and North Carolina. Though these controlled more than a majority of electoral votes, they constituted only half the number of states in the union. The party, though active, was noticeably less vigorous in New Jersey and Delaware (where, interestingly enough, old Federalists were the principal leaders of the Jackson party and where the General would be defeated), while Tennessee suffered that neglect which often befalls the home of the favorite son. New England showed excellent starts in those areas where former Radicals operated, particularly Maine,

Massachusetts, Connecticut, and a few counties in Vermont. Organizational weaknesses were most apparent in the South—Virginia, Louisiana, and North Carolina excepted. Perhaps central to the difficulty in that section was the near-total absence of Coalitionists, for nothing stimulates party-building like a healthy political brawl between rival slates of candidates.

Another weakness among Democrats was the difficulty they manufactured for themselves over the vice presidency. Certain unforgiving Radicals, mainly in the South, injured the ticket by their unsuccessful attempts to substitute Crawford or Nathaniel Macon for Calhoun as Jackson's running mate. Several state conventions failed to nominate the Vice President and left the second slot vacant rather than stir up trouble among their die-hard Radicals. Even some professional politicians were confused. "Unless I hear something to the contrary from you," Caleb Atwater wrote to Major Lewis, "I shall oppose any nomination for the vice President by our convention" and "shall leave the V.P. to our friends in Washington this winter—to manage as they see fit." Naturally, this snub infuriated Calhoun's friends. Many of them wrote scorching letters to the correspondence committee demanding his nomination, irrespective of personal feelings. "Let no divisions exist," stormed one New Englander. "Get into no quarrel about the Vice Presidency. . . . You have but one object, that is to put down the coalition, and to restore to the people their full rights." To escape their predicament, a couple of states took an easy way out: they left the selection of the Vice President to their electors. Most of the others, however, fulfilled their responsibility and nominated Calhoun, whether they liked him or not.

The failure to hold a national nominating convention as suggested by the Vice President and agreed to by Van Buren may have been another indication of organizational weakness. Just why the convention was not held is difficult to explain. There were repeated references to it in the newspapers all during 1827, but after January 1828 nothing more was said about it. Perhaps the leaders feared a fight over the vice presidential nomination, which would jeopardize the alliance with the Radicals, or over certain issues such as the tariff and internal improvements. Perhaps they judged it unimportant (considering the action taken by so many state con-

VP- many disagreed, but most nominated Calhoun

ventions) and, unlike Calhoun and Van Buren, failed to understand its value in directing Jackson's popularity to the service of the entire organization. But whatever the reasons, the national convention was postponed until the next election, at which time it became an integral component of the electoral mechanism.

Factionalism also broke out among Jacksonians, particularly in those places where the old Federalists joined the Democratic party and tried to lead it. One New York Bucktail was outraged by their behavior. "We dont like such counsellors," he snapped. "We are not anxious of their company tho their assistance may be welcome." The trouble seemed to stem from the fact that Federalists expected full payment for whatever assistance they rendered. If there was victory, they demanded "a fair proportion of its honors & profit." Later, to the accompaniment of loud snorts of disapproval, most of the politically wise Democrats—and that included Andrew Jackson—paid off the Federalists in full.

It soon developed that there was trouble between Jacksonian Federalists and Republicans in Boston when the new Democratic organization split into two groups in a feud over future patronage. Theodore Lyman (the leader of the Jacksonian Federalists in Massachusetts) headed one group, while the druggist David Henshaw (the leader of the Jacksonian Republicans) headed another. Fortunately, in the summer of 1828, the two factions subordinated their greed to the common cause, accepting a truce that was probably arranged by Vice President Calhoun. In the election, the southern and western counties of the state succumbed to Democratic persuasion, due almost entirely to the inexhaustible energy of Marcus Morton.

Other states may not have had such factional problems, but they were nonetheless disturbed by the continued confusion over issues. Hence, certain leaders simply ignored national questions in favor of local, state, and regional problems. Georgia, for example, wrapped up the election over the removal of the Indians; Missouri condemned President Adams for allegedly opposing the state's admission into the Union and for reserving various lead mines and alternate sections of iron lands from public sale. In Massachusetts, the issues of free bridges, lotteries, and the sale of liquor took precedence over all others, while New Jersey voters contended over the question of the Delaware and Raritan Canal.

Perhaps this confusion over the party's public policy, the factionalism, and the other weaknesses and deficiencies were to be expected in a young party, still growing, still learning, still exploring the hidden sinuosities of public favor. When compared to its strengths—committee system, newspaper chain, intersectional alliances, congressional leadership, and improved electioneering techniques—these flaws, in the over-all view, seem trifling and unimportant. They were imperfections, to be sure; but they would be corrected in time.[23]

XI

The improved electioneering methods that the Jacksonians developed to manipulate votes on a mass scale were the most obvious signs of the "great political revolution in progress." "Our true object," Duff Green had written, "is to . . . induce all aspirants for office to look to the people . . . for support." And to win that support, Democrats once more revealed their flashing astuteness by launching a novel campaign of song, slogan, and shout. In the process they inaugurated some of the worst barbarisms of American electioneering, but they also advanced the cause of democracy in the country, whether they intended to or not.

On the whole, voters in the United States do not think very deeply about political matters. They simply respond to stimulation. The bigger the stimulation, the bigger the response. Jacksonian Congressmen, in cooperation with state leaders, newspaper editors, publicists, and stump orators, were now about to create a monumental stimulation—the first of its kind in presidential politics—and the degree to which the voters responded to it measured the extent of Old Hickory's victory in 1828. Thoughtful discussion of the qualifications of the two candidates was virtually discarded during the canvass in favor of more effective tactics, such as barbecues, tree plantings, parades, public rallies, dinners, jokes, cartoons, and propaganda guaranteed to induce mass enthusiasm. This was the first election in which "gimmicks" were extensively employed to arouse and maintain popular interest in the activities of the party. Hereafter, all presidential contests would include a large dose of ballyhoo to amuse and delight an otherwise "lethargic" public.

In their campaign oratory and publications the Democrats did not hesitate to invoke religious bigotry or national prejudice whenever such tactics braced their cause. They teased special-interest groups with vague promises, and they trifled with the fears of minorities or recent immigrants who exercised the suffrage. To one and all they offered Andrew Jackson as the symbol of a rising popular democracy, the symbol of an electorate grown to political maturity. In each issue of his "Extra" *Telegraph,* Duff Green hammered out the principal Democratic theme: "Andrew Jackson is the *candidate of the People.*"

John Quincy Adams, on the other hand, was the candidate of the aristocracy who preached that "the few should govern the many [and] that the will of the Representatives should not be palsied by the will of his constituents." Should a man, thundered the Democratic press, who obviously despised republican institutions, who conducted himself like a king as he strolled around the White House, who recklessly spent the people's money on the trappings of royalty—should such a man enjoy popular favor? "We disapprove," ran several resolutions passed by Jackson conventions, "the kingly pomp and splendour that is displayed by the present incumbent."

And Henry Clay was no better. He talked grandly of American democracy, his American System, but he was just as enamoured of expensive foreign products as Adams. He even used English writing paper in the State Department! "O fie, Mr. Clay—*English* paper, *English* wax, *English* pen-knives, is this your *American* System?" mocked Green. "However, let us be just towards Mr. Clay in one respect—his playing Cards are of American Manufacture. They are all made in New England—the 'land of steady habits.'"

To prove the Administration's "royal extravagances," the Jacksonians whipped up a great storm over an account of White House expeditures submitted to the Congressional Committee on Retrenchment. The report stated that public funds had been used to equip the East Room with gambling furniture, in particular a billiard table, cues and balls, and a set of expensive chessmen made of ivory. Although Adams later corrected the original statement to show that he paid for these games out of his own pocket, and although the Register of the Treasury Department certified that the White House account contained no appropriation for billiard equipment, the Jacksonians did not alter a single lying accusation They went right on beating Adams over the head with his own cue stick. In a letter entitled, "The East Room," written anonymously by Thomas Hart Benton and published in Ritchie's *Enquirer*, the President was pilloried for spending 25,000 dollars of public money on a wide assortment of gambling equipment, including billiard table, balls, cues, backgammon board, dice, chess, and "soda water."

A few Democrats, disturbed by the vulgarities of modern campaigning, objected to the "East Room" piece. "I am against all *foul play*," wrote one Southerner. "The Author of that letter ought to be ashamed of himself." Most Jacksonians, however, thought that the letter made beautiful propaganda. Its charges were restated in the web of newspapers that covered the country. The state organizations came alive to its implications, and advice poured into Congress to subject Adams' personal finances to a careful and thorough investigation. "Push the enquirers about the money," commanded one delighted New Englander. "Bring John Q's account before the Congress again if you can get them there—the *whole* from the commencement of the govt to the present day." Some Democrats also demanded an inspection of the first John Adams' expense allowance: between father and son, perhaps it could be proved that the public had been bilked of a fortune.

In adding up the pay "John Q" received from the moment he left the United States as Minister to Russia in 1809 until he became Secretary of State in 1817, the Jacksonians discovered that it came to the grand total of nearly 105,000 dollars, or better than 12,000 dollars a year. A kingly sum for a servant of a Republic; if this did not convince the voters of "rottenness in our institutions" —nay, corruption, charged the Democrats—nothing ever would.

The debates in Congress over executive expeditures were conducted with such serious concern for the preservation of frugality and thrift in government that they succeeded in fostering a general

impression around the country of extraordinary waste and extravagance by the Adams Administration, an impression that worked
wonders in the West, especially among the German, Dutch, and
recent immigrants. John Blair of Tennessee, chairman of the House
Committee on Expenditures in the Department of State, along
with his fellow committeemen, James Trezvant of Virginia and
Robert Letcher of Kentucky, combed through Henry Clay's pur-
chases and requisitions for propaganda titbits. They found nothing to equal the billiard table and soda water, but they took exception to several insignificant items, such as pictures, prints, and
medallions.

To attract the vote of the several nationalities in the country,
the Jacksonians utilized a wide variety of techniques—a few ra-
tional and legitimate, a few devious and underhanded. As a start,
they reminded immigrants that John Adams was the well-known
"author" of the Alien and Sedition Acts, and that there was always
a distinct possibility that John Quincy Adams might revive them—
apparently for no other reason than that he was the son of John
Adams and, as everyone said, like father like son. The Dutch in
New York, New Jersey, Pennsylvania, and Delaware were solemnly
assured, as though every word were true and could be documented,
that the friends of the Coalition "have heretofore spoken of the
Dutch, calling them 'the Black Dutch,' 'the Stupid Dutch,' 'the
ignorant Dutch' and other names equally decorous and civil."
The Hero, naturally, "revered" the Dutch for their many virtues,
their steady habits, and their patriotism.

Far more legitimate as a campaign device was the approach used
to win the German vote in Pennsylvania. Party leaders published
tracts, handbills, and pamphlets in German. They sent German-
speaking lawyers into the heavily populated communities to organize rallies and public meetings. They lashed the President with
charges of extravagance, corruption, treachery, and support of
higher taxes, achieving such a phenomenal success that Pennsylvania Germans were reportedly voting for Jackson long after his
death, even after the Civil War!

In Boston, the leaders, "proclaiming Jackson as an Irishman . . .
planted their flag on the meagre of Broad Street; and holding him
up as the champion of the poor against the rich, they received with
'hugs fraternal' the tenants of poorhouses and penitentiaries."

West— responded to supposed waste in
Adams Administration.

Meanwhile, in New York, that darling of the Irish, De Witt Clinton, reminded them of their patriotic duty to vote for Andrew Jackson. He reminded them so well that for safety's sake 1,000 illegal ballots were reportedly added to the Hero's tally in 1828. "Terence," wrote one obviously delighted Democrat, voted for Jackson twice in every ward, "making 28 times, and at each time he drank a pint of beer."

But the master political propagandist among the several nationalities in the country—especially among the Irish and the Scotch-Irish—was Duff Green. "General Jackson, it is well known," he wrote, "is the son of honest Irish parents. . . . That natural interest which all true hearted Irishmen feel in the fame of one who has so much genuine Irish blood in his veins, has drawn down upon the heads of that devoted people, the denunciations of the partisans of Messrs. Adams & Clay."

"While on this topic," Green continued, remembering still another voting bloc, "we are induced to notice a most excellent and appropriate toast offered at the Jackson Celebration on the 8th January in Charleston, S. C. by the Roman Catholic Bishop of that Diocess [sic]." Said the Bishop, "England" by name: "The Land, under the influence of whose atmosphere the *Shamrock* becomes a *Hickory!!!* (Received with great cheering.)" But "Rough" Green was not content to score a point in Jackson's favor unless he also smeared the President. "Mr. Adams," he charged, "denounced the Roman Catholics as bigots, worshippers of images, and declared that they did not read their bibles." Worse, "Johnny Q. the tory" was secretly working to "unite CHURCH AND STATE after the manner of the English monarch." In the West, poor Adams was accused of hobnobbing with Catholics, conversing in Latin with nuns and priests, and visiting their schools and universities to address the faculty and the student body. Or he was labeled a "Unitarian," not because the Jacksonians knew that this was indeed his religion or even cared, but because in many parts of the country it was just a polite way of calling a man an "atheist." Meanwhile in puritan New England, Isaac Hill published a report that the President was seen "travelling through Rhode Island and Massachusetts on the Sabbath, in a ridiculous outfit of a jockey." What was the country coming to, worried the pious Mr. Hill?[24]

Even the gentle Quakers were sold a bill of goods. They were told that the Hero of the Battle of New Orleans, when a member of the Tennessee constitutional convention, advocated a proposition "to exempt Quakers from military duty" because of his sympathy for their belief in nonviolence. Although the Quakers found this very hard to believe, they were assured that it was so.

How thoroughly these Jacksonians understood the political game and how brilliantly they played it is best exemplified in a single question on the "religious issue" asked of James A. Hamilton by Martin Van Buren. "Does the old gentleman have prayers in his own house?" he queried. "If so, mention it modestly." Now Hamilton, who had been sent by the Magician to do liaison work in Nashville, had recently seen Jackson ask for a gun so that he could take a pot shot at a riverboat pilot who was annoying him. Nevertheless, the reply that Hamilton sent back to New York and which was subsequently published went like this: "[Jackson] is a sincere believer in the Christian religion, and performs his devotions regularly with his family in his own House, and in a Presbyterian Church in his neighborhood." In the New Hampshire *Patriot*, Isaac Hill went Hamilton one better. He had Jackson saying prayers "every morning and night, also table prayers." Future presidential candidates in search of mass support were well advised to cast a public image of deep religious belief—even if only recently acquired.

The nation's war veterans were not forgotten by these fast-stepping political innovators. Like many office seekers in each generation, the Democrats viewed the veteran as a chronic beggar perpetually looking for a government handout; or they feared him and hoped to buy his friendship with a subsidy. In deference to the veteran's sizable influence at the polls, the Jacksonians issued flat statements that if the General was elected President, "the officers and soldiers of the revolution might the more readily have their claims upon the government allowed."

To build their majority the Democrats even courted the Federalists, although that voting bloc was supposedly tainted with treason. No matter; one quick rub with a Republican cloth and they were as good as loyal Democrats. Such former Federalists as Roger B. Taney, Robert G. Harper, and Virgil Maxcy of Maryland; Louis McLane of Delaware; James Buchanan of Pennsylvania;

Theodore Lyman of Massachusetts; and John Berrien of Georgia
and Littleton W. Tazewell of Virginia appealed to their former
political comrades to follow them into Jackson's organization. Duff
Green, as an official party spokesman, welcomed all except those
he conveniently termed the "Hartford Convention Federalists." At
the same time Van Buren commissioned James A. Hamilton, son of
the great Alexander, to write several political tracts for Federalist
consumption which he planned to distribute throughout New England, Maryland, and Delaware. Many Federalists responded sympa-
thetically to the Democratic appeal because they thought that
through Jackson they could regain their lost political power. As
Democrats, they even mingled with the masses, which must have
caused Alexander Hamilton to turn violently in his grave. "The ad-
herents of Jackson in New Jersey," wrote one critic, "are all led on
by the ultra feds of the most incorrigible of the aristocrats who by
vociferation—impudence & abuse lead on a rabble and try to
intimidate weak men." They were the same men, he continued,
"who in the year 1800 were tools of the late Genl Hamilton &
wished to circulate his pamphlet on the subject of the then pending
Presidential election and to join him in denouncing the then President Adams."

The most concentrated Democratic propaganda, however, was
aimed at the vast numbers of farmers and yeoman throughout the
nation. Jackson was described to them as a man of the soil who
dropped his tools in the field like Cincinnatus of old and instantly
responded to his country's call to duty. But that scion of the
House of Braintree, that aristocrat, he never worked a day in his
life, never toiled, never knew suffering and hardship. As long as
he remained President his corrupting influence would spread like
a disease over the land. Indeed, an epidemic had already begun.
"We are sorry to learn," lamented the editor of the Winchester
Virginian in May 1827, "that owing to the ravages committed by
[the Hessian Fly] the wheat crop . . . begins to wear a sickly as-
pect, and that a general failure of it in this quarter is to be apprehended. Everything seems to go wrong since the birth of the
present Administration. Contemporaneous with that event . . . the
Weevil first made its appearance; both of which have since been at
work to the no small annoyance of the farmer."

farmers + yeoman — said 1 of them

To all muscular patriots, to all who thrilled at the cannon's roar, to all who cherished the image of the British retreating before an army of aroused Americans protecting their homeland, the Hero of New Orleans was portrayed as a second George Washington. He was the soldier boy of the Revolution, cruelly mutilated by a British officer; he was the veteran commander of the War of 1812, criminally betrayed by corrupt politicians. When the Coalition editors countered by attacking the General for the cold-blooded murders of innocent American militiamen, the Democrats replied with a "crushing and blinding argument": "Cool and Deliberate Murder. —Jackson coolly and deliberately put to death upward of fifteen hundred British troops on the 8th January, 1815, on the plains below New Orleans, for no other offense than that they wished to sup in the city that night."[25]

Presumably, all this propaganda helped to identify Jackson with the American people (whether they were farmers, veterans, Protestants, Catholics, Irish, Dutch, German, or members of some other enfranchised group) and induced the electorate to vote the Democratic ticket. But soon this approach was supplemented by other electioneering techniques—those gimmicks and tricks which gave the election its original style, its wild "delirium." Voters were completely unprepared for some of the stunts initiated in 1828, but once the original shock was absorbed, they asked for more.

One of the earliest and shrewdest moves of the Democrats was to adopt a symbol to represent their candidate. Since the Hero was already known as "Old Hickory"—had been since 1813— there was no problem in making a choice. Hickory brooms, hickory canes, hickory sticks shot up across the country, at crossroads, on steeples, on steamboats, in the hands of children—almost everywhere. Poles made of hickory were erected "in every village, as well as upon the corners of many city streets. . . . Many of these poles were standing as late as 1845, rotten momentoes [sic] of the delirium of 1828." Local Jackson Clubs and militia companies also organized ceremonies to plant hickory trees in the village and town square as part of their campaign to "enlighten the public mind."

"Planting hickory trees!" snorted the opposition press. "Odds

HICKORY TREES.

nuts and drumsticks! What have hickory trees to do with republicanism and the great contest?" Predictably, the Democrats did not stop their planting to tell them.

Another technique that proved almost as effective as the hickory symbol in arousing popular response was the public rally or street demonstration organized to honor the Hero. In Baltimore, a day set aside to commemorate the successful defense of the city against British attack during the War of 1812 was appropriated by the Democrats and converted into a Jackson rally. A "Grand Barbecue" was arranged by Roger B. Taney and his associates to climax the demonstration. "I am told by a gentleman who is employed to erect the fixtures," Jackson was advised, "that three Bullocks are to be roasted, and each man is to wear a Hickory Leaf in his hat by way of designation." On the appointed day, "gentlemen of the exchange, blacksmiths, tanners, carpenters, masons, butchers and the men from all trades . . . in fact the best part of the bone and sinew of the town was there—good Jackson sinew into the bargain." The festivities commenced with the firing of a cannon, followed by a "thrilling" parade of 700 marshals. Someone then called for a cheer—for the brave defenders of the city?—but the crowd responded with three cheers for the Hero of New Orleans. After that the crowd quaffed "their bumpers to his health" and listened to a lengthy and spine-tingling oration about his exploits against the British and the Indians. When the speeches ended, the congregation sang a new song entitled "Hickory Wood" and settled back to the splendid repast provided by the party.

On the pretext of honoring the victory of Oliver Hazard Perry in the War of 1812, the Jackson Committee in Frankfort, Kentucky, arranged a public celebration and dinner for September 10, 1827. The General was invited to participate, but because of limited time he was obliged to decline. However, in his place he sent a toast to be read during the ceremonies. "Kentucky!" he wrote. "Steadfast in principle, and valiant in war." Not a word about Perry or his victory! At the dinner all the toasts and resolutions extolled the virtues and the heroism of Andrew Jackson. Poor Perry was forgotten.

Not that the great Hero was the only man to receive the toasts of the Democrats at these celebrations. Sometimes Adams and Clay were remembered. On one occasion a toastmaster in Kentucky raised his glass to—"The Administration! Foisted on the people contrary to their wishes; dying while it lives. No cheers, no guns." Then he raised his glass again. "Henry Clay!" he trumpeted. "Kentucky mourns his loss as a mother weeps for her first born, while his captors exult in the prize. Three groans."

On two successive Fourths of July, 1827 and 1828, the patriotic ceremonies in many cities and villages were quietly converted into Jackson rallies. New England towns began the day with a military parade, followed by chapel meeting, hymns, toasts, and the public reading of the Declaration of Independence. Once the reading was out of the way, the Jacksonians pushed forward to wave the flag and the hickory stick, calling the General the nation's great defender of liberty and reminding the people how he preserved it for them at New Orleans. Then all were urged to huzza the name of Andrew Jackson.

Many of the demonstrations and banquets in the West—whether Fourth of July celebrations or not—were explosively boisterous, delighting the leaders who arranged them. In one state the Central Committee supervised the installation of a "Hickory pole at every cross road." Barbecues were advertised where the voters were told they could eat beef and pork and swill hard liquor "under the shadow of a hickory bush." "Those who fear to grease their fingers with a barbecued pig," chortled one Democrat, "or twist their mouths away at whisky grog, or start at the fame of a 'military chieftain' or are deafened by the thunder of the canon [sic] . . . may stay away."

In the Middle Atlantic states a touch of elegance was often added at large but select party functions. "The Jackson Dinner," commented one reveler at a New York City celebration, "was truly magnificent & was in every respect worthy of the occasion. Owing however to the mismanagement of one or two of the committee the expenses of the entertainment will unfortunately exceed the amount calculated by at least five hundred dollars. The Champagne was dealt out too liberally; 400 bottles were drank [sic]: a much greater quantity than I have ever known to be consumed at any Public Dinner in the City of New York." These scenes of unrestrained joy and enthusiasm over the party's presidential candidate stirred the hearts of the most cynical politicians. "Van Buren has learned you know," reported one observer, "that the *Hurra Boys* were for Jackson and . . . all the noisy *Turbulent Boisterous* Politicians are with him and to my regret they constitute a powerful host." The Magician did indeed appreciate the Hurra Boys; but more than that, he realized how fortunate the Democrats were to have Andrew Jackson as their candidate, a man whose career and personality automatically set off public demonstrations, a man whose character blended perfectly with their efforts to build a party. Americans had never before experienced a candidate quite like the General, not even in 1824 when he made his first bid for the presidency. Still, it was the same Jackson in 1828, but with greater attractiveness somehow, greater appeal.[26]

Democrats in the South imitated their Northern and Western organizers in rousing the electorate's interest. "Considerable pains were taken," remarked one of them, "to bring out the people . . . flags were made and sent to different parts of the county, and the people came in in companies of fifty or sixty with the flag flying at their head, with the words 'Jackson and Reform' on it in large letters." This outpouring of people, like all demonstrations in the General's honor, whether they were parades, rallies, barbecues, or dinners, was carefully planned and staged. Spontaneous gatherings were rare, because without organization and planning the crowds never materialized, the people never showed up in the numbers demanded by the party. To whip up enthusiasm prior to a public meeting, local committees frequently sent out squads of men on horseback "with labels on their hats" to identify their party and their candidate. In the Baltimore 12th Ward these riders threw small coins among the crowds that gathered, and called to the boys "to huzza for Jackson" as they rode by. Not a few times such street demonstrations indulged in unbecoming pettiness. For instance, the Hickory Club in Randolph, Massachusetts, which was adjacent to Quincy, organized a small parade to march past the President's home and shout, "Down with the House of Braintree, Hurray for Old Hickory."

Before long, several of the more imaginative Central Committees began toying with the possibility of including Jackson himself in their meetings and rallies, although this clearly violated tradition and ran the risk of outraging public decency. Still, many politicians were willing to chance it. "A visit from you," Congressman T. P. Moore told the General, during the first week in August, "would be productive of much good. We could advantageously contrast the time of your visit with that of Mr Clay & it is the period at which the Springs are most resorted. Your presence would convene thousands from all parts of the state. If you will write me by return mail, I will endeavor so to arrange the matter as to make your reception at once flattering & *serviceable*." But Jackson replied that such politicking was really against his principles. Besides, a bolt of lightning had killed his horses and destroyed Mrs. Jackson's carriage.

Other state committees kept after Jackson. Indiana asked for an appearance; Ohio, too. "If hard pressed," Atwater wrote the Hero, "you *must*, yes I say, you *must* visit us next autumn in person." However, Jackson appreciated that such campaigning would be regarded in many quarters as undignified, if not improper, so he politely but firmly declined.

At length the Louisiana Democrats succeeded in luring the wary General out of Tennessee, and they did it by inviting him to a celebration in New Orleans on January 8 to honor his great military victory. Surely no one could criticize him for taking part in a patriotic affair. But, as one committee member subtly reminded him, "The effect thro the Union would be such as would dispose all to feel grateful for your manifold Services." Apart from that, there were several other reasons for accepting which Jackson found most compelling. First, Louisiana was a "doubtful and troublesome state" whose vote had been split in 1824. It behooved him to "concentrate" it. Next, the legislature of the state refused to recognize his services in 1815 and this honor, though belatedly offered, would tend to wipe away all past unpleasantness and misunderstanding. Finally, according to one observer, it was felt that the "enthusiasm" such as this celebration could provide would "effect in the southwest what management was accomplishing in New York." Under the circumstances, therefore, Jackson could not decline the invitation. Besides, "His blood was up," said one man. "He was resolute to win."

In their letter urging the Hero to come to New Orleans, the

Louisiana Committee assured him that the reception, both on and off the battlefield, would be worthy of his presence—that he would be "hailed with enthusiastic demonstrations of respect and regard." Nothing would be left undone to provide him with every courtesy and accommodation befitting the high position he held in the public esteem. Moreover, to lessen the inconvenience of the journey, they would dispatch the ship *Pocahontas* to convey him to New Orleans.

In accepting the invitation, Jackson laid down one condition: the celebration must be completely nonpolitical. The Committee replied that they were more than happy to abide by his terms. Nevertheless, they went right ahead with their plans to secure national attention in the event, all the while insisting that the celebration had nothing to do with politics.

Once these preliminary problems were out the way, the Hero notified Major Lewis and the Nashville Junto to begin preparations for the trip and to schedule a stop at Natchez, Mississippi, on the way down. He wanted to "receive the [Jackson] committee" in that city, he said, though he had every intention of avoiding "the appearance of electioneering." Then he added a postscript to his letter: "Have Judge Overton informed of the arrangements."

Not only Overton, but the entire city of Natchez, was informed. And the schedule of events programmed by the Tennessee, Mississippi, and Louisiana state committees for the Hero's two personal appearances could not have been more elaborate, more thrilling to the people, or more commanding of national interest. Major Lewis even arranged to have a second steamship stand by, in case the *Pocahontas* was delayed on account of weather, river conditions, or some other calamity. "The importance of the occasion," Lewis wrote his chief, "requires absolute certainty with regard to our movements."

Late in December, Jackson boarded the *Pocahontas* and headed south to New Orleans. With him on this "non-political" trip were Judge Overton, John Coffee, William Carroll, Houston, Lewis, and deputations from the Ohio, Kentucky, New York, Pennsylvania, and Mississippi state delegations. When the group finally arrived at Natchez, a great crowd turned out to greet the warrior; cannons boomed; a public dinner and ball were given; and Jackson heard himself called the benefactor of his country whose services could never be forgotten. After thanking the good people for their recognition of his "humble" accomplishments, Jackson returned to his ship and proceeded south.[27]

January 8, 1828, dawned cloudy and dark over New Orleans, a chilly day that threatened to ruin in an instant what had taken months to prepare. But at ten o'clock, as though on signal, the thick mist that had covered the land and water rose into great clouds. The sun broke through and bathed the scene in brilliant light. The clouds scurried off to the east.

On that "never to be forgotten day," the city was packed with people from as far away as New Hampshire, Illinois, New York, and Ohio. They crowded along the river bank, hung from windows and balconies, and stood on the roofs of their homes. The tops and riggings of ships at the wharves were alive with spectators. And wherever they stood or sat, the people stared upstream, watching for Jackson's coming, their hearts palpitating "at the sound of his name, and the anticipation of his arrival in the city." As they waited they saw a flotilla of steamboats get under way to serve as an escort. In all, eighteen ships of the "first class" maneuvered into position. Finally, the *Pocahontas* rounded the bend of the river and came into sight, preceded by "two stupendous boats, lashed together." The flotilla signaled its presence with a continuous fire of artillery, answered by several ships in the harbor and from the shore.

Then the crowds saw him standing on the fantail of the *Pocahontas*, his head uncovered. They let loose with wild screams. They waved to him, shouted his name, and finally in unison set up a cry: "Huzza! Huzza! Huzza!"

At the precise moment that General Jackson's foot touched the shore a signal was given. Artillery blazed away. The fearsome noise "thundered from the land and the water" as the erect commander strode forward to meet the welcoming committee. Generals Planché and Labaltat with soldiers of the Revolution and the remnants of the "old New Orleans Battalion" stood stiffly at attention, forming a line in his honor. The governor moved forward and greeted the Hero with a long laudatory address, customary on such

BIG FUSS AT JAN. 8th 1828 PARTY

occasions. Then the General reviewed the troops, his shoulders squared, chin high, looking every inch the proud commander and savior of his country. Mrs. Jackson, with a small group of Tennessee ladies, hung back to avoid being noticed, but the adoring crowd spotted her and shouted their welcome.

That night a magnificent dinner was tendered the General and his lady. But it was more than a local affair, more than an aggregation of tired politicians and old soldiers paying tribute to a man who had spared the city from British capture. It was an entire nation expressing homage to a brave soldier, a dutiful son, a living legend. Men from every section of the country proposed extravagant toasts in his honor. And despite the injunction against mentioning the presidential election, the toasts had one common theme:

ANDREW JACKSON
His Titles are his Services
His Party the American People

When the shouting, drinking, speechmaking, and huzzahing were over, the members of the Central Committee congratulated themselves for organizing what was probably "the most stupendous thing of the kind that had ever occurred in the United States." One man said it was "like a Dream. The World has never witnessed so glorious, so wonderful a Celebration—never has *Gratitude* & *Patriotism* so happily united, so beautifully blended—& it will form a bright page in American history."

Although other state committees could not match the glory and splendor of the New Orleans shindig, still their ability to organize giant rallies improved as the campaign wore on. Naturally, the Democrats claimed that their meetings were always packed because their candidate represented the people, and just as naturally such claims invited peppery comments from the Adams newspapers. "The multiplication of Jackson meetings," sputtered Peter Force, editor of the Washington *National Journal*, "and the number of which they are composed, are favorite themes with the Opposition papers. . . . If we go into one of these meetings, of whom do we find them composed? Do we see there the solid, substantial, moral and reflecting yeomanry of the country? No. . . . They comprise a large portion of the dissolute, the noisy, the discontented, and designing of society." Perhaps the Democratic claim that only Jackson was the "candidate of the people" was in fact so much political blather; even so, it was imprudent of the Adams press to refute the claim by describing the people who attended the meetings as dissolute, discontented, and designing. Instead of sneering, the Adams men would have been better advised to imitate the Democrats, at least in trying to identify their own candidate with large numbers of voters. "The Jackson men," sighed one Coalitionist, "are extremely active devoting themselves, soul and body to their cause. They have advertised a meeting to be held on Monday eveng. next, which I have no doubt will be numerously attended as great pains have been taken to court the *rabble*, and to bring them out." There were thousands in every city who came out because efforts were taken to bring them out, and yet the Coalitionists continued to call them the rabble. Small wonder, then, that Jackson's name became synonymous with the democracy.

To prove the Hero's unrivaled popularity, the Democrats began conducting public opinion polls. Militias, grand juries, readers of certain newspapers, bridal parties, and other groups were asked to state their preference. And, as politicians soon learned, published polls had a tendency to create votes. Since many men will only run with the pack, polls served the useful purpose of indicating the direction in which the pack was headed.[28]

Early in the canvass the leaders noticed the delight with which the people responded to their new brand of electioneering, how the parades, barbecues, tree plantings, and rallies "amused and entertained" them. The favorable reaction encouraged the Democrats to program a wider assortment of entertainments, which soon included songs, jokes, cartoons, funny stories, poems, and puns. Songs like "Hickory Wood" and "The Battle of New Orleans" (the latter sung to the tune of "Hail to the Chief") became popular at rallies, causing some anxious men to tremble at the possibility of presidential elections turning into singing tournaments or popularity contests. At length, special wearing apparel was introduced— such as hats sporting hickory leaves, canes, vests, and buttons—to designate the user's allegiance to General Jackson.

In several issues of Green's "Extra" *Telegraph* some of the best jokes and funny sayings were reprinted as part of the political entertainment. To wit:

"Hurrah for *Jackson*," said one man.

"Hurrah for the Devil," said a spunky Coalitionist.

"Very well," retorted the Jacksonian. "You stick to your candidate, and I'll stick to mine."

One story was told of a man who found the Adams supporters like the Frenchman who strutted and boasted that King Louis had spoken to him.

"What did the King say to you?" asked an awed friend.

"He told me to get out of his way," replied the happy Frenchman.

All the puns were pretty ghastly, as puns usually are, but they, too, served the people's cause:

Question: "Why is Adams on ticklish grounds?"

Answer: "Because he stands on slippery Clay."

Question: "Why has Adams an aversion to the Postmaster General?"

Answer: "Because he dislikes to McLean the Augean Stables."

Several "funny" stories were salacious, resulting in part from the unfortunate discussion in the campaign of the strange circumstances surrounding Jackson's marriage and the feeling among Democrats that they must reply to verbal filth in kind. In what now seems like the funniest joke ever recounted in campaigning history —funny because it is so totally incredible—the Jacksonians claimed that President John Quincy Adams of Massachusetts was once a practicing pimp. Probably the chief executive's old enemy, Jonathan Russell, who served with Adams at the peace negotiations in Ghent that ended the War of 1812, furnished the details for this uncommon tale. The story first appeared in a short campaign biography of Old Hickory published by Isaac Hill and entitled *Brief Sketch of the Life, Character and Services of Major General Andrew Jackson* in which it was stated that Adams, while Minister to Russia, procured an American girl for Tsar Alexander I. The facts behind this libel, as reported by the President in his diary, were obviously quite different. The girl in question was Martha Godfrey, a chambermaid to Mrs. Adams and nurse to young Charles Francis Adams. In her letters back home Martha entertained her friends by narrating the gossip of the Russian court. One such letter, which recounted the Tsar's reputed love affairs, was intercepted by Russian postal authorities and turned over to Alexander. Apparently the letter amused the sovereign and he expressed a wish to see the girl. Just why the Tsar of All the Russias would want to meet a gossipy nursemaid from Boston, and meet her in the presence of his wife, is difficult to understand. Adams said that Alexander was curious. In any event, as it developed, the Tsarina's sister, the Princess Amelia of Baden, asked to meet young Charles, so he was sent to her accompanied by his nurse. During the visit the Tsar and his wife chanced to come by and passed ten minutes talking to the child and finally meeting good old Martha, whose letter, said Adams, "had afforded them some amusement." She was a girl of irreproachable conduct, wrote the President, who returned to the United States, married a man who played a "very respectable musical instrument made in Boston," and died there some years later. "It is from this trivial incident that this base imputation has been trumped up," he added.

That Isaac Hill would publish this story or that anyone would believe John Quincy Adams a procurer is an extraordinary commentary on American politics in 1828. Not only was the canard widely circulated but some desperate men chose to give it credence. In the West the Democrats mocked the President as "The Pimp of the Coalition" whose fabulous success as a diplomat had at last been explained.

When Mrs. Jackson was slandered as an adulteress and a bigamist, the Democrats, operating on the principle that one "dirty" story deserved another, charged that Mrs. Adams had had premarital relations with the President. Later, they said that she was illegitimate. Duff Green led the assault against Mrs. Adams and was amazed when it earned him the contempt it deserved. ". . . I was denounced," he admitted, "in the most bitter terms for assailing *female* character by those very men, who had rolled the slanders on Mrs. Jackson under their tongues as the sweetest morsel that had been dressed up by peter Force and Co during the whole campaign."

There can be no question that this election splattered more filth in more different directions and upon more innocent people than any other in American history. No one was spared, not the candidates, not their wives, not their friends and supporters. To some extent the sudden appearance of an army of Hurra Boys in active politics accounted for much of this nonsense. True, they had participated in earlier campaigns, but never in such numbers nor with such approval and encouragement by state and national leaders. And never had they such license to say and publish whatever they supposed would swell a majority at the polls. Had the leaders honestly sought to engage the ordinary citizen in the operation of American politics rather than simply win his vote, had they truly sponsored the "rise of the common man," the country would have been better served. Older and wiser heads wondered if these men had any conception of the dangers that threatened the nation on account of their "revolution." At stake was not some minor post to be fobbed off on a popular entertainer, but the office of the President of the United States, an office occupied for nearly forty years by the most distinguished men the country could produce. Should the "revolution" succeed, it would mean for the future that any amiable incompetent clever enough to attract popular support might presume to occupy the chair of Washington, Jefferson, and Madison. "God help the nation," said one, "I am afraid it will run mad."[29]

XII

By the spring of 1828 the electorate, prodded by the politicians, started to take their places around the party banner. National and state tickets were headed with Jackson's name, a procedure that in some places had not been practiced in a presidential contest in over a dozen years. Governor James B. Ray in Indiana narrowly escaped defeat for re-election in 1828 by running as an independent. The slowness of newspaper deliveries in advertising his independence saved him from almost certain defeat. In the East, Pennsylvania Democrats warned Governor J. Andrew Shulze either to "come out or go out," while in Massachusetts David Henshaw proposed Marcus Morton for governor and published a list of "Republican Jackson" candidates for the state senate with his own name at the top of the list. As early as 1827 the state contest in Kentucky "turned on our preference for the Presidential candidates," said Charleton Hunt; the same was true in Ohio, where "Jackson and Reform," wrote Atwater, was the "test at this election for members of the Legislature."[30]

While state leaders were quick to link Jackson's name with local candidates in the hope that his popularity would rub off on them, they were not so quick to explain the Hero's intended program. But whether they chose to include or exclude national questions, whether they fabricated history or not, whether they blackened Adams' name by calling him a pimp, gambler, or aristocrat, depended upon their analysis of popular approval or disapproval. The remarkable skill of so many Democrats in avoiding the problems that would divide them and in concentrating their efforts on "union and concert of action" lightened their task of raising a national party out of the wreckage of factionalism.

In seeking—and ultimately winning—popular approval for their labor through their conventions, committees, increased newspaper coverage of the election, popular campaigning, and such, the Jacksonians indirectly advanced the cause of democracy in America. The General's striking personality and character, his reputation as a hero, his career as an Indian fighter, and, most important, the fact that he was a self-made man, dovetailed perfectly with their party work. Hereafter, the availability of a presidential candidate would depend to a large extent on his personal attractiveness, irrespective of his governmental experience. In 1828, Jackson's attractiveness was the result not merely of an heroic past but of the strenuous, imaginative, often unscrupulous labors of a remarkable group of first-rate politicians.

Dem. — GOOD AT AVOIDING ISSUES!

4. The National Republicans

I

IN A LETTER to a friend written some twenty years after this campaign, Jabez D. Hammond, the politician-historian of New York, recalled joining the Coalition because he approved its principles and program and respected the President's talent and integrity. On the other side of the political fence, however, he said he found a "military chieftain," an upstart, a man totally devoid of a "literary, legal and statesmanlike education." Certainly the White House was no place to acquire such an education; so, like a great many other thoughtful men, Hammond enlisted in what he called the "National Republican" party. "By the by," he added, "that party received its name from a series of numbers written by me and published in the Albany Daily Advertiser and republished in the Boston papers, signed 'National Republican' in, I believe, 1827."

Age dims the memory, and Hammond no doubt forgot that in 1828 both parties used the name indiscriminately. Even Duff Green adopted it at the tail end of the campaign, designating the Jackson-Calhoun ticket in his newspaper as the "National Republican Party." Eventually the label stuck to the Adams-Clay group, but by that time the Jacksonians were happy to call themselves "Democrats."

In this election the Coalitionists had a solid claim to the disputed title. They were less fearful of centralized government and less concerned about the constitutional limitations of the federal authority. Their program of aid to all the partners of the social compact was specific and intelligible. In speeches and public pronouncements both Adams and Clay had clearly defined their intentions: federally sponsored public works, including those that would advance the intellectual and cultural life of America; protection and stimulation of industry through higher tariffs; improved banking facilities; and the distribution of federal surpluses to the states to implement the national program. Thus, as far as principles and program go, the Coalition was a more developed party than its rival. Only in the vital areas of organization and leadership did it suffer by comparison. And by 1828 that suffering became an agony.

Henry Clay undertook most of the work involved in erecting a national party, yet his limited success was achieved without the assistance, encouragement, or interest of the President. Several members of the Cabinet helped Clay, along with a handful of Congressmen, most notably Daniel Webster and John W. Taylor of New York. But their labors crumbled before the Jacksonian wrecking crew of Calhoun, Eaton, Van Buren, Benton, and a half-dozen others, each an expert in political in-fighting or a master parliamentarian or a publicist.

It is a pity that the rigidly correct and high-minded Adams could not see his way clear to lighten the burden of his friends. Nothing could persuade him to abandon the candidate's traditional silence; nor would he essay the role of President as party leader, invoke his many powers, and electioneer in his own behalf. The mere suggestion by Webster that he show a courtesy to his friends in Philadelphia so annoyed the proper Adams that he planned to bypass the city on a trip back home to Quincy. Only the tact of his wife, Louisa, persuaded him to change his mind; but his physical presence in Philadelphia hardly disguised his intense annoyance and irritation. On this same homeward journey he reacted coldly to any display of public affection and brushed off state leaders who invited him to attend rallies in his honor.

These trivial incidents were part of a larger picture of the President's unfortunate public relations. Even when he tried to be friendly, he invariably landed on his face. For example, in Baltimore on October 16, 1827, Adams was present to help commemorate the successful defense of the city against British attack during the War of 1812. And, in due course, he was asked to propose a toast.

"Ebony and Topaz," he responded. "General Ross's posthumous coat of arms, and the republican militiamen who gave it." As he paused, members of the audience stared at one another, searching for the meaning. What had he meant, "Ebony and Topaz," and what was the business about a coat of arms? Seeing their bewilderment, Adams quickly explained his meaning, and what he said left his audience dumfounded. The allusion was taken from Voltaire's *Le Blanc et Le Noir* (a savagely anti-Christian work, hooted the Democratic press) in which Ebony stood for the spirit of evil, represented by the British Robert Ross whose coat of arms received a posthumous addition by the king, while Topaz was the good spirit represented by the American militiamen.

This ridiculous toast and its explanation, when published, rocked the Democrats with laughter. At first, said the New York *Evening Post*, "we supposed it to have been the production of some wicked Jacksonian wag who had undertaken to burlesque the clumsy wit and unwieldy eloquence of the ex-professor." But the realization that it actually came from "Old Ebony" himself was almost too good to be true. Duff Green said that he would reserve comment because he was not as versed in "Oriental literature" as President Adams.

Naturally, the National Republicans were mortified. In a letter to Clay, Charles Hammond wrote: "I wish Mr. Adams's *ebony and topaz* were submerged in the deepest profound of the bathos. You great men have no privilege to commit [such] blunders." But before Adams quit his office, his blunders were legion. And perhaps the worst was his refusal to assist Clay in purging the government of those men who opposed the Administration. The appointees of the former Secretary of the Treasury, William Crawford, were everywhere, faceless creatures who were impossible to remove because they could not be indicted for disloyalty to the satisfaction of President Adams. So they remained, and there was nothing Clay could do but look to the future. "Henceforth," he announced to Webster in April 1827, "I think the principle ought to be steadily adhered to of appointing only friends to the Administration in public offices. Such I believe is the general conviction in the Cabinet." Had the principle been invoked two years earlier and commanded the President's wholehearted support, it might have boosted the Adams campaign in 1828. As it was, a small army of government appointees went about their business, indifferent (if not hostile) to the Administration's future. "I do not know an officer of the Gen Govt in the District," wrote one Coalitionist, "upon whom we could confidently call for five dollars to print a pamphlet." Small wonder; many of them had already contributed to the Jackson campaign. The Postmaster General, John McLean, for instance, was quietly subsidizing Green's *Telegraph* with Department favors. "I am the servant of the people," he sanctimoniously wrote Jackson, "not of the administration. The patronage placed in my hands is to be used for the public benefit."[1]

Because Adams refused to sanction any measure to counteract the growing strength of the Democratic organization or involve himself in any action to encourage the men who sought party support for him, he was the principal architect of his own defeat. He would not even say in some public manner that he liked being President and wanted to keep his job. He turned his head away from the hard fact that politicians all around him were engaged in party activity, whether he liked it or not, whether he approved or not. Stubbornly, resolutely, he resisted what his own stern conscience disapproved, however much he would benefit personally from a less scrupulous concern for political proprieties. Lacking any real capacity to distinguish between vice and expediency, he judged them equally immoral, against which Christian men, like himself, must constantly war.

The President's contribution to Democratic success was not all indirect, however. As an Adams, true to the tradition of his father, he could not resist the temptation to do himself an injury. His handling of the Indian removal problem in the Southwest became in fact "a recommendation of Jackson to the voice" of the entire region. Even in the field of foreign relations, where his genius had been revealed when he was Secretary of State under James Monroe and where all but the most partisan Democrats were prepared to acknowledge his skill, he severely damaged his public reputation. The United States and England had adopted restrictive policies regarding trade with the British West Indies, yet both recognized that this reciprocal ill will hurt their own nationals. By the middle of the 1820's, Britain was disposed to compromise. But not Adams.

He pressed for preferential treatment of Americans entering West Indian ports, refusing, at the same time, to allow the removal of American duties on British ships engaged in the same trade. His demands were preposterous, and before the American Minister to London, Albert Gallatin, could be authorized to withdraw them, the British government broke off the discussion and once again closed the West Indies to American ships.

The Jacksonian newspapers pounced on Adams for his senseless obstinacy and stupid trifling with American economic interests. "Our diplomatic President," they mocked, had ruined "colonial intercourse with Great Britain." Seemingly blind to the consequences of failure, they said, he sacrificed an extremely lucrative market, which Southern agricultural and Northern shipping interests had once enjoyed.

Democrats pretended that there would be no further criticism of Jackson's qualifications now that Adams had raised a question of his own fitness for office. Surely the General could do no worse, they guffawed, than the "experienced diplomat" from Braintree. Though this was wishful thinking, nevertheless Van Buren's political instincts told him that the game was over. *"You may rest assured,"* he advised a friend, *"that the re-election of Mr. Adams is out of the question."*

While the Democratic press roared at the President for his alleged faults and vices, Adams maintained his public composure. Unlike Jackson, he refused to roar back at these "vile calumniators," no matter what the provocation. Instead, he spilled his hurt and bitterness over the secret pages of his diary. Seated at his desk, in the quiet of his study, writing furiously, he dispatched his tormentors with the business end of his pen, calling them all "skunks of party slander."[2]

II

In the spring of 1827, just as the Jacksonians were inaugurating their grand alliances, a general meeting of the friends of the Administration was called in Boston for the purpose of forming a new national party. Both Clay and Webster urged the obliteration of "old political landmarks" and the "amalgamation" of former factions into a modern organization responsive to the changing economic needs of the American people. "It appears to me to be important," Clay explained to Webster, "that we should, on all occasions, inculcate the incontestable truth that now there are but two parties in the Union . . . and that all reference to obsolete denominations is for the purpose of fraud and deception."

In the hope of actually starting a second party, local Republicans and former Federalists trooped to the Boston meeting, led by Governor Levi Lincoln. Attentively, they listened to the massive voice of Daniel Webster intone all their hopes and interests. His swelling oratory about the goals to be achieved through a national program sponsored by the federal government may not have altered party history, but it most assuredly clinched his own election to the United States Senate.

The meeting disappointed its promoters, however, because it drew only a local crowd. Yet the earnest talk of tariffs and improvements and sound banking ultimately reached the ears of rising capitalists, manufacturers, entrepreneurs, and some farmers and mechanics clear across the nation. These men believed that their financial status would swell to an unprecedented level of prosperity once the American System became law.

The task of transforming this enthusiasm into a majority of electoral votes rested principally with the leaders of the Coalition in Washington; and Clay and Webster turned to it zestfully. One of their first actions was to begin a search for that essential ingredient of party-making—money. "It seems to me," Clay advised Webster, "that our friends who have the ability should contribute a fund for the purpose of aiding the cause . . . You stated, I think, last winter that such a fund would be raised, and that I was authorized to address you on the subject. . . . If you coincide in these views, would it not be well for you to give an impulse to the creation of a fund for the above objects by conversation or other communication with some of our friends?" Thus, with little more than a friendly exchange of letters and a remembrance of an earlier conversation, Webster was unofficially appointed the party treasurer. And a good choice it was, too. Few Republicans in the country matched his keen sense to locate tappable pools of liquid resources. In a reply that might be regarded as acceptance of his appointment, Webster sent Clay 250 dollars with a promise of additional money as soon as he contacted "some of our friends." Whereupon the Secretary advised him that John Pleasant, editor of the Richmond *Whig*, required immediate financial assistance but to remit the money to the "Hon J.S. Johnston," who corresponded with the editor. This circumvention would avoid messy embarrassments in the transferral of funds.

Webster and Clay made quite an effective financial team. Through "conversation" and "communication" Webster pursued what money was available; then Clay told him where it could be sent to do the most good. For instance, a newspaper in Ohio edited by Charles Hammond attracted national attention in 1827 by carrying stories that Jackson's wife was an adultress and his mother a prostitute. Immediately, Clay alerted Webster to the opportunity. "C. Hammonds paper in Cincinnati," he wrote, ". . . is I think upon the whole, the most efficient . . . gazette that espouses our cause. . . . I think he is every way worthy of encouragement and patronage. . . . Perhaps he might receive a present of a new set of types." The Massachusetts statesman agreed that Hammond's sheet "is certainly ably & vigorously conducted." Such vigor surely deserved a present, and Webster thought he could obtain a set of types "for abt. 5 or 6 hundred Dollars" which he would ship to Cincinnati forthwith.[3]

Webster's thorough canvassing of possible financial backers and his persistence in obtaining large contributions fattened the treasury by many thousands of dollars. But costs mounted so quickly that other methods had to be introduced to supplement his work. Fund-raising committees were organized at the county level, and party meetings and conventions became occasions to solicit cash contributions. The 200 men at the Adams state convention in Virginia, for example, taxed themselves five dollars each to foot their publication bill. An additional financial advantage was enjoyed by the Coalition on account of Clay's position as Secretary of State. He designated public printers to publish the laws and notices of the government. Using his power with considerable restraint, Clay nonetheless removed Jackson printers whenever he could identify

them and find suitable substitutes. Thus, he replaced Amos Kendall's *Argus* with the Kentucky *Commentator* and Isaac Hill's
Patriot with the New Hampshire *Journal*. Since few established
editors were so incautious as to jeopardize their federal largesse,
removals were comparatively few.

Much of the money that Webster and Clay raised (and between
them they raised a great deal) was spent buying newspaper support. "The course adopted by the Opposition, in the dissemination
of Newspapers and publications against the Administration and
supporting presses," declared Clay, "leaves to its friends no other
alternative than that of following their example, so far at least as
to circulate information among the people." Before long, the Administration had an excellent press that radiated the richness and
variety of its national program. In Washington, the *National Intelligencer*, edited by Joseph Gales and William W. Seaton, and
the *National Journal*, edited by Peter Force, were powerful organs
whose voices carried as far as the best Jacksonian sheets. In the
states, they were echoed by the New York *American*, the New
Jersey *Patriot*, the Cincinnati *Gazette*, the Virginia *Constitutional
Whig*, the Maryland *Republican* and the Baltimore *Marylander*,
Niles Weekly Register, the Massachusetts *Journal*, the Kentucky
Reporter, the Illinois *Gazette*, the Missouri *Republican*, and many
others. Out West, probably a majority of established journals stood
four-square behind the Coalition, while in New England, Administration newspapers by themselves rubbed out most of the gains
of the Democratic organizations. "Why Sir," stormed Francis Baylies, the tireless Jacksonian publicist from Massachusetts, "all New
England believes that . . . Jackson left N. Orleans in a huff on the
night of 8th January. That Jackson wrote a mispelt letter to the
Editors of the Journal. That John Marshall said every man who had
any regard for the Constitution must oppose Gen Jackson. . . . Our
people are honest and mean well but they are deluded by con-
tinual falsehoods."

To propagate these "falsehoods," quite a few Administration
journals were established in 1827 and 1828, although nothing compared to the number of Jacksonian sheets. In North Carolina (to
use a Southern and therefore uncommon example), two new Adams
papers were founded at the beginning of the campaign to bring that

state's total to six. Ohio, Kentucky, New York, and Pennsylvania made similar additions, each succored in part by government patronage. By the end of 1828 the country was so well papered (if not actually littered) with opposing journals that enterprising farmers took to stringing the sheets between poles to serve as scarecrows.

One of the most basic tactical errors committed by the Adams men was their failure to rivet their high-powered newspapers to the emerging state organizations as the Jacksonians had done. Where the Richmond *Enquirer*, the Albany *Argus*, the Boston *Statesman*, the New Hampshire *Patriot*, and the Kentucky *Argus* were real mouthpieces of their state parties, the Administration presses were much too independent of local organizations. In addition, some of the Adams editors were politically inept and unconsciously abetted the Jackson cause. For the want of a better term, they frequently dubbed the Administration conventions "Anti-Jackson meetings." They played up the glamorous General (mostly his supposed vices) to the neglect of Adams' considerable virtues. Of course they mistakenly saw Old Hickory as a gun-toting backwoodsman, and as such Jackson made better copy than the scholarly Adams. Writers had no trouble finding descriptive phrases to spring the Hero to life, but they were stumped by the sour-faced intellectual. In desperation they resorted to repeated commonplaces about his education, his experience, and his talents. But American voters found no vicarious pleasure in the triumphs of the President to compare with those of the General. The trouble with Adams, complained several Coalition editors, was his remoteness, the fact that little was known about him except for his public career. Even in Massachusetts, few people "are acquainted with the person of John Q," noted one politician.[4]

To overcome their disadvantage in this age suddenly fascinated by personality as a qualification for the presidency, Clay, several members of the Cabinet, Webster, and other Congressmen hit the campaign trail as official representatives of the Administration. They deployed over a wide area to preach the American System and to extol Adams' unique presidential attributes. They journeyed from state to state, winding in and out of the major sections, attending rallies, meetings, and public dinners. They busied themselves collecting campaign contributions and writing political propaganda. Eventually, they stitched together a national party that was active in all the important states in the East, West, and upper South.

As soon as Clay found it possible to escape his duties in Washington he started a long campaign trek. He went to Baltimore to attend an affair in his honor. Then up to Philadelphia to combine politicking with a medical checkup by the celebrated Dr. Philip S. Physick. Later he swung south to Virginia to speak at several dinners; from Virginia he headed west to Kentucky, Indiana, and Ohio. When he reached Cincinnati a crowd estimated at 5,000 turned out to roar their welcome. He even stood in the town courtyard for three straight days during the 1828 state election in Kentucky to shake the hand of every man who came to vote. So unsparing were his efforts that, had he been the candidate himself, he said, he could not have labored more.

Unfortunately for the National Republicans, there were too few Henry Clays, otherwise the organizational imbalance between the two great parties might not have been so great. Clay prepared nine separate and lengthy addresses to the public in defense of the Administration against the libels of the Democrats. Almost monthly he corresponded with a large corps of politicians, including Peter B. Porter and John W. Taylor of New York, John Sergeant and Philip S. Markley of Pennsylvania, Levi Lincoln of Massachusetts, John Crittenden of Kentucky, Josiah Johnston of Louisiana, Francis Brooke and John Pleasants of Virginia, and others. He exhorted their fullest energies to establish newspapers, form local committees, and organize state conventions. "It is a part of the system of the friends of General Jackson," Clay said to Francis Brooke, "to make demonstrations—speak boldly—claim every body and every State, and carry the election by storm. The circumstance most to be deprecated is that this system has too much success in dispiriting our friends. You ask my opinion as to the project of a convention in Virginia to nominate, in January next, electors for Mr. Adams. It appears to me to be an excellent project, and one that can not fail to have good effect."

At the same time he reminded his friends of the urgency of creating county organizations. "I submitted your paper on the subject of a County meeting," he was told by one leader, ". . . to a small party of friends at my house . . . who approved of the suggestions & promised their cordial cooperation in carrying them into execution." Clay also insisted that the American System be treated as the party's platform. He explained to Webster that the question of internal improvements must be supported in New England "and that the West and Penna. should be made *sensible* of that support. . . . We must keep the two interests of D.M. & I.I. [Domestic Manufactures and Internal Improvements] allied, and both lend to the support of that other great & not less important interest of Navigation." As early as 1827 he was advising the party's hierarchy that "the time has come when demonstrations should be made, and made in N England as well as elsewhere."[5]

Daniel Webster was another diligent campaigner, but he was not as personally and as intensely involved in the election as Clay. He even allowed that Jackson was "a very honest man" and "a good soldier"; nevertheless, "some of us think him wholly unfit for the place to which he aspires," he concluded. Along with raising money for the campaign, Webster toured New England to ensure its loyalty to the President, and later accepted speaking engagements in the crucial states of Pennsylvania and New York. Fearful that the Keystone State might swing with the "Dutch" vote, he arranged for the publication of a *"pamphlet,* for the especial benefit of Pennsylvania" to be printed both in English and German. But perhaps his greatest work was in convincing Federalists that they belonged behind the President, something he had been doing since the early months of 1825.

While other members of the Cabinet imitated Clay's barnstorming, they scheduled more limited tours, usually concentrating on particular sections of the country. Apparently they enjoyed unexpected success because the Democrats, snarling derision, started calling them the "juggling or traveling Cabinet." The Secretary of the Navy, Samuel Southard, for instance, whipped through Maryland, Delaware, and New Jersey, harassing the Jacksonian organizations in each community he visited. His words were so sharp and cut so deeply that the General felt the lacerations clear out in Tennessee and bellowed his pain.[6]

Although the efforts of these Cabinet officers and Congressmen, plus the meaningful program of economic and intellectual progress that they presented to the electorate, combined with the excellence of their newspaper campaign, were all of them mighty supports to Adams' candidacy, more important than these were the organizations formed within the states to direct and control the popular vote. Like the Democrats, the National Republicans held local rallies, county meetings, and state conventions. "Political meetings are continually taking place in the different Towns of the State," Samuel Southard was told by a New Jersey politician, "where Resolutions are passed and Delegates appointed to attend at Trenton to fix on the Electoral ticket." In addition, they printed pamphlets, handbills, and broadsides; appointed Central Committees and committees of correspondence; and scheduled "public commotions" in the President's favor. They were most active in the Middle Atlantic and Western states, where unflagging energy was required to keep pace with the fast-stepping opposition. In Maryland, both parties were reported "fairly in the field, under *'whip & spur'!'* In Kentucky, John J. Crittenden informed Clay that the Central Committee had at last reached its stride. Letters had been written to influential men in every county of the state "invoking the utmost exertion of their activity & zeal." In New Jersey, this zeal was so well directed that the Adams men probably had a better organization than the Jacksonians.

Like the Democrats, the National Republicans climaxed their work with the convocation of a state convention. "What party," asked William C. Rives of Virginia, "is so poor as not to have its *convention* in these times." Even in the South, where Adams' prospects were next to hopeless, partisans of the Administration called conventions in Virginia, North Carolina, and Louisiana; however, they were content to stage local "meetings" in Alabama and Mississippi rather than gamble on anything more elaborate. At most of these conventions the precedures were fairly similar. The Virginia meeting, for example, met in January 1828 with 200 delegates in attendance, presided over by Francis T. Brooke. The first order of business, after organizing the convention, was the nomination of Adams and his running mate, Richard Rush of Pennsylvania. Then the electoral ticket was composed and a committee appointed to prepare an "Address to the People," of which 30,000 copies were ordered. Next, a Central Committee and a committee of corre-

1828 Virg - Richard Rush JQA's running-mate

spondence were formed and instructed to communicate with the "National General Committee" in Washington for the distribution of documents and messages emanating from the office of Henry Clay. What gave this convention additional interest was the attempt of the managers to glamorize the electoral ticket by heading it with the names of James Madison and James Monroe. Unfortunately, both ex-Presidents declined the honor, much to the distress of the Secretary of State. "It will for the moment, produce a bad effect," worried Clay, "but I am persuaded that it will soon pass off."

These conventions for Adams were usually well attended, although the Democrats insisted that "they did not represent the people." Several of them unofficially adopted the oak tree as a symbol of the National Republican party, and while this was a move in the right direction, the oak, unlike the hickory, did not capture the popular fancy, perhaps because its relation to the presidential candidate was rather obscure. At a few of the conventions the Coalitionists also stumbled over the vice presidential nomination, not because of personal vendettas or factional feuds, but because of their earnest attempt to support the one man who would strengthen the ticket. "We understand from Washington," wrote a Pennsylvanian, "that this is a matter that cannot be settled until after the meeting of Congress & consultation with our friends from the Western & Southern States." Most National Republicans, after consultation, seemed to think that the Vice President should come from Pennsylvania, Virginia, or New York. Although several states nominated Richard Rush, a few others left the slot vacant and simply charged their electors to vote for that man most acceptable to the majority of Adams men throughout the nation.

In addition to their many other problems, the National Republicans were troubled by sectional conflicts over the issues—just like the Democrats. They were chagrined to learn that the Virginia convention frankly admitted that it could not approve all the Administration's policies—and this moments after Adams had been nominated and the delegates pledged to support him. It was that old devil the tariff which bothered them, and they wanted Adams and Clay to understand how they felt about protection and what they could be expected to do if higher rates were introduced in Congress. Similarly, the friends of the President discovered that

oak tree—symbol of nat'l Repub. party
sectional conflicts!

the congeries of factions united behind them varied from state to state, that the electorate did not respond to their appeals in any set pattern. It was impossible to identify a Coalitionist according to his past record, or reckon from earlier preferences those individuals most likely to vote for Adams—at least not with any degree of certainty. Former Federalists and members of old political factions paraded into both parties, depending on local conditions and the calculated advantages to be obtained in supporting one candidate over another. So there were Republicans and Federalists voting for Jackson, and nationalists and states' righters voting for Adams.

During the campaign most of the Central Committees appointed by the Adams conventions engaged crack speakers to entertain the crowds. But foolishly the Coalitionists in the West relied almost exclusively on the persuasiveness of their speakers, on their newspaper support, and on the value of their program as understood from Adams' presidential messages to Congress. More county committees, more public demonstrations of enthusiasm for Adams and Rush, more local meetings, and more tax assessors turning in lists of voter preference, as the Jacksonians were doing, would have been more helpful. It soon became quite evident that the National Republican party as an organization was distinctly outmatched by the Democrats. In many places the Adams men were exasperatingly slow in erecting the party apparatus; Central Committees seemed unconcerned about union and concert of action; and in too many important cities and states there was no organization worthy of the name. When Henry Clay sent out a detailed paper on the necessity of large committees of vigilance, he received an acknowledgment from one state leader that questioned the advisability of such a committee. "It was apprehended by some," the letter read, "that the appoint. of such a comm. would excite the animadversions of our adversaries." Exciting animadversions in politics, according to this man, apparently fell within the category of unsportsmanlike conduct. However, he allowed that "the plan in effect will be carried out"—one way or another. This was the sort of thing that Clay was continually up against. Several times he was lectured by pedants that "in a country like ours where freedom of opinion and of action are secured . . . to organize a disciplined corps who will submit to the drill of some half dozen interested demogogues" was impossible.

AJ – got Repubs + Federalists
JQA – got nationalists + states' righters.

These shortcomings among the Adams men, serious though they were, did not invalidate the excellent start they made toward the formation of a national party. The course of governmental action advocated by the Administration and the slate of candidates put forward to steer that course attracted voters in every section of the country. Webster, Taylor, Brooke, the traveling Cabinet, all of them worked strenuously to create among state politicians a sense of joint responsibility for the election of the national ticket. Together, they succeeded in providing the American people with a party of principle and purpose—one committed to a presidential candidate of proven talent, integrity, and experience.[7]

III

To convert all this integrity and purpose into a winning majority in the electoral college remained the central problem. And where was Adams going to find the 131 votes he needed for re-election? Admittedly, New England was fairly safe and would start the party off with a minimum of 51 electoral ballots. By adding Kentucky, Ohio, and Missouri—all won by Clay in 1824—the total would be brought to 84. Then, if Adams picked up a substantial portion of the 17 votes from New Jersey, Delaware, and Maryland, the election could be successfully concluded in New York and Pennsylvania, both highly susceptible to the tariff argument. There were many variables in this calculation, but the National Republicans were not without political advantages in 1826 and 1827. Unfortunately, they frittered most of them away. By superb miscalculation they lost the biggest prize of all—New York.

In the election of 1824, Adams had won 26 of New York's 36 electoral votes, and there was every reason to hope he could duplicate that victory now that the people, rather than Van Buren's legislature, chose the presidential electors. The fact that Clinton and Van Buren, the two most powerful politicians in the state, were Jacksonians did present a serious obstacle, but certainly not an insurmountable one. Luckily for the Administration, Clinton died in February 1828 and most of his followers (who had silently suffered his Jacksonianism) now crowded into the Adams camp.

In Washington, Clay breathed a deep sigh of relief when he received the doleful news. "All accounts concur," he enthused, "that the political effect of Mr. Clinton's death will be favorable to the administration; and intelligence generally from that State . . . is very cheering."

But far more "cheering" than the governor's "fortuitous demise" was the sudden outbreak of Anti-Masonry in the western counties of New York. Virtually overnight the Coalition became the beneficiary of a wild frenzy that threatened to crush the Democratic organization and annihilate Jackson at the polls. It all began when one William Morgan mysteriously disappeared in the fall of 1826.

Morgan was an itinerant stone mason who eventually settled down in Batavia, New York, where he took up his work and lived quietly with his family. He belonged to the Masonic Order but apparently did not get along too well with his brethren. After one dispute Morgan swore revenge against the order and threatened to write a book revealing the secrets of the first three degrees of Masonry. He found a publisher for his manuscript in David C. Miller, the editor of the Batavia *Advocate*. Although his friends begged him to disavow his intention and abide by his earlier promise to protect the Masonic secrets, Morgan would not listen. So his friends had him arrested for stealing a shirt and tie, just to let him know they meant business. At the same time they seized the page proofs of the book and fired Miller's office.

When the charge against Morgan was not sustained, he was rearrested for a debt owed to another Mason. Someone then paid his bail. As he emerged from jail he was hustled into an awaiting carriage and taken to Fort Niagara, where, according to Thurlow Weed, he was held captive for several days and then drowned in the Niagara River. Whether this is a true account of Morgan's final days still remains in doubt; probably the full history of his disappearance and death will never be known.

Yet one thing was certainly known. The frustrated author had vanished. Within a matter of weeks the western counties of New York were ablaze with excitement. What had the Masons done to this unfortunate man? Where had they taken him? Who were the criminals? Sensing more than a local disturbance, Governor Clinton issued a proclamation for the apprehension of the kidnapers.

Public meetings were called, prosecutors gathered evidence, and indictments were handed down against several Masons. As the trials of these men began, witnesses against them suddenly disappeared, like Morgan, or were hurried out of town. Excitement and curiosity gave way to anger, and the entire fraternity of Freemasons was charged with sabotaging the machinery of the law, with daring to place their secret organization ahead of human life.

A year later a body was washed up on the shores of Lake Ontario. Morgan's widow was requested to examine the remains, and to her horror she recognized her late husband. Despite the fact that the body had been in the water for a little more than a year, she was positive of her identification because of the "double teeth all around." Later several more bodies were fished out of the lake, all of them identified by someone as the late, lamented Morgan. After a while the Jacksonians became pretty annoyed with these shenanigans. "Some dead body is always dug up," complained one, "and examined, two or three times, in order to excite into activity all the old prejudices against the masons and masonry."

The discovery of a "good enough" body rekindled the Anti-Masonic torch. The pious, Bible-oriented Yankees, who had recently moved from New England to western New York, vowed to eradicate the order. It was a conspiracy of aristocrats, they preached, bound together by fearful oaths and committed to the advancement and protection of Masons at all cost; it was a threat to social stability, a menace to the public safety. Determined to halt this threat, the inflamed citizens of the west commenced a political witch hunt. They crowded into public meetings where they voiced their resentment and fear. No Masons, they decreed, would be supported for public office, and those already occupying seats of power would be removed.

While the Anti-Masonic outbreak appeared to some as a democratic movement to terminate the alleged privileges of an elite, to others it was a sudden release of violence produced by "the disturbed and unsettled state of the public mind" during a period of rapid economic and political transition. Unquestionably, deep psychological and possibly religious forces were at work. But even more fundamental in explaining the "disturbed" state of the public mind may have been the economic strangle hold that Albany and

New York City bankers exerted over western expansion and speculation. One of the most important institutions controlling and, on occasion, thwarting western growth was the Regency-operated Mechanics and Farmers Bank in Albany. Several years later a director of that bank remarked, "Now you cannot imagine, without more knowledge of the business transactions of the M & F Bank, how interwoven the prosperity & even existence of the Western Banks in this state, are with that Institution." Other "eastern" bankers repeatedly applied the financial brake to western speculation for sound business reasons, an action that demonstrated how completely they controlled the prosperity of the outlying districts of New York. Naturally, this control and interference infuriated westerners. Perhaps, then, the cold-blooded murder of Morgan and the conspiracy to protect his kidnapers unleashed a pent-up fury against all those exercising economic and political advantage in the west. Many bankers and businessmen were Masons. So, too, were their political friends in Albany and New York City.

At the height of the disturbance someone discovered that Andrew Jackson was a "grand king" of the Masonic Order. For the moment the announcement nearly flattened the Democrats, especially when it was also learned that John Quincy Adams was free "from all imputed criminality of that sort." The New York Jacksonians threw up their hands in despair. Old Hickory had joined one organization too many.

After the initial shock wore off, the Regency, in its typical businesslike manner, set about repairing the damage. First off, they dispatched a letter to the Jackson party in Boston, urgently requesting information that would brand Adams with the hot iron of Masonry. The Boston men were apprised of the seriousness of the request and asked to find something—anything—that would help. Meanwhile, other letters went "to our Friends at Washington" with a plea to direct their attention to the problem in order to "determine on the best course" of action and to notify the Regency immediately of their concerted opinion. Quite frankly, they expected the Little Magician to conjure up the formula that would rescue them from the disaster.

Van Buren responded by return mail, but he had nothing con-

AJ - MASON!

crete to propose. He simply charged his friends to await the progress of events and to exploit the first mistake the Anti-Masons
committed. Shortly thereafter, the long-awaited report from the
Boston organization reached New York and, like many long-
awaited reports, it contained both good and bad news. The good
news was that Major Russell of the *Centinel* claimed he had positive
information that Adams had been initiated into a Masonic Lodge
in 1791 and again in 1794. Splendid. But with it came the bad news
that Russell was a congenital liar who would do anything to attract
attention and that his testimony was practically worthless. Naturally, the Regency discarded the uncalled-for report on Russell and
released the story of Adams' Masonic initiation to several western
newspapers. Duff Green picked it up, added an embellishment of
his own, and printed the lie in his October 18 issue. He claimed
that Russell had actually seen with his own eyes *"Adams made a
mason"* in Boston. The President categorically denied the published
story. "I state that I am not, never was, and never shall be a freemason," he said. Unfortunately for the Jacksonians, most New
Yorkers believed him.[8]

When Van Buren returned from Washington he made a hurried
tour through the western counties to inspect for himself the extent
of the disaffection. He was stunned by what he saw. Nevertheless,
in a letter to Andrew Jackson, the Senator pretended that all was
well. He reassured the General that the "politics of this State . . .
are yet governed by Old Party feelings." Although Anti-Masonry
was a setback, "I am sure I cannot be mistaken in believing, that
we shall be able to give you a very decided majority of the votes."

Just how he intended to manage this feat in the face of rising
dissatisfaction with his party, the cautious Senator did not explain.
As always, he depended on the Regency. And, as always, they did
not fail him. They demonstrated their mettle by uncovering the
heartwarming information that Henry Clay was a bona fide, 100-
per-cent Freemason. "I have just been told," Gulian C. Verplanck
gleefully wrote Jesse Hoyt, "by a distinguished Western member
[of Congress] that Mr. Clay is a Mason of rank. He has been in
Lodges, Chapters &c., with him. Cannot this be so used with Clay's
friends in our Western Districts, or with the people, as to divert
that question from mingling with the Presidential one? Suggest

these matters to those who will use them to advantage." The information was indeed used extensively, but its advantage was voided almost entirely by Jackson's personal "criminality."

The logical consequence of these political developments should have been the formation of a coalition between the Anti-Masons and the National Republicans in New York. Such an alliance would have strengthened the entire Administration state ticket down to the lowest seeker of public favor. Yet nothing of the sort occurred. On the contrary, the Anti-Masons and National Republicans started bickering over petty differences instead of emphasizing their common objective: the defeat of the "grand king," Andrew Jackson.

Thurlow Weed, one of the first men to direct the political force of Anti-Masonry through the establishment of a Rochester newspaper, the *Anti-Masonic Enquirer,* struggled to unite the two groups to form a single party. But his work was constantly obstructed by many Adams men who were themselves Freemasons. Still, a compromise could have been reached at almost any time if the National Republicans had shown a modicum of political sense.

Francis Granger was the link between the two parties. A champion of Anti-Masonry, a loyal supporter of the Administration, and a confidant of Thurlow Weed, he was the odds-on favorite for the gubernatorial nomination of the Anti-Masonic party. Had the Adams men accepted him to head their own state ticket, a coalition between the two anti-Jackson groups would have been assured. On July 23, 1828, in Utica, the fateful decision was reached when the National Republicans held their convention. Undismayed by the predictable consequence of their act, they nominated Smith Thompson, an associate justice of the United State Supreme Court, for governor. Then, in what appeared to westerners as a studied and deliberate insult, they chose Granger for lieutenant governor.

The Anti-Masons dismissed the Thompson nomination with a simple statement that the judge was not "radical enough" to suit their taste. Instead, at their convention on August 4, they nominated Granger and "Honest" John Crary of Washington County.

Weed argued with the National Republicans that there was still time to effect a fusion with Anti-Masons, provided they dumped Thompson in favor of the more radical Granger. In reply, they

sectionalism still occurred btwn Anti-Masons + National Repubs.

offered the lame excuse that such action would offend many Administration men and "jeopardize not only the State, but the electoral ticket." However, if the Anti-Masons were so anxious for cooperation, they conceded, let them show their good will by adopting the Administration slate of candidates. Apparently fusion was fine, as long as the National Republicans did nothing to bring it about.

Since the Administration men would not budge, Granger tried to move the Anti-Masons around. He respectfully declined their nomination and asked them to accept Thompson in his place. But the Anti-Masons were as stubborn as the Adams men. They called a second convention and replaced Granger with the farcical and slightly addled Solomon Southwick. Under the circumstances, they huffily announced, it was *"expedient . . . to disregard all national & State politics"* in determining their slate of candidates. So, what might have been a powerful anti-Jackson coalition in New York ended with the two parties feuding with each other and supporting two weak candidates for governor.

The Democrats howled their delight. As the Magician had predicted it was just a matter of waiting "until we have the full advantage of all the follies" of the "bad men" who led the movement. "I presume," laughed one Jacksonian, ". . . Mr. Van Buren's long fingers will be found in it by the sage editors of the Intelligencer. As the time rolls on, and the period of active engagement approaches, the cause of Jackson improves." In any event, the "anti-masonic snake" was scotched—at least for the moment.[9]

But the National Republicans had not yet completed the task of snatching defeat from the jaws of victory in New York. They were given a second opportunity in the spring of 1828 when a movement took shape in New York City that contained elements that were anti-Tammany, anti-Regency, and anti-Jackson. It concerned the auction system, which dated from 1815 when the British chose New York as the best American seaport to unload their surplus manufactures. These goods were sold at auction; but the right to sell at auction was a licensed monopoly restricted to about fifty individuals appointed by the governor though actually controlled by a dozen men. The opponents of the system argued that these sales destroyed competition, injured domestic manufactures, and encouraged fraud. Importing merchants unanimously condemned the auction, and since their interests were linked to those of many mechanics, tradesmen, and clerks, a representative segment of the city's working population agitated for reform. On May 2, 1828, they held an anti-auction meeting in Masonic Hall to frame their grievances within a series of written resolutions. One of these resolutions declared, "Auctions are a monopoly . . . giving to a few, that which ought to be distributed among the mercantile community generally." One proposed solution was the increase of tariff duties by the federal government to bar British imports.

The mention of protective rates should have jolted the National Republicans to attention. A common ground existed by which a city party could be formed in opposition to the Jacksonian Tammany Hall. Yet the Adams men made no serious attempt to identify their own program with the resolution of May 2.

Again, in October, over 2,000 people in New York City attended another anti-auction meeting. Politically, it was a mixed crowd, with both the Administration and Jackson parties well represented. The importance of the gathering was further signified by the presence of several Congressmen, including Churchill C. Cambreleng and Gulian C. Verplanck. At one point in the proceedings, Cambreleng and Verplanck were asked to make a statement, and both frankly refused to support any measure that would abolish sales at auction. Politics and the tariff, they insisted, must be divorced from the discussion. The audience was shocked by their attitude. Since both men were Jacksonians, and Cambreleng a lesser member of the Regency, their words were interpreted as the official position of the state's Democratic party. Hence, it seemed to some observers that the Jacksonians, by their defense of the auction, virtually handed over the vote of the city's merchants and mechanics to the National Republicans.

A few weeks later, another meeting was called by the mechanics of New York. In strongly worded resolutions, Cambreleng and Verplanck were castigated for refusing to heed the expressed will of their constituents. Support for their re-election to Congress was withdrawn; and, after obtaining the approval of the merchants, the mechanics nominated Campbell P. White, Thomas C. Taylor, and David B. Ogden for Congress. White, however, had already been nominated by Tammany Hall, and he was the only candidate of the three to win election.

Unfortunately, the Adams men never took full advantage of the opportunity presented them in New York City. They failed to recognize and act upon the attraction their national program held for some members of the urban working class; they appeared victimized by the Jackson propaganda that depicted them as a party of aristocrats repudiated by the people at large. Nevertheless, for a party of supposed aristocrats, they polled an extraordinary number of votes from western farmers and city mechanics.

Indeed, the interest of urban workers in the program of the National Republicans caused the Democratic managers deep concern. One Eastern politician regretfully concluded that "the real Jackson party . . . is in the country." Westerners shared that opinion. "Our Towns are most aristocratic," Felix Grundy was told. "Our country people mostly republican." In such "aristocratic" cities as New York and Philadelphia, what shielded Andrew Jackson from defeat was his unrivaled personal appeal among recent immigrant groups and among certain nationalities such as the Irish and the Germans. Had the Adams men given adequate attention to the business of party-building in these cities, the final election returns would have been quite different.[10]

IV

The palsied condition of the Adams party in New York was unhappily duplicated in Pennsylvania. The enormous advantage that the Administration held over the Jacksonians in the Keystone State on account of their unqualified advocacy of the tariff was wasted by a do-nothing organization. According to all serious observers, no one could campaign successfully in Pennsylvania without endorsing the program of the National Republicans. It was rumored as early as 1827 that unless Jackson himself accepted public works and a higher tariff as his platform, and accepted them without double talk, Pennsylvania would shift to Adams. ". . . In other words [he] should eat the *whole hog* as the condition of her support of him."

Jackson never did eat the whole hog, but still he won Pennsylvania in a landslide. A clue to the reason behind it was suggested in the 1827 state elections, when the Democrats won decisively in most counties but lost Philadelphia. They lost the only contest for a seat in Congress. John Sergeant, the Administration candidate, trounced Judge Hemphill, though the latter had the solid backing of George Dallas, one of the state's leading Democrats. The defeat was a stinging loss to the Jacksonians, who fretted over their continued failure to attract city voters. But Sergeant's victory was easy enough to explain inasmuch as he had the support of the Federalists, and the Federalists controlled Philadelphia. In terms of the next presidential election, it should have been incontrovertibly clear even to the most witless politician that "amalgamation" between the Federalists and the National Republicans was mandatory. Still, the Adams men were reluctant to accept open amalgamation. Would it not, they asked, "have a tendency to drive the *uncommitted* . . . into the Jackson ranks." They struggled with the question. Finally they held "a sort of council of ancients," at which time it was discovered that a "large majority of the company were ready to write the federalists to fraternize with us." But seven argued against such action and argued so successfully that the final decision was a rejection of amalgamation. And with that bold decision, Adams' defeat was guaranteed.

Everywhere else in Pennsylvania the election results of 1827 were dramatically opposite that of Philadelphia. In Lebanon County "the activity of the Jackson men, and the inertness of their opponents," wrote a newspaper reporter, provided a stunning Democratic victory. For one thing, the Jacksonians nominated for the General Assembly only those men who were well known, widely respected, and therefore practically certain of election; for another, they required from their candidates, in every instance, "a pledge that they will vote for the General, as the indispensable condition on which they will be supported." This "superior management and activity . . . gave them the machinery of the Democratic party," and with it they "returned a majority of members to the General Assembly."

The machinery of party! Obviously, such machinery was powerful enough to carry a state election and carry it handsomely. But could the machinery go the distance of a presidential contest, especially when national issues such as the tariff were involved? Jacksonians were extremely vulnerable on the question in Pennsylvania, and the leaders were reduced to making absurd statements about how the

General would raise protection rates every time he passed his hand over them.

With each new session of Congress the issue was obviously getting hotter. As recently as the spring of 1827 Daniel Webster had guided a Woolens Bill through the House of Representatives. When it arrived in the Senate, the Democrats schemed to defeat it but feared to do so openly. Their problem was resolved by Senator Robert Y. Hayne of South Carolina who moved that it be laid on the table. Since Congress was scheduled to adjourn in three days, the motion would quietly kill the measure without requiring the members to vote against it directly. Several Jacksonians bolted through the Senate door as the vote was taken on the motion. A tie resulted, and Vice President Calhoun cast the deciding ballot that sent the bill into limbo.

The Senate's cynical handling of this important measure roused protectionists to renewed efforts to force the government into a more realistic attitude toward American trade and industry. The old 1824 schedule of rates on iron, hemp, woolen goods, and glass, they averred, was ineffectual and meaningless. New Yorkers and Pennsylvanians were particularly distressed, and William Marcy warned Van Buren that the congressional dodge would create "infinite mischief to the cause of General Jackson in this State."

Hezekiah Niles, editor of his own *Weekly Register,* and Mathew Carey undertook the task of organizing a campaign for higher tariff rates, but it remained for Henry Clay to provide the excellent idea of a national convention to dramatize the needs of American manufacturers and farmers. "Let all persons," he wrote on March 18, 1827 "(friends of D.M.I.I. and the Admin) without regard to party denominations heretofore existing, be brought out. . . . Let the meeting publish an address, well drawn, temperate in language, but firm in purpose, and eloquent and animated in composition. The meeting will form a nucleus."

A nucleus, indeed, and more than that. The meeting might have served to unite the demands of the farmer and manufacturer in the Western and Middle Atlantic states in a general platform designed to support the candidacy of John Quincy Adams. It could have been a genuine national nominating convention, had the managers of the enterprise dared to throw off the guise of nonpartisanship. Instead, they avoided all reference to the approaching presidential election, presumably to ensure the success of the measures proposed.

In May 1827 the Pennsylvania Society for the Promotion of Manufacturers and the Mechanic Arts sent out a call to farmers, manufacturers, and "friends of both branches of industry" throughout the country to hold state conventions and appoint at least five delegates to meet in Harrisburg, Pennsylvania, to chart a course of action. On July 30, one hundred delegates arrived in Harrisburg representing all but nine states. As might be expected, no one showed up from Georgia, the Carolinas, Mississippi, Alabama, and Tennessee. The failure of Missouri and Illinois (and possibly Louisiana as well) to send representatives resulted probably from the distance of these states from Harrisburg and the limited time allowed for the selection of delegates.

The most active participants at the convention were Mathew Carey and Charles J. Ingersoll of Pennsylvania and Hezekiah Niles of Maryland. The presiding officer was Joseph Ritner, also of Pennsylvania. The near-perfect accord that characterized the meeting produced a memorial and a petition to Congress within a matter of days. In addition, a schedule of increased tariff duties was suggested for flax, hemp, iron, distilled spirits, and other commodities; but both the memorial and the schedule emphasized the dire need of the woolen industry for greater protection.

In all this talk about government aid to industry and agriculture there was no mention of the presidential election. Clay's letter suggesting the meeting called on the "friends of D.M.I.I. and the Admin" to form a nucleus. At Harrisburg, domestic manufactures were thoroughly discussed but nothing was said about the "Admin" —no endorsement, no approval, nothing. In a simpering letter to the Secretary of State, John Sergeant of Pennsylvania said: "I was in hopes . . . that something would have been done in Harrisburg, but there is no sign of movement." No sign of movement! even though a number of prominent Administration Senators and Representatives sat bold as brass in the front ranks of the delegates. At an earlier time and under friendlier circumstances, Martin Van Buren once told Henry Clay that to have an efficient party it was necessary to "drill" the members, but apparently the National Republicans preferred "hopes" to "drill."

The memorial and the recommended duties were signed on Friday, August 3, by ninety-seven men. Hezekiah Niles and a committee of eight were given the job of drafting an address in time for the first meeting of Congress in December. The report was subsequently published in October, and Niles reiterated the convention's appeal to the government to redress the grievances of American manufacturers and farmers. Throughout the North there was general satisfaction with the Harrisburg proceedings, attested to by the additional meetings called in some states to approve the recommendations of the convention. In the South, however, the reaction was predictably opposite. The tariff laws of 1816, 1820, and 1824 were lumped together and condemned as a monumental violation of the Constitution. In Columbia, South Carolina, Dr. Thomas Cooper electrified an audience by predicting that the South would soon be forced to "calculate the value of the Union."

After the appearance of Niles' address, Jacksonian politicians in the North made a careful distinction when evaluating the Harrisburg Convention. Manufacturers and wool growers, they cooed, were all honest and well-intentioned men. Of course they were. But the managers of the convention, those sly agents of the Administration, were base deceivers who sought to make the convention a "political stalkinghorse" for the President. "The whole phalanx of the Opposition papers," reported one Adams journal, "are in great trouble about the Harrisburg Convention. They see in it a thousand political evils on every side. They think there is some cabalistic meaning in the phrase—American System—something which is to seduce . . . Pennsylvania in the next election." Indeed, that was precisely what they saw. "The Harrisburg Convention," cried the New York *Evening Post*, "is considered in its true light, as a contemptible political strategem to bring over Pennsylvania to the Adams party."

If this was truly the strategem of the Administration men, it was thunderingly unsuccessful. All the political sounds they produced at Harrisburg were so muted that only the sharp-eared Jacksonians could hear them. By the close of 1827, despite the Harrisburg Convention, the tariff initiative was lost to the National Republicans.

When Congress reconvened in December, both Houses contained a majority of Jacksonians, and the leaders promptly began the task of writing a tariff that would pacify the Middle Atlantic and Western states and thereby ensure Jackson's election to the presidency.

In New York and Pennsylvania, the two states that were pivotal in all their calculations for a successful campaign, the National Republicans dissipated their natural advantages. The ultimate penalty came to forty-eight electoral votes—enough to swing the election.[11]

V

In not a few states, 1828 marked the end of some old political wars and the beginning of some new ones. And neither the ending of the one nor the beginning of the other favored Adams in any way, as can be seen by what happened in Kentucky and Pennsylvania. Kentucky was a sort of ending, an ending to a political feud that went back almost ten years and had its origins in the Panic of 1819. Because of the acute financial distress brought on by that depression, the Kentucky legislature passed a series of relief measures: stay laws to prevent immediate foreclosures, abolition of imprisonment for debt, and a bill chartering the Bank of the Commonwealth and authorizing it to issue 3,000,000 dollars' worth of paper for circulation. The inflation of the currency and the stay of replevin promptly divided the Republican party into two opposing factions: Relief and Anti-Relief. The Anti-Relief party was composed of large farmers, the mercantile class, and the inevitable contingent of lawyers. Together, they brought suit against the new laws and won a judgment from the Court of Appeals, the highest court in Kentucky, invalidating the replevin stay law. Whereupon the Relief party, consisting of debtors, small farmers, and a second contingent of lawyers, gained control of the legislature, abolished the Court of Appeals, and created a New Court. This Relief–New Court party (the terms were almost synonymous after 1825) elected Joseph Desha to the office of governor over his Anti-Relief rival, Christopher Tompkins. In his efforts at fiscal and judicial reform,

Desha, a charming, ambitious courtier, was aided by the chief justice of the New Court, William T. Barry, a trim, sallow, neatly dressed, and modest little man, and by the first clerk of the New Court, Francis Preston Blair, an associate of Kendall on the *Argus* and later an officer of the Commonwealth Bank. Other leaders of the Relief party included John Rowan, a short, corpulent, unscrupulous demagogue, and George M. Bibb, an uncompromising, no-nonsense advocate of states' rights.

The leadership of the Anti-Relief–Old Court party, on the other hand, included Charles A. Wickliffe, a rich lawyer who debated under the mistaken notion that bombast was oratory; his cousin, Martin D. Hardin, also a lawyer, whose wit John Randolph of Roanoke had once described as "like a butcher's knife whetted on a brickbat"; and John J. Crittenden, a homely, crooked-toothed, very civil and obliging gentleman who was only mildly Anti-Relief.

By the time the presidential election of 1828 rolled around, the old political fires had banked considerably. The New Court had been abolished by the legislature and the old judges reinstated. Although most Relief–New Court men were Jacksonians, there were notable exceptions, such as William Gerard, who supported Clay and the Administration. Since the political fires no longer scorched, both the National Republican and Democratic parties sought to "amalgamate" the Old and New Court advocates in time to influence the presidential election. But the Jacksonians were much more successful in winning converts, for, as one observer reported, men like Moore, Kendall, and Bibb were constantly arranging dinners and private meetings "to produce a union, as far as practicable, among relief and anti-relief men in favor of Jackson." But they made one mistake. They nominated William Barry for governor, and because he was so intimately associated with the New Court, "hundreds, nay thousands, of Genl. Jacksons old court friends," wrote the ever-watchful Major Lewis, "could not be prevailed on to vote for Barry." Nevertheless, Lewis discounted the gubernatorial contest as a true "test of strength of parties." One of the "travelling corpsmen," Felix Grundy, had recently been through Kentucky and had reported to the Nashville Committee that "Jackson will most unquestionably get its electoral vote."

The Hero did indeed win Kentucky in 1828. While his personal popularity and Western background were considerable assets to him, he was helped in no small measure by politicians like Bibb, Kendall, Moore, and Blair who managed his campaign and ultimately succeeded in amalgamating the former factions through their committees, private meetings, and dinners.

Meanwhile, in Philadelphia, a new and most significant development took shape late in July 1828. It was the formation of a Workingmen's party, composed of laborers, intellectuals, physicians, merchants, speculators, lawyers, politicians, and others. In the beginning, the party agitated against several "abuses," including legislative aid to those who monopolized "the wealth creating powers of modern mechanism," "excessive distillation" of liquor, and the lottery system. It also advocated improvements in general education. Later, it demanded reforms respecting the auction system, imprisonment for debt, mechanics lien laws, monopolies, and paper money. While the movement actually drew considerable strength from middle-class capitalists, it does seem probable that the party included a bona fide labor group contending for the interests of the wage-earner. In time the party spread to New York, Boston, Newark, and Baltimore, and during the course of its history shifted its support from one party to the other, crossing political lines almost at will in order to achieve its objectives.

Since the Federalists controlled the city of Philadelphia, the appearance of the Workingmen's party in 1828 necessarily weakened that control. And the Federalists were already laboring under the disadvantage of the vote taken by the National Republicans at their "council of ancients" against amalgamation. Hence, to protect their domination of Philadelphia, the Federalists tried to absorb the Workingmen's party, but their motives were so blatantly selfish and obvious that all such attempts were abortive. Meanwhile, the Adams men just stood by, watching, doing nothing. The Democrats, on the other hand, were frightened by the sudden appearance of the Workingmen and, in typical fashion, began hacking at the new party in order to split it into several factions and thereby dissipate its political strength. In the 1828 Philadelphia election, both parties, in an effort to join what they could not destroy or absorb, ran candidates as Workingmen. When the final returns were in, the city and the county were swept clean by the Democrats; all the Workingmen candidates who also ran on the Jackson ticket were likewise elected.

The failure of the National Republicans to do much of anything with the Workingmen, along with their refusal to amalgamate with the Federalists, were distress signals of acute organizational weaknesses. This plus the strong German, Irish, and recent immigrant vote cast for Jackon and his ticket and the backing of a machine that had repaired the single disaster of the previous year were too much for the National Republicans. In sum, the political beginning in Pennsylvania, like the political ending in Kentucky, helped Adams not at all. He lost both states.[12]

VI

The campaign waged by Administration writers in the press and in pamphlets, books, handbills, and other media contained all the power and drive that the state organizations too frequently lacked. So much power, in fact, that local politicians did not always trouble themselves with other forms of campaigning except to engage a few stump speakers now and then and to arrange an occasional parade. By the time the Coalition writers completed their tasks, they had accomplished a miracle of propaganda in portraying Jackson as a ruffian, killer, duelist, and butcher, a man whose temperament, lack of education, and lack of experience in government totally disqualified him for the high office he sought.

Perhaps the most "delectable" story injected into this contest concerned Jackson's marriage, the details of which Charles Hammond, editor of the Cincinnati *Gazette*, uncovered on a research trip he made to Kentucky and Tennessee. His findings (by no means original) allegedly proved that Jackson prevailed upon Rachel Robards to desert her husband and "live with him in the character of a wife." Anyone else would have been jailed for "open and notorious lewdness," cried the outraged Coalition, but not Old Hickory. He was rewarded with a presidential nomination.

The story shocked and confounded the electorate, as such stories are intended to do. Certain points in the twisted account given by

Hammond came close enough to the truth to lend credibility to the whole. Technical adultery and bigamy had been committed, although Rachel and Andrew were guiltless of intentional wrongdoing.

The story began with Rachel Donelson's unhappy marriage to Lewis Robards. At the Robertson settlement in Tennessee on the Cumberland River the couple lived with Rachel's widowed mother until such time as the Indians had been sufficiently subdued in the area to permit moving outside the settlement. But before that happened, young Andrew Jackson arrived on the scene. The year was 1788 and the widow Donelson welcomed him into her house as a boarder for the additional protection he could provide against marauding Indians. Yet his mere presence aroused Robards' deepest suspicions and jealousy. Husband and wife quarreled constantly, and on one occasion Robards threatened to whip the intruder. Finally Rachel could stand the abuse and mistreatment no longer. She deserted her husband and fled with Jackson to Natchez, chaperoned by the elderly Colonel John Stark. Later, in the mistaken notion that Robards had obtained a divorce, Rachel and Andrew were married in August 1791.

Not for some time did the happy couple learn the awful truth. Robards had no divorce; rather, he had an enabling act from the legislature of Virginia permitting him to bring suit against his wife in a court of law. The act stated that if a jury found Rachel guilty of adultery and desertion as charged, then the divorce would be granted. Because Robards had not exercised the privilege conferred by the enabling act, Rachel, who had remarried in the interim, was a bigamist. In September 1793, at Robards' request, a jury in Mercer County, Kentucky, finally dissolved the first marriage; four months later Rachel and Andrew recited their wedding vows a second time.

In itself, the true story contained enough ammunition to kill a regiment of presidential candidates. Whether provoked or not, Rachel had deserted her lawful husband and lived in technical adultery with Jackson. "Ought a convicted adultress and her paramour husband to be placed in the highest offices of this free and christian land?" fumed Charles Hammond. "If General Jackson should be elected President," wrote another, "what effect, think you, fellow-citizens, will it have upon the American youth?" Presumably no one with a sense of decency needed an answer to that frightening question.

It was one thing for Hammond to publish the unwholesome story, but quite another to garnish it with enough distortions so that Jackson emerged from the pages as a seducer and home-wrecker. Hammond brought out a small edition of the romance entitled *A View of General Jackson's Domestic Relations* and later, in 1828, he established a special journal, *Truth's Advocate and Monthly Anti-Jackson Expositor*, to advance his attempted assassination of the Hero's character. Both productions drove Jackson into a volcanic rage. And because the National General Committee in Washington gave them wide circulation and because he had information from a correspondent in Kentucky that Hammond had communicated with the Secretary of State during his research trip, Jackson was convinced that Adams and Clay were the villains responsible for the story in the first place. Immediately, he commissioned William B. Lewis and Judge Overton to prepare a statement for the newspapers to correct the Hammond account. During the preparation the old Hero stood at Lewis' side, handing him documents, giving him advice, and hurrying him on to the completion of his task. The final statement was published in 1827, replete with affadavits, letters, and sworn testimony. Sadly, angrily, Jackson was forced to reveal to his countrymen certain details of his private life and his wife's unending agony.

Then, using the types Webster so generously sent him, Hammond struck again:

"☞ General Jackson's mother was a COMMON PROSTITUTE," read the opening sentence of the piece, "brought to this country by the British soldiers! She afterwards married a MULATTO MAN, with whom she had several children, of which number General JACKSON IS ONE! ! !" In a succeeding section, Hammond stated that the Hero's eldest brother was sold as a slave in Carolina.[13]

Along with assailing Jackson's moral behavior in the courtship of his wife, the opposition newspapers tried to prove that he was a cold-blooded murderer and butcher, a sadist who took pleasure in ordering military executions. One particular incident in the General's life excited their best prose and most outraged manner. It concerned six militiamen—John Harris, David Morrow, Jacob Webb, Henry Lewis, David Hunt, and Edward Lindsey—who were executed on the Hero's orders during his campaign against the Creek Indians. The story of John Harris was usually singled out from the group to illustrate graphically Jackson's cruel and pitiless nature. As reported by the Coalition press, Harris was a "Preacher of the Gospel" who, through no fault of his own, was unable to support his wife and nine children. So he volunteered as a substitute in the Tennessee militia and was told by his officers at the time of his enlistment that his tour of duty would expire on September 20. When that day arrived, he surrendered his musket to his captain, bade him a friendly adieu, and started back home. But "fearing he might have erred" somehow—one was never quite certain about military regulations—he returned to the camp and was promptly arrested and court-martialed. Then, at the insistence of Jackson, this innocent man, this father of nine helpless children, this gospel preacher, along with five others, was "shot dead."

In a flash of political inspiration, John Binns, the editor of the Philadelphia *Democratic Press,* conceived a means of dramatizing the executions in such a way as to confound and horrify the American people. He printed a handbill, bordered in black and bearing the title, "Some Account of some of the Bloody Deeds of GENERAL JACKSON." The names of the six victims were posted across the top of the page, and under each he affixed a ghastly picture of a huge black coffin. This "Coffin Hand Bill," as it was known, also carried a short description of the "murders," followed by a tearful "poem" entitled "Mournful Tragedy."

> O! Did you hear that plaintive cry
> Borne on the southern breeze?
> Saw you JOHN HARRIS earnest pray
> For mercy, on his knees? . . .
>
> "Spare me"—he said—"I mean no wrong,
> "My heart was always true:
> "First for my country's cause it beat,
> "And next, great Chief, for you.

"We thought our time of service out—
"Thought it our right to go:
"We meant to violate no law,
"Nor wish'd to shun the foe. . . .

"At home an aged mother waits
"To clasp her only son;
"A wife, and little children—this arm
"Alone depend upon. . . ."

'Twas all in vain, John Harris' pray'r
'Tis past the soul's belief!
Hard as the flint was Jackson's heart;
He would not grant relief. . . .

Sure he will spare! Sure JACKSON yet
Will all reprive but one—
O hark! those shrieks! that cry of death!
The deadly deed is done!

All six militia men were shot:
And O! it seems to me
A dreadful deed—a bloody act
Of needless cruelty.

Choking with indignation, the Jackson Central Committee in Nashville countered with its own version of the incident. At a time, read the Committee's address to the public, when Jackson was fighting desperately to subdue the rampaging Creeks along the southern frontier, Harris hatched a mutiny among 200 militiamen. The miscreants broke into a commissary storehouse, stole supplies, and then deserted. When the ringleaders were finally captured, they were legally tried and sentenced to be shot. Their constitutional rights had been protected in every particular, even to the manner of execution.

In publishing the address, Duff Green tongue-lashed those responsible for the Coffin Hand Bill. The public could now discern, he said, the thorough corruption of the Administration and all its works. Adams and Clay conceived this despicable broadside "to strip the honored laurel from [Jackson's] brow." As for Harris, that "professed ambassador of Christ," he deserved death for his crimes of "robbery, arson and outrageous mutiny."

The Adams press was not at all impressed with the Jacksonian version of the bloody deed and reprinted a circular signed "Truth," which contradicted the Nashville address at several significant points. In a feat of rare journalism they even managed to elicit sympathy for the Indians by describing in vivid prose Old Hickory's brutal treatment of the Creeks.

But the Jacksonians had the last word. After the election a group of Philadelphia citizens decided to punish "Undertaker Binns," as he was now called, for his indecent handbill. They planned to kidnap him from his office, deposit him in an open coffin, and carry him through the streets on a tour of the city. As the rumor spread through town and the mob formed, Binns bolted his office doors and fled with his wife to the roof. Soon the mob surged to the building, carrying over their heads an enormous black coffin. They stormed the doors but could not force them. Stones were hurled. "After two or three hours' screaming and screeching," reported Binns, "the rioters slunk away in squads, taking with them the coffin and whatsoever else they had brought." But they returned the following night, again yelling and screaming for the "Undertaker," again inviting him for a moonlight ride in an open-topped coffin. After three nights of disappointments the mob finally gave up. Obviously Binns was a poor sport.[14]

Newspapers frequently augmented their accounts of the murders of "innocent American boys"—there were several others in addition to the six in the Coffin Hand Bill—with stories of Jackson's reputation and record as a duelist. The most famous duel they recounted was the one the Hero fought against Charles Dickinson in 1806. Several versions of the incident were published, few of them approximated the truth, but all agreed that Dickinson was the "best shot in Tennessee" until he met sudden death in the person of Andrew Jackson.

The fight had been brewing for a long time. On repeated occasions, when drunk, Dickinson had uttered "offensive words" against Mrs. Jackson, though he never failed to apologize in the dawn's sobering light when he glimpsed the approaching form of the infuriated General. What finally provoked a challenge, however, was a dispute over a horse race wager in which Jackson's horse, Truxton, had been matched against Captain Joseph Ervin's Plow Boy, with the stakes set at 2,000 dollars and the forfeit at 800 dollars. The day before the race was scheduled, Plow Boy was withdrawn and the forfeit paid by Ervin and his son-in-law, Dickinson. Later, it was said that the notes offered by Ervin in payment of the forfeit were different from those that Jackson had agreed to receive. Dickinson denied this; charges and countercharges were exchanged couched in formal but insulting language; finally Jackson wrote out his challenge.

The two men met on the dueling grounds one bright May morning. They stood under the tall poplars arranging the ritualistic form by which they would attempt to kill each other. Eight paces were measured off, and Dickinson and Jackson took their position. When the signal was given, the "best shot in Tennessee" raised his pistol quickly and fired. The ball broke Jackson's rib and raked his breastbone, yet the Hero stood perfectly still and merely raised his left arm and pressed it tightly against his throbbing chest.

"Great God!" Dickinson screamed, "have I missed him?" As the young man stood waiting for the return shot, Jackson aimed his gun carefully and then squeezed the trigger. Nothing happened. The trigger had stopped at half-cock. Jackson drew it back, aimed a second time, and fired. The ball tore through Dickinson's body just below the ribs. As he reeled, his friends rushed forward to catch him. Gently they lowered him to the ground and stripped off his clothes. But nothing could be done to stop the rush of blood. The wretched man, hardly twenty-seven years of age, bled to death.

This was not the only gunfight described in the campaign to discredit Jackson and prove him unfit for the presidency. The brawl with the Benton boys drew considerable attention, since Senator Thomas Hart Benton was now one of the General's staunchest advocates in Congress. The incident had a long history, beginning with a duel between Benton's brother Jesse and Billy Carroll. Jackson had acted as Billy's second. During the duel Jesse apparently panicked, for, after firing his gun, he turned around and bent over. Then, with embarrassing accuracy, Carroll dropped his shot into the broad expanse of flesh.

Thomas Benton was outraged by Jackson's participation in the humiliation of his brother. After all, the General was an older man and had no business involving himself in a duel between two young bucks. The matter rested without further incident until late that summer, when Thomas and Jesse went to Nashville to take care of some personal matters. They were anxious to avoid Jackson, so they found quarters at a tavern the Hero never frequented. Next day the General went for a stroll with Colonel John Coffee which would take them past the post office where they could collect their mail. As they walked down the street they spotted Thomas standing in the doorway of his hotel. "Do you see that fellow?" asked the surprised Coffee. "Oh, yes," replied Jackson, without turning his head. "I have my eye on him."

The two continued to walk on, the Hero shifting his riding whip to get a better grip on it. After picking up their mail they started back to their lodgings, only this time they went out of their way to encounter the Bentons. Both brothers were waiting. As Jackson rushed at Thomas, he brandished his whip and shouted, "Now, you d———d rascal, I am going to punish you. Defend yourself." Thomas reached into his breast pocket, presumably for his pistol— at least that was the General's impression. Jackson drew his own gun and backed Thomas to the rear door of the hotel, all the while aiming the gun at Benton's heart. Meanwhile Jesse scrambled for a forward position in the barroom to ambush his brother's assailant. Once in place, he fired two balls and a large slug straight at Jackson. One ball shattered the General's left shoulder, another grazed the fleshy part of his left arm, while the slug went wide and splintered the partition beside him.

Jackson fell to the floor across the entry to the passage, his arm soaked in blood. By this time Coffee came racing into the room, firing at Thomas as he entered. He was joined by three other men, one carrying a sword cane, the others knives. During the kicking, jabbing, and knifing, the Bentons were slashed several times about the arms and hands. The gunfight finally ended when Thomas went crashing backward down a flight of stairs at the rear of the hotel as he attempted to ward off the knife thrusts of his attackers.

The General was immediately rushed to his hotel where several doctors worked over him to stanch the shoulder wound. He soaked through two mattresses before the physicians finally stopped the flow of blood. "I'll keep my arm," ordered the determined General, unaware of the seriousness of his condition or the difficulty of removing the deeply imbedded bullet. Meanwhile, down in the public square, Thomas and Jesse strutted before a gathering crowd, daring Jackson to come out and renew the fight. They would finish the assassin off, they boasted, were he to show his face in front of their hotel again. Thomas concluded the performance by waving a sword aloft (presumably Jackson's) and then breaking it in two over his knee.

The wounded Hero finally fell into unconsciousness from the considerable loss of blood. No attempt was made by the doctors to remove the bullet and it remained in his arm for more than twenty years. The wound was dressed with poultices of elm and other wood cuttings as prescribed by the Indians, but it was several long weeks before Jackson could venture from his bed.

The value of the incident in the presidential compaign of 1828 was to help create the impression that the great Hero of New Orleans was a common barroom brawler. What degree of idiocy did it take, asked Administration editors, to prefer such a man in the White House? Not only was he a ruffian and a bully, they argued, but a gambler, a promoter of cockfights and horse races, a profaner, and a Sabbath-breaker. Indeed, the entire corps of Jacksonians were little better than wastrels and street fighters, they contended, the flotsam of American society. Had not Russell Jarvis, one of Duff Green's associates on the *Telegraph*, waylaid and assaulted the President's son while the latter was on official business carrying documents from his father to the Congress? Had not Green himself swaggered through the Capitol several times, armed with a "bludgeon" and snarling threats at the Coalition men who challenged his right to appear on the floor? Green admitted an attack upon one Senate reporter, said Peter Force, yet the Jacksonians voted down all motions to censure him or restrict his movements.

As the campaign intensified, the Administration press even dared to disparage the Hero's victory at New Orleans, claiming that he left his army to visit his home at the precise moment the British invaded Louisiana; that James Monroe, the then Secretary of War, ordered him to return and repel the invasion; and that the ultimate victory, therefore, properly belonged to Monroe, not Jackson.

Naturally, the General exploded over the attacks on his military record. Neurotically suspicious of a plot, he pounced on Monroe as the author of the report, although Eaton assured him that the former President had done everything possible to avoid implication in the controversy, indeed that he was Jackson's friend.

The driving assault on all aspects of the General's military and public career soon broadened to include the Seminole War and his tenure of office as governor of the Florida Territory. With respect to the latter, the National Republicans maintained that it was so wretched that Congress was obliged to abrogate every one of his ordinances as governor. Without Eaton and the Nashville Central Committee to advise him and correct his errors, they insisted, he was incapable of conducting the affairs of state; in short, he lacked "wisdom and judgment."

The Seminole War triggered another controversy. In 1817 the Indians in the southern district of Georgia conducted a series of raids against white settlements, after which they retreated into Spanish Florida. The War Department, in a vaguely worded dispatch, authorized Jackson to pursue the Indians across the border and "attack them within its limits . . . unless they should shelter themselves under a Spanish post. In the last event, you will notify this Department." As a muscular patriot of the first water, Old Hickory offered to compound the fracture of American-Spanish relations and seize Florida. Rather generously, he took the President into his confidence and suggested that Monroe signify his consent to the plan through John Rhea, a member of Congress from Tennessee. For a man who severely punished all infractions of military discipline, Jackson himself had no compunction against ignoring the War Department and its Cabinet officer, John C. Calhoun. In any event, he received a rather cryptic note from Rhea shortly thereafter which he chose to interpret as the approval he wanted. He smashed across the border, burned Indian villages, hanged several of their chiefs, ejected the Spanish governor from Pensacola, and, to top it all off, executed two British subjects, Alexander Arbuthnot and Robert Ambrister.

Needless to say, a monumental headache was created in Washington by the burnings and hangings and killings; but Jackson's exploit resulted eventually in the acquisition of Spanish Florida. At the time, however, many Americans, including Clay and Calhoun, urged the General's censure and the immediate tendering of apologies to Great Britain and Spain. Ironically, it was Adams, then Secretary of State, who defended the Hero and convinced the President that Spain should be pressured into selling the troublesome territory. The controversy was revived during the presidential campaign to demonstrate that Jackson, in exceeding his authority to war against the Spanish, had substituted his own judgment for that of the President and the United States government. It was another example of his arrogant disregard for any law not his own. Jackson denied this. He had proper authority from Monroe to invade Florida through the letter from Rhea, he maintained; he searched his correspondence for documentary proof, only to discover that many of his letters dealing with the Seminole affair had disappeared. Although Monroe emphatically denied endorsing any such scheme as the General propounded through Rhea, Jackson directed his Central Committee in Nashville to interrogate several witnesses for corroborating evidence and then prepare a formal public statement for distribution to the correspondence committees.[15]

The final attack upon the Hero's career was the public assertion that he directly participated in the Conspiracy of Aaron Burr. The indictment was first leveled at the Virginia state convention where it was charged that he coaxed one Nathaniel Williams of Tennessee to join Burr's army. From that beginning the story soon grew to include a variety of specifications: that he levied troops for Burr by calling on governors of the several states for their militias; that he was one of Burr's chief officers; that he was slated to command all the Kentucky and Tennessee troops once the Conspiracy was under way; that he was privy to Burr's schemes and entertained him in his home from December 14 to December 22, 1806; and that he was a confidant of Mrs. Harmon Blennerhasset, whose husband's island in the Ohio River had been used by Burr as a springboard for military operations.

Jackson's reaction to the treason charge was impulsive, immediate, direct, and typical. He wrote to Nathaniel Williams and demanded to know "whether you are or are not the author of this calumny, before I expose it as such." Simultaneously, he summoned the Nashville Committee to prepare his defense; letters and documents were hastily stitched together in the form of a brief and dispatched to the state correspondence committees. In an address entitled "Statement to the Public," quotations were cited from Jackson's letters to President Jefferson and Generals Claiborne and Smith which warned them that Burr was involved in something mischievous. According to the Committee, these communiqués were the first tangible evidence Jefferson received that a conspiracy was brewing in the West.

Despite the seriousness of the accusation, the Hero was not nearly as upset about it as he pretended in public. He now had an organization working full tilt in his behalf, with an apparatus equipped to handle the problem quickly and decisively. "On this Burr business," he wrote confidently, "my friends at Washington and Richmond, are prepared to meet it, whenever the attack is made." And meet it they did—by swinging hard and low at Henry Clay. They had no difficulty in finding evidence to prove Clay's involvement in the Conspiracy. The Secretary had defended Burr before a grand jury in Kentucky, which was all the evidence the Democratic press needed to justify the headline, "Henry Clay, A Traitor!" Although Jackson and Clay had indeed been associated with Burr at one time or another during the Conspiracy, the possibility of treason on the part of either man was about as likely as John Quincy Adams pimping for the Tsar of Russia.

By the close of the campaign the Coalition had thoroughly explored and publicized every phase of the General's career and every charge that documented his immorality, incompetence, and illiteracy. But the accusations were most unfortunate. Unfortunate not simply because they were indecent or untrue or a mockery of presidential politics, but because many of them suggested ridicule of Jackson's personal success against heavy odds, his services to the nation, and his intense love of country. This the American public would not abide. Similarly, the electorate would not condone ridicule based upon his "frontier" character and exploits or his lack of formal education.

If the Coalition press wished to drive Jackson to the defensive, they would need something better than his victories and honors and relentless patriotism. And something better than prurient sensationalism.[16]

VII

The summer and fall elections of 1827 were ominous warnings to the National Republicans. While there were encouraging signs in Delaware, New Jersey, Pennsylvania (Sergeant's election), Maryland, and, of course, New England, elsewhere they were all bad. In the Northwest, smooth-running machines were setting up a Jackson victory in Ohio and Indiana. Illinois looked safely Democratic, once Governor Ninian Edwards' friends started their movement into the General's camp. Edwards himself kept in touch with the Central Committee in Washington through his brother-in-law, Duff Green; and several Illinois Congressmen, notably Senator Elias K. Kane, found Van Buren attentive to their special interests. At first there were three factions jockeying for political control of Illinois: the "whole hog" Jacksonians; the Adams men, consisting of Northern anti-slavery elements for the most part; and the "milk and cider" men who eventually separated into the Democratic and National Republican parties. By 1828, many observers agreed that the Jacksonians were too well organized to be defeated, and no political judgment was more final than that. Meanwhile, in Kentucky, the situation worsened for the National Republicans after they foolishly consented to set up a legislative investigating committee to inquire into the corrupt bargain charge. Such a committee boded nothing but trouble, for enough evidence existed to arouse suspicions throughout the Northwest that Adams and Clay had violated the spirit (if not the letter) of the Constitution in the House election. "Your friends," Crittenden unhappily explained to Clay, "allowed themselves to be goaded & precipitated into the measure without much reflection." Amos Kendall, who probably conceived the idea of an investigation, promptly furnished the committee with a staggering array of facts and documents about Adams' election.

He proved nothing, yet he raised in the West the kind of doubt that makes men talk of smoke as a sure sign of fire.

In New York, the Democrats prevailed upon their "idol and pride," Martin Van Buren, to head the state ticket as their gubernatorial candidate in order to counteract the Anti-Masonic movement and safeguard Old Hickory's election. Once they agreed that he might resign the office if called into Jackson's Cabinet, he submitted to the nomination. Thus, New York had three candidates for governor, two of whom shared the Adams vote.

In New England, the National Republicans fared better. To the shock of some Democrats, Isaac Hill was defeated in the spring of 1828 in his bid for a seat in the United States Senate. Close by, in Vermont, Anti-Masonry seeped into the state and undermined the small Jackson organization that Hill had helped to set up. Because of Old Hickory's association with an exclusive and secret society, the General's party in Vermont was tagged as "anti-democratic." Several new weekly journals were established to expose the "Masonic aristocracy," progress reports were fed to them from New York, and the excitement took on the character of a national movement.

Sitting in his office in Washington, Henry Clay scrutinized the letters written by his lieutenants from the field to explain the many defeats in 1827. All of them repeated the identical weakness. "We are in the same disjointed state here as formerly," wrote a Pennsylvanian. "A great many well wishers . . . but no organization." A Westerner explained it in terms of Jacksonian strength. "The opposition," he said, "are an organized corps, active and well disciplined." In the South, one of Clay's pensioners predicted that the "organization of the other side . . . *will be* stronger than all." Even in New England an alarm was sounded by Daniel Webster. For the last two years in New Hampshire, he wrote, "the attempt has been to put down Mr Hill by the organization of the *Republican party*. It has not been done, & cannot be done. . . . Hill himself, & a few other cunning & indefatigable Caucus men control the movements, & arrange the organization of the party."

Over and over, from each section of the nation, the single complaint: lack of adequate party organization. Still, Clay could scarcely believe that the American people would succumb to the blandishments of the Hurra Boys and their machines, that they would approve the "military principle," especially in "the person of one devoid of all the graces, elegancies and magnaminity of the accomplished men of the profession." Since the foundation of the Republic, the presidency had been reserved for men of major and tested talents, not illiterates of questionable morality. The country would yet remain faithful to its great tradition, thought Clay, and re-elect John Quincy Adams. [17]

5. Political Brokerage

I

WITH THE COMMENCEMENT of the Jacksonian-controlled Twentieth Congress in December 1827, Washington was jammed with Democrats in a mood for some high-level horse trading to win the electoral votes necessary to place Andrew Jackson in the White House. If the presidential contest could be settled in Congress on a *quid pro quo* basis, men like Van Buren, Calhoun, Benton, and Eaton were open to any legitimate scheme. They started with the assumption that the New England and Southern states were irrevocably committed to their respective candidates and therefore in no position to bargain for congressional favor; their problem, therefore, consisted of wooing Kentucky, Ohio and Missouri, which had voted for Clay in 1824, along with Indiana, Illinois, and all the Middle Atlantic states. To the extent that these states could be influenced by legislation and converted to Jackson by congressional favor, the Democrats meant to devote their energies. For the next six months, legislation was framed with the single purpose of ousting Adams from the presidency and replacing him with Andrew Jackson.

Political brokerage at so high a level and among so many skillful and experienced traders demanded precise and detailed planning, and none planned so adroitly as Martin Van Buren and his Albany Regency. As his first move he called a congressional caucus on December 2, 1827, to devise Jacksonian strategy. While majority rule was invoked at the meeting, there was no question that the representatives from Tennessee (Eaton), Pennsylvania (Ingham and Buchanan), Kentucky (Moore and Richard M. Johnson), and South Carolina (Calhoun or one of his henchmen) and New York were in control. Their first order of business was the selection of a Speaker of the House of Representatives to replace the Administration's incumbent, John W. Taylor of New York. Since this officer by his committee assignments and general policing of House business plotted the course of congressional legislation, his selection preceded all others in importance. He was pivotal in any Democratic scheme to buy or trade votes.

Apparently, a great deal of discussion went on in the caucus over the selection of their candidate. Van Buren was disposed to give the post to a Southerner, in particular a Virginian, as another prop for his North-South alliance; but he did not want to dictate a choice. After all, this was not a caucus of New York Bucktails eager to rubber-stamp his slightest suggestion, and he had to be careful when treating these highly sensitive and privilege-conscious Congressmen. Apart from everything else, Van Buren was genuinely fond of Southerners (which they recognized) and deferential to them. It was Southern support, in the final analysis, that gave him a real claim to national leadership. Perhaps, too, he foresaw the terrible pain he would have to inflict upon them during the session in order to win important votes in the Northwest and therefore wanted to ease the hurt beforehand by giving them the speakership. In any event, when the general discussion ended, two names were in formal nomination before the caucus and both came from Virginia: Philip B. Barbour and Andrew Stevenson. Either man was acceptable to the Magician, although he preferred Stevenson because of their friendship of many years. Someone then remembered—perhaps at Van Buren's prodding—to ask the chief of the Richmond Junto what he thought of the choice, since both candidates came from Virginia. Ritchie sent back word that he liked Stevenson, and that settled the matter. On the first caucus ballot Stevenson was elected. A short time later one Congressman remarked how the smooth hand of Van Buren seemed to be everywhere, never conspicuous, just there.

The decision of the caucus was duly approved by the full House of Representatives on December 4. Stevenson received 104 votes against 94 for Taylor. As possibly another indication of the profound changes going on in American politics, Taylor was not permitted to bow out quietly. As he exited he was pelted with charges of philandering! It did not matter that his extra-curricular activities had nothing to do with his duties as Speaker; it did not matter that Taylor belonged to the opposition and that the Jacksonians now had the majority and simply followed normal political procedures by removing him. The chance to cite additional corruption inside the Coalition as well as make jokes about how the speakership was no place for philanderers was too good an opportunity to neglect. Few could resist the temptation to muddy Taylor. Even Jackson yielded a little, and he should have known better. "I rejoice to hear that Mr. S is appointed speaker," he informed Major Lewis. "It is evidence at least that Congress has some respect for itself, by moving a man of good morals over it."

Stevenson's first task was to fill up the House committees with reliable and capable Jacksonians, as dictated by the party leadership. According to the Adams men, no appointment was conferred without the approval of the Little Magician. In the Senate, presided over by Vice President Calhoun, responsible Jacksonians took immediate charge of the important committees. By the time Congress was ready to begin its debates, both Houses were thoroughly organized and disciplined. Differing views among Jacksonians were quickly resolved, thanks to the prompt intercession of Van Buren. "You will have seen the arrangement of our committees & the new Speaker," wrote one Representative. "A difference of opinion existed among the leaders but the course taken was conformable to the advice of Van Buren to them." Under the circumstances, the Administration abandoned any claim to legislative leadership. "The opposition party," commented Senator John Tyler, "constitute in fact the *administration*. Upon it rests the responsibility of all legislative measures."[1]

With so many politicians gathered together in one place, with the political climate so favorable, and with the Congress about to commence its task of President-making, several imaginative Democrats proposed bringing Andrew Jackson himself to Washington to send the campaign roaring into high gear. Such a public demonstration of party unity and enthusiasm would constitute a major triumph. Its advantages in displaying the vigor and energy of Democrats were not lost on the leaders. The staging in Washington was also compelling. Yet such a departure from the traditional behavior of candidates might unduly agitate the people and needlessly provoke sympathy for President Adams. Already there were loud complaints that Old Hickory had overstepped the bounds of propriety by openly soliciting support throughout the Western states.

Jackson kept silent about a trip to the capital, although rumors of his arrival spread rapidly through Washington and "hints" of his coming appeared in the *Telegraph*. Duff Green was one of the sponsors of the scheme, backed enthusiastically by the Washington Central Committee. Earlier, he had asked Edwin Croswell and Mordecai M. Noah, his newspaper colleagues in New York, for their opinion of the scheme. Predictably, both men turned their letters over to Van Buren with requests for instructions. They received a resounding negative. The Senator thought the proposal too callous toward public sensitivity, too nonchalant about the traditions of the party—in sum, too risky. "The reasons agt. such a step are manifold," he wrote to Jackson, "and to my mind conclusive. To that effect have our editors written to Genl. Green. I forbear to assign these reasons because I cannot but think that it will strike you as it has me."

It struck Jackson to heed the advice and stay home, which was probably what he meant to do all along. He just wanted confirmation from his "safest and most prominent friends in other states" before sending Green his refusal. Although he was not averse to making public appearances under the proper circumstances (such as the New Orleans jubilation), he was too good a politician to miss the possible danger to his dignity as a candidate. It was enough that he went to New Orleans in January. Anything more might give the people the uncomfortable impression that he would stoop to electioneering to win the presidency.[2]

II

From the start of the session the Democratic Congress addressed itself to a single problem—that of providing crucial states with substantial reasons for voting the Jackson ticket in 1828. Subsidy was the time-honored approach to their good will, and appropriations for harbor installations, lighthouses, public buildings, and roads were passed with little comment. While several of these measures fractured orthodox Republican principles, no outcry was heard from the Radicals; not one of them rose in his place to call down the wrath of the sainted Jefferson. They simply registered their "Nays" and then took their defeat as philosophically as circumstances allowed. When Calhoun was forced to cast the deciding vote against one such bill, he rushed an explanation of his action into the pages of the *United States Telegraph* so that no one could misunderstand his motives. The Coalition dubbed it "a speech made for the West; a bait thrown out to catch the votes—the despaired of votes, of Illinois and Missouri."

The Revolutionary War veterans were not overlooked by the Jacksonians in the general outlay of government monies. An appropriation to raise pensions by several hundred thousand dollars was voted without distinguishing between those veterans who needed the pension and those financially well off. Wealthy or not, a veteran owned a key to the public treasury during a presidential campaign.

Land grants were another guaranteed route to the gratitude of the states. The legislative hopper was stuffed with bills to give away the public domain, most of which, mercifully, were lost in the shuffle. Nonetheless, Alabama received 400,000 acres to improve navigation on the Tennessee, Coosa, Catawba, and Black Warrior rivers; and Illinois and Indiana were authorized to sell land previously restricted. But the fattest land grant went to the state with one of the largest electoral votes. Ohio was awarded 800,000 acres of land to aid her in the construction of canals, the sale of which was expected to yield approximately 1,000,000 dollars.

The enormous size of the grant was quite accidental, one of those quadrennial accidents to which the Congress is so regularly prone. In this particular instance the Jacksonians and National Republicans decided simultaneously that Ohio deserved special consideration in the distribution of the federal largesse, and both rushed to sponsor the necessary legislation. The Jacksonians moved faster and entered their land grant on the House calendar first. But the Adams men were not to be outmaneuvered so easily, and before anyone discovered their "treachery" they slipped their own land bill onto the calendar ahead of the Jacksonian grant. To the surprise and consternation of the Democrats, the Administration measure came before the full House first; naturally, they could not vote against it because that would mean voting against Ohio and her sixteen electors. So the bill passed. When the Jacksonian measure finally came up a while later it had to be rejected, since there could not be two bills for two grants of land to one state. Badly stung by the defeat and worried over its consequence, the Democrats went to their friends in the Senate and dejectedly explained what had happened. It was too late to repair the mismanagement in the House, but perhaps the Senate might force the Adams men to share Ohio's gratitude. If two bills were impossible, what was wrong with one bill giving the state a double grant of land? And just think how happy it would make Ohio. All they had to do was reintroduce the lost Jacksonian measure into the Senate as an amendment to the House bill. No other solution seemed feasible or practical, so the Democratic leadership approved the scheme. The bill was amended accordingly, both houses agreed to the change, and Ohio was richer by several hundred thousand dollars.[3]

III

But the supreme example of political horse trading in this Twentieth Congress was the passage of the Tariff of 1828, most often referred to as the "Tariff of Abominations."

After the Harrisburg Convention adjourned, a powerful lobby began operating in Washington, and Northern Congressmen were harassed to support the principle of protection. Yet the opponents of the tariff were not without articulate and energetic friends. Certain commercial groups in the cities opposed any curtailment or interference with foreign trade; and Southerners, almost without exception, regarded protection as ruinous to their economic system. These colliding forces, political and economic, made it almost impossible to arrive at a satisfactory schedule of rates. But the Democrats, when they began to write their new tariff, never intended to resolve such problems. Their bill had one objective: the election of Andrew Jackson. "I fear this tariff thing," warned a Coalitionist; "by some strange mechanical contrivance or legerdemain, it will be changed into a machine for manufacturing Presidents, instead of broadcloths, and bed blankets."

The House Committee on Manufactures was responsible for framing a suitable bill, and its members had been chosen by Speaker Stevenson to conform to the party's grand objective. A majority of them were Northern and Western Jacksonians, although a Coalitionist, Rollin C. Mallary of Vermont, was retained as chairman because Stevenson owed him a political debt and could not honorably remove him. The other members included James S. Stephenson of Pennsylvania, T. P. Moore of Kentucky, Silas Wright, Jr., of New York, Lewis Condict of New Jersey, William Stanbery of Ohio, and William D. Martin of South Carolina. The most important figure on the committee was Silas Wright, a solid, squarely built man with an impassive and ruddy face, a Regency lieutenant, thoroughly partisan, smart, alert, and Van Buren's trusted henchman. At first he was reluctant to serve on the committee because he was totally ignorant of tariff matters; furthermore, Richard Keese of New York wanted the assignment and "had fixed his mind to be on that committee." However, the Congressional leaders smiled away Wright's touching modesty; then they signaled Keese to back off. As Wright later explained to the Regency, "In order to bring our arrangement about, I had to consent to go on it myself, as Stevenson [sic] of Pa. made it a condition of his going onto it that he might select his men from N. Y. Ky. and Ohio." So an "arrangement" had been made among Pennsylvania, New York, Ohio, and Kentucky even before the members were chosen!

As dedicated Jeffersonians and practical politicians, a majority of the committeemen were prepared to assist the farmer with higher schedules for raw materials; yet they would not accord the manufacturer similar treatment unless he happened to come from a favored state. The least favored were New England manufacturers, especially the manufacturers of woolens. The committee was purposely selected, raged one protectionist, "to keep up *appearance* of friendship to the Tariff but really to destroy it so far as *Wool* is concerned."

Before preparing the "arranged" bill for presentation to the House, the committee listened to a parade of witnesses who detailed their reasons for increased protection. Petitions and memorials were submitted; documents and reports were subpoenaed in order to weigh both sides of the question and arrive at "an honest and fair" rule by which to determine the schedule of rates. A great deal of time was expended by the investigation before the specific recommendations were finally laid before the House of Representatives in February 1828.

The result was a ghastly, lopsided, unequal bill, advantageous to the farmer but wholly inadequate to the manufacturer. Every section of the measure showed marks of political preference and favoritism. A duty of ten cents per gallon was levied on molasses, while that on distilled spirits was raised ten cents. Sail duck was established at nine cents per square yard, and hemp and flax were fixed at forty-five dollars per ton, to be increased five dollars annually until a maximum of sixty dollars was reached. But the best was reserved for raw wool. A duty of seven cents per pound was suggested, plus a 40 per cent ad valorem rate, which would be increased 5 per cent yearly until it amounted to 50 per cent. On manufactured wool, however, the rates were ridiculously disproportionate. An involved set of schedules were drawn, depending on price range, not one of which met the basic needs of the manufacturer.

As soon as the bill was brought into the House the worse suspicions of the National Republicans were confirmed. "They do not really desire the passage of their own measure," said Henry Clay, "and it may happen in the sequel that what is desired by *neither party* commands the support of both." Others accused the Jacksonians of writing a bill to force the New England Representatives into joining Southerners on the final vote to kill the entire measure. The blame for the defeat would then rest upon the friends of the President; the filthy mess would be splattered all over the National Republicans.

It was perhaps typical of the Adams men to lack appreciation for the more subtle forms of political manipulation. They convinced themselves that this "abominable" tariff had been designed to be defeated and that they were expected to shoulder the responsibility. Doggedly they clung to this belief, ignorant of the strategy of the Democratic leaders.

Silas Wright divulged the true intentions of the House committee in one of his many letters to the Regency. "Why did we frame the bill as we did?" he wrote. "Because we had put the duties upon all kinds of woolen cloths as high as *our own friends* in Pennsylvania, Kentucky & Ohio would vote them. Why did we put the duties upon Molasses so high? Because Pennsylvania and our friends west of that State required it to induce them to go for the woolens. The Hemp and flax duty was also inserted for the same reasons, and the duty on Irons are the Sine qua non with Pennsylvania." So the bill was not aimed at satisfying the nation's farmers or manufacturers; nor was it introduced to be defeated. It was concocted to suit the interests of "our friends" in the Middle Atlantic and Western states whose combined electoral vote was sufficient to decide the presidential election in Jackson's favor. Specifically, it was expected to reverse the 1824 results in Ohio, Kentucky, and Missouri and secure the important votes of Pennsylvania and New York. Actually, the bill served a double purpose: it rewarded producers of raw materials and certain manufactured goods such as "Irons" in favored states and penalized New England distillers, shipbuilders, woolen manufacturers, and commercial groups.[4]

Southerners were also penalized. This was unfortunate. But Wright and Van Buren knew that their Southern colleagues regarded Adams as the "acknowledged leader" of all manufacturing interests and therefore could not bolt the Democratic party. They also knew that the Southerners would kill the measure if possible, since no other choice remained to them.

Calhoun's rough-talking henchman, George McDuffie, probably devised the Southern plan to defeat the bill. The object was to remain silent during the debate and vote down any amendment that would improve the duties on manufactured goods. In this way Southerners felt they could compel the "Eastern" New England Representatives to join them on the final roll call and kill the entire tariff. "Its fate rests on our ability to preserve the bill in its present shape," wrote Senator John Tyler of Virginia. "If we can do so, it will be rejected."

The "Eastern" Representatives had a different plan, however.

According to Silas Wright, they agreed to vote down the hemp, flax, molasses, and iron duties and then sit back while the "Jackson tariff men from our State, Pennsylvania, Ohio & Kentucky" defeated what remained. "They are *determined* to kill any bill," he exclaimed, "but they wish to make *our friends* do it."

Both these murderous plans revealed the particular interest and worry of their respective sections. Yet the inability of the Southerners and the Easterners to get together on a single course of action worked to their mutual disadvantage. The Southerners went to Wright, so he reported, and solemnly assured him that they were "willing to sustain the shape of the bill as it is, but frankly say if we increase their burdens by a still further increase upon the woolens, they must go with Eastern men in their motions to strike out." Then, said Wright, "away goes your Molasses, Iron, Hemp, Flax etc and you have again a *woolens bill* which our own friends *will certainly kill.*"

Southerners picked the wrong man to bluff. Wright was not readily fooled by their professed willingness to "sustain" the bill or their threat to join the Easterners. As he said earlier in the session, "The politicians here are many of them genuine men, but bad managers. They do not understand doing these things, after all, as well as the Albany Regency." What, then, did his great manager-friends in Albany suggest he do to protect the tariff from defeat? The clerkish Azariah C. Flagg, "senior member of the Regency at home," urged him to hold the line. "The Boston folks are right mad," he chuckled. "They say that New England will go against it, unless altered to suit them. That the bill is worse than nothing, and [that] . . . some *arch magician* must have framed the bill for the purpose of annihilating the manufacturers. . . . My notion is, that you should press the bill, as you are doing."[5]

IV

When the recommendations of the Committee on Manufactures were placed before the House, Chairman Mallary disclaimed any connection with the bill, since all his suggestions had been disregarded by the other members of the committee. To improve the measure, therefore, and give the manufacturer a fair degree of protection, he proposed a long list of amendments, several of which lowered the rates on raw materials.

In the ensuing debate the Southerners sat grim-faced, hardly uttering a sound. It was a penitential hair shirt to keep silent, but they dared not risk exposure of their scheme. Finally, on April 9, a vote was taken on the Mallary amendments, and each one of them was defeated in turn. Then, just as the last amendment went down, the Southerners jumped up, shouting and applauding. Off came the hair shirt as they foolishly babbled about how clever they were, how potent their scheme, and how total their victory. Without Mallary's amendments they were positive that the entire bill was doomed. Childishly, they taunted the New Englanders with the details of their cunning. They told "the Gentlemen of the East that they voted for molasses, & some other articles with a view of making the Bill odious to them." Now the measure was dead, and the Adams men would have to share the responsibility.

Stunned by what they heard, the "Gentlemen of the East" glared at their tormentors. If Southerners thought that they could trifle with New Englanders and get away with it, maneuvering them into voting against the tariff and then saddling them with its defeat, they did not appreciate the Yankee spirit. When George McDuffie saw what his Southern colleagues had done in revealing the purpose of their action, he exploded in a torrent of "curses." He cursed them individually and collectively; he cursed them until he was exhausted. Back and forth between state delegations he raged and roared, his hands fisted in anger. Their stupidity and haste had ruined their single hope of killing the tariff in the House. "We have not only disclosed our plan," groaned Augustine H. Shepperd of North Carolina, "but defeated its success."

Western Jacksonians were also shocked by the antics of the Southern Representatives, especially their admission of having voted for molasses, hemp, and flax in order to bring about their ultimate defeat. McDuffie's performance was particularly outrageous, since he seemed to be the author of the conspiracy. Several Western delegations began muttering that the actions of the Southerners could possibly hazard Jackson's election in their states, and they purposely muttered loud enough to be heard by their Northern friends.

After the defeat of Mallary's amendments and the disclosure of McDuffie's plan, many New Englanders searched their minds for a sufficient excuse to accept the tariff. "Can we go the hemp, iron, spirit and molasses," asked Daniel Webster, "for the sake of any woolen bill?" On April 22, they gave their answer. By the vote of 105 to 94 the measure carried through the House, courtesy of these abused "Gentlemen of the East."

In the Senate, the measure received rougher treatment. It was first referred to the Committee on Manufactures, composed of representatives from the states of Pennsylvania, Ohio, Delaware, and Rhode Island and chaired by Senator Mahlon Dickerson of New Jersey. When it was finally reported out, the bill was again loaded down with corrective amendments to increase the duties on certain manufactured articles and lower the rates on selected raw materials. Southerners made no attempt to hide their strategy since it was now generally known. Besides, in the Senate they were in greater numbers proportionately and there seemed no need for pretense. They also relied on Vice President Calhoun to dispose of all tie votes in their favor. New Englanders, for their part, served notice that without a change in the woolens schedule they would reject the tariff on the final vote. And their strength combined with that of the Southerners would be sufficient to kill the bill outright.

During the voting on the separate amendments that would reduce the duties on molasses, hemp, flax, and other indispensable provisions, the Jacksonians closed ranks and voted them down. Senators Benton, Eaton, Johnson of Kentucky, McLane, Van Buren, and Woodbury generally acted together. But on the fourth amendment—an amendment to increase the duty on manufactured wool to a 40 per cent ad valorem rate with a 5 per cent increase each year until it reached 50 per cent—Van Buren and Woodbury switched sides and the amendment passed, 24 to 22. This switch spelled the difference between passage and defeat for the entire tariff. It was Van Buren's accommodating way of compromising the issue to prevent defeat; it was "a concession to the wants and wishes of the Eastern States." Now Pennsylvania could have its duty on iron and Ohio and Kentucky their duties on flax, hemp, and molasses, just as the House Committee had "arranged."

With the increased woolen rates, the New Englanders consented to swallow the bill whole. Southerners barked their disappointment, later insisting that they were deceived by Northern Jacksonians into believing the tariff was marked for death from the beginning. On May 13, the entire measure came up for final action, and by the count of 26 to 21 it passed. The Jacksonian leaders—Van Buren, Benton, Eaton—voted with the majority and were joined by the New Englanders Webster, Foot, Silsbee, Wiley, Knight, Chase, and Seymour.

The dissatisfied promptly dubbed this tariff "abominable." But abominable or not, it would harvest a crop of votes for Jackson in the presidential election. The Kentucky *Watchtower* of May 10 said that the "American People are indebted for the Tariff bill which has just passed," while the Albany *Argus* hailed members of Congress for giving "the country a national tariff, which protects, with a just and natural equality, all the great interests of the nation."

In the South, reaction bordered on violence, with talk of secession not uncommon whenever crowds gathered. Once home in South Carolina after the adjournment of Congress, John C. Calhoun set about writing his *Exposition and Protest,* enunciating the doctrine of nullification. The work asserted the state's constitutional privilege to void the tariff if it was not repealed. At a dinner given to George McDuffie on June 19 at Columbia, South Carolina, the tariff was toasted as "The bone of contention, pulled at one end by our friends, and at the other by our enemies. Which does us the most harm?"[6]

The chagrin and sorrow that most Southern Congressmen felt over the treatment they received from their Northern Jacksonian friends prompted Senator Levi Woodbury of New Hampshire to ask Van Buren to help sooth "their fears & sufferings." The Little Magician was much respected in the South because of his orthodox Jeffersonian views; and since he was the author of their suffering, he was urged to ameliorate it in some suitable way. Woodbury also wrote to Robert Y. Hayne of South Carolina, warning him that the "anti-Tariff movements" in the South could seriously injure the Democratic party in the North and West and suggesting "the propriety of keeping things quiet at least for the present." Still smarting over the whipping inflicted on his section, Hayne snapped back that the action of Congress was "chargeable to *Eaton* & others . . . who in their anxiety to conciliate other sections of the country, have wholly disregarded the South." Nevertheless, like the good party man he was, he said "I shall . . . endeavor to keep things quiet till the next meeting of the Legislature (before which time the Presidential election will be over)."

Duff Green was another worrier over Southern excesses. In a letter to Calhoun he faulted McDuffie for his wild behavior in Congress. Not only had the hothead risked his own leadership, but he had jeopardized the Jackson campaign throughout the Western states. "His course last winter," wrote Green, "was calculated to estrange from him the most active members of our party, and should we be hard pressed during the present canvass in the west, he will have to bear all the burden of his own indiscretion." To repair the damage, the editor suggested that McDuffie write something, anything, as long as it was conciliatory and would relieve and please the Western mind. "I could republish it here," said Green, "and throw it upon the west in time to produce the best results in Ohio and Kentucky."

Despite their grievance and anger and pain, Southerners had no wish to endanger Jackson's election. Indeed, they looked to him as the future President to redress the wrong inflicted against their section. Nor had they any intention of antagonizing Westerners, whose political support was essential to the South's defense against the growing power of an industrial North. In the remaining months of the campaign, Calhoun, Hayne, and McDuffie attempted to mollify Westerners, principally through the good offices of Duff Green. They wrote several articles reassuring the West of Southern good will. Meanwhile, that kindly Little Magician from New York heeded Woodbury's suggestion and applied soothing words to the "fears & sufferings" of his Southern allies.

Elsewhere in the nation, Jacksonians tallied the electoral votes purchased by the abominable tariff. If the principle of protection once threatened the Democratic ticket in Indiana, Ohio, Kentucky, Illinois, Pennsylvania, and New York, it threatened no longer. The

Democratic leadership in Congress had seen to that. "On the subject of the Tariff and internal improvements," commented a New Yorker, "the feelings of the western states the middle & N England states are *in almost perfect* consonance."

The passage of the Tariff of 1828 was the last and possibly the most successful of all the concerted acts taken by Democrats to arrange the election of Andrew Jackson. As triumphant political brokers, they might now return home with every expectation of a handsome commission from a satisfied public. It was simply a matter of waiting out the time until the people spoke their appreciation and their will at the polls.[7]

6. Triumph of the Politician

I

"TO THE POLLS!" commanded Duff Green. "To the Polls! The faithful sentinel must not sleep—Let no one stay home—Let every man go to the Polls—Let not a vote be lost—Let each Freeman do his duty; and all will triumph in the success of

JACKSON, CALHOUN and LIBERTY"

Let the Freeman speak! After years of shrieking into his ear, after pouring a fortune into a campaign of song, slogan, and nonsense, after spending arduous months constructing political machines to ensure the proper majorities, the politicians now submitted it all to the absolute test of popular approval.

Both parties exuded confidence on the eve of the election, as all parties must do. Local leaders spoke with certainty that they had a national winner and invited all to join them on a sure bet. Money was wagered by those who believed what they said or were pressured into proving their belief. In his customary fashion Van Buren spread his wagers with a prodigal hand, reminding his lieutenants in the leading counties of New York not to "forget to bet all you can."

With so much money at stake, with so many people expected to vote in this election, the possibility of fraud was not overlooked by the men responsible for their party's success. Indeed, the possibility became an invitation. None of the states used a secret ballot, and in many areas the voice vote was still practiced. The oppor-

tunity, then, to correct individual "misjudgments" was limitless unless proper precautions were taken. And the precautions actually
devised were another sign of organizational growth. In the Kentucky election of 1827, for example, it was reported that 250 Ten-
nesseans crossed the state line and voted in the 8th Congressional
District, with the Hero himself privy to this "gross outrage." Wagon-
loads of men were taken to several polling places and given the
names of deceased citizens with which to commit their fraud. In
the presidential election, these floaters voted three and four times,
receiving fifty cents a day (in most states the polls were open for
three or four days) plus expenses from the party. If Tennessee,
complained an Ohioan to Henry Clay, "disgorges 1000 voters upon
us, we are gone. We shall have two or three thousand illegal ones
of our own." So certain were the Jacksonians that the Coalition
would tamper with the ballots that many county organizations set
up special committees to attend the polls as "watchers."

The election of 1828 set a record for the number of frauds and
attempted frauds committed in a presidential contest up to that
time. To be sure, it was a record that did not stand for long. As the
parties grew, as they perfected techniques of operation, and as the
numbers of participating voters increased, the problem of fraud
became more acute. Adding to the voter's difficulty and challenging
the politician's managerial skill was the failure of the states to
provide an official ballot. The parties printed their own ballots, distributed them to friends, and employed high-pressure salesmen or
tough-talking ward heelers at the polls to harass the voter into accepting their ticket. It was not unusual for an individual to be
accosted by several men at the same time and threatened, sometimes with physical violence, if he refused to take the proffered
ballot. Fistfights between rival hawkers and between voter and
hawker were common whenever partisan spirit ran high or the
liquor dispensed by the party flowed too freely.

In those states with active organizations, much attention was
given to "bringing out the vote" on election day. Certain committeemen were selected to herd the party faithful; others were commissioned to arrange festivities, usually at the local tavern. As one
of their final acts, county Central Committees distributed flags and
bunting to the local clubs for use in the election-day parade. Not
a few organizations brought the voters to the polls in companies of

fifty or sixty marching behind a banner blazoned with the words "JACKSON AND REFORM." And whenever a genuine two-party battle developed within a state, voter participation in the contest was unusually high.

The procedures for voting in the election of 1828 differed considerably throughout the twenty-four states. In South Carolina and Delaware, the electors were chosen by the state legislatures. Everywhere else, they were selected from a general or district ticket by an electorate that was roughly equivalent—except in Rhode Island, Virginia, and Louisiana—to the adult white male population. New York, Tennessee, Illinois, Maine, and Maryland employed the districting system, which meant that their electoral votes could be split between the candidates on a proportional basis. In all other states where the general ticket was used, the candidate with the highest popular total received all the electoral votes. Rhode Island and Virginia continued to restrict suffrage with property qualifications, and Louisiana maintained tax payments as a requirement for voting. Four states—New York, Vermont, Georgia, and Louisiana—changed their election laws between 1824 and 1828 to permit, for the first time, popular selection of presidential electors. Previously, this privilege was exercised by their legislatures. Hence, this single reform increased the total number of voters participating directly in a presidential contest by several hundred thousand.

Balloting was stretched out over several months, beginning in September and ending in November. As the polls opened—and all polls within a state did not necessarily open at the same time—the electorate assembled around the standard of one or the other major party as represented by Jackson or Adams, something they had not done in a presidential contest in over ten years. And, as they assembled, the two-party system reappeared in American political life. To the accompaniment of flag-waving, parades, speechmaking, and loud huzzas, national politics replaced factionalism and party cannibalism. The long months of preparation in organizing state committees and conventions, in establishing newspapers, in raising money, in distributing campaign literature, and in arranging the sectional combinations and coalitions was about to be tested in the crucible of a national and popular election.[1]

II

About the middle of October, partial returns began to trickle into the newspaper offices of the leading cities. And, suddenly, it appeared that the "revolution" predicted by so many politicians had actually materialized. Almost upon receipt of the first returns the American people seemed overwhelmingly in favor of General Andrew Jackson. In an age before the invention of political science and the critical scrutiny of first returns, the early Jackson totals from doubtful states looked like the beginning of a landslide. Months and years later this initial impression continued to characterize the entire election.

The first state in New England to submit a final result indicated what lay ahead. The Democrats had expected to lose the entire section, yet Maine, with nine electoral votes, awarded one of them to Jackson. In Cumberland and York counties, a spunky little Democratic organization—remodeled from an old Radical clique—outfought the Administration men and succeeded in winning one elector. Since Maine used the districting system, that lone vote obliterated the anticipated solidarity in New England for Adams. The land of steady habits was not as steady as everyone thought, cheered the Jacksonians.

Yet the surprise in Maine hardly excited the professionals among Democrats or unduly agitated the National Republicans. Hezekiah Niles, in his *Weekly Register*, conceded the loss of the solitary vote but reminded his readers that the President had won 8 others and expected to add 42 more from the rest of New England. Massachusetts, Vermont, and Connecticut would surely pose no serious problem for Adams, although a two-party battle, in varying degrees of intensity, broke out in all three states. As for Rhode Island, the resolution passed by the General Assembly in support of the President was tantamount to a commitment of the state's electors. Only in New Hampshire was there real danger to the National Republicans, but the general ticket system was expected to wipe out the Democratic successes achieved in those counties under the sway of Hill's machine.

The Jacksonians, therefore, hardly glanced at the first New England totals. They were far more interested and concerned over the returns from the Middle Atlantic and Northwestern states. Their concern was groundless. Around the second week in October, returns came dribbling out of Pennsylvania which not only delighted but surprised them. At first they could scarcely believe what they read. Jackson was running ahead of his opponent by 2 to 1. In a state so deeply committed to the protective tariff and the American System and whose last congressional election appeared to reemphasize that commitment, these totals seemed incredible. Yet each day brought new figures that enlarged the dimensions of Adams' defeat; the President was being mauled, flattened, and kicked from one end of the state to the other. Specifically, it meant that 28 electoral votes were well on their way into the Jackson column.

"All Hail Pennsylvania," trumpeted the ebullient Duff Green. "Good old Pennsylvania. Victory! Victory! Victory!"

Hard on the heels of this splendid news came word from Ohio that Jackson had scored a second triumph. The contest in the Buckeye State was much closer than the one in Pennsylvania, but the final outcome was identical—and it took place right in Henry Clay's back yard, among improvements men and protectionists and transplanted New Englanders.

When the Ohio tallies reached the desks of Jacksonian newspapermen in the East, they again broke out in a chorus of wild shouts and exaggerated claims. "GLORIOUS TRIUMPH IN OHIO," they announced. "THE COALITION ROUTED, BEATEN, and DEFEATED." In a letter to Jackson, the ecstatic Green interpreted these early results as the beginning of an unprecedented popular revolution. "It will be a Triumph," he predicted, "such as never was before achieved in the country and permit me to unite with the millions of free men who cheer the 'Hickory Tree.' . . . Excuse my dear Sir the overflowing of a heart which is almost too full to rejoice."

It was still the middle of October, still time to gain added mileage from these heart-filling victories. New Yorkers, for instance, had several weeks left before going to the polls, and if properly informed of the Pennsylvania and Ohio results, they might be induced to run with the pack. In all those states where the polls had not yet opened, Green swiftly notified their Central Committees to circulate the news of Jackson's early triumphs as quickly as possible. His *Telegraph* beat out the refrain:

JACKSON'S COMING JACKSON'S COMING
Ohio is for Jackson
SPREAD THE NEWS

Even Old Hickory was amazed by what he called his "overwhelming majorities," and he summoned Major Lewis to pass the information along to the other Western states so that they could use it to advantage. "This is a change that my friends did not calculate upon," he admitted. Lewis, as a matter of fact, had already acted on this latest information by dispatching it to the New York Committee with a note that it be used immediately. In reply, he was patiently advised that the news while significant and very serviceable would nonetheless not be incorporated into the campaign until "about 10 days before the Election which takes place on the 3rd 4th & 5th Nov." Proper timing in utilizing the information, the Committee implied, was almost as important as the information itself.

Such was the efficiency of the Democratic machine in some states; no wonder, then, that the Hero's victory swelled with each new return. State after state fattened his total, until by the closing weeks of November 1828 the result of the election was all but official. Andrew Jackson had soundly defeated John Quincy Adams and defeated him in the only place it really mattered: the electoral college. The voting, as published in Duff Green's "Extra" *Telegraph* and later revised, proved Jackson a national President elected by a national party:

STATES	POPULAR VOTES		ELECTORAL VOTES	
	Jackson	Adams	Jackson	Adams
Maine	13,927	20,733	1	8
New Hampshire	20,922	24,134		8
Vermont	8,350	25,363		7
Massachusetts	6,016	29,876		15
Rhode Island	821	2,754		4
Connecticut	4,448	13,838		8
New York	140,763	135,413	20	16
New Jersey	21,951	23,764		8
Pennsylvania	101,652	50,848	28	
Delaware ...... (electors chosen by the legislature)				3
Maryland	24,565	25,527	5	6
Virginia	26,752	12,101	24	
North Carolina	37,857	13,918	15	
South Carolina .. (electors chosen by the legislature)			11	
Georgia .... (no contest)	19,363		9	
Alabama	17,138	1,938	5	
Mississippi	6,772	1,581	3	
Louisiana	4,603	4,076	5	
Kentucky	39,397	31,460	14	
Tennessee	44,293	2,240	11	
Missouri	8,272	3,400	3	
Ohio	67,597	63,396	16	
Indiana ....,	22,257	17,052	5	
Illinois	9,560	4,662	3	1

Jackson received a total of 178 electoral votes to Adams' 83. His sweep included practically everything south of the Potomac River and west of New Jersey. Adams carried New England, Delaware, New Jersey, and most of Maryland. Together, the two candidates shared New York, with the Hero taking the larger portion.

In the vice presidential contest John C. Calhoun was re-elected over Richard Rush, but he received seven fewer electoral votes than Jackson because Georgia—still carrying a grudge—awarded the seven to Senator William C. Smith of South Carolina.

Jackson's overwhelming victory in the electoral college resulted directly from the general ticket system then employed by most states. Had Maine, New York, Maryland, and Illinois used the system, his total vote would have been even greater. These states split their votes, giving 29 of them to Jackson and 31 to Adams; under a general ticket Old Hickory would have received an additional 11 ballots.

Jackson's popular majority was not as impressive, however; nor was Adams' defeat quite as devastating. The Hero polled 647,276 to his opponent's 508,064, or approximately 56 per cent of the total vote cast. Percentagewise, this was a stunning victory, unequaled or bettered in any presidential election during the nineteenth century; but it was not as spectacular as the Jacksonians had hoped. One Democrat offered what seemed to him a plausible explanation. "Our majority," he predicted, "will not be . . . great . . . as it is impossible to bring all the Country people to the Polls & the Towns are generally against us." This was an oversimple explanation, which may have applied to a few Western towns but in no way characterized urban voting in the majority of states.

Some 1,155,340 white males voted in the election out of a total population in the country of nearly 13,000,000 people, representing a jump of more than 800,000 actual voters over the previous presidential election of 1824. In Pennsylvania alone the number rocketed from 47,000 in 1824 to 152,000 four years later. Several reasons account for this phenomenal rise. First, the party system had been re-established in a great many states, thus limiting the race to two men, not four as in 1824; secondly, politicians in the most populated regions expended time and money in "getting out the vote"; there was also heightened interest in national politics whipped up by an exciting campaign; lastly, the action of four states enlarged the voting population in presidential contests by transferring the selection of electors from their legislatures to the people. The number of voters affected by this single change exceeded the total number of those who directly participated in the previous election. Although this reform, enacted by the four states, was important, it did not create surging mobs at the polls intent upon electing the democratic Jackson over the aristocratic Adams. A substantial proportion of "plain citizens," men who were farmers, merchants, industrialists, and workers, voted for the President.

The paramount reason for Jackson's towering success in 1828 was the overwhelming strength of his party in a sufficient number of states to control the election. The Democrats were thoroughly organized in Ohio, Indiana, Kentucky, Missouri, Illinois, Virginia, North Carolina, New Hampshire, Pennsylvania, and New York. Among them, they awarded Jackson 128 electoral votes, 3 less than the necessary majority. Had New York and Illinois employed the general ticket, this total would have reached 145. By adding such "sure states" as Tennessee (11 votes), Georgia (9) where there was no contest, and South Carolina (11) cast by the legislature controlled by Calhoun's friends, the total spiraled to 159. Against such odds, Adams never had a chance.

Of the ten states where the Democrats were especially active, New York, Virginia, New Hampshire, Pennsylvania, Ohio, Kentucky, and Indiana reported record turnouts at the polls. In Ohio, Indiana, Kentucky, and New York, the National Republicans waged a desperate battle, but their ultimate defeat did not stem solely or simply from Jackson's reputed popularity or Adams' lack of it. As John Pleasants, editor of the Richmond *Whig*, told Clay in 1827, the Administration men were numerous in his state, but the Democrats had the overriding advantage of superior party organization.

The extent to which the electorate responded to the appeals of the major parties to exercise their suffrage right varied sharply across the nation. Wherever rival political committees took "considerable pains . . . to bring out the people," the results were heartening and instructive. In Ohio, Indiana, Kentucky, Maryland, New Hampshire, New Jersey, and New York, the electorate responded in unprecedented numbers. But they voted for Adams almost as frequently as they voted for Jackson! In New York, Van Buren was aghast at the President's strength. While he had won his own election for governor and had helped to capture 20 of the state's 36 votes for the Hero, he nonetheless resented—and resented deeply—the 16 taken by Adams. Anti-Masonry was not a good enough explanation for Van Buren, since that poison appeared to him to be restricted to the western countries. He finally blamed it on the Federalists—his usual excuse to explain a setback. "It seemed," he muttered, "as if old '98 Federalists had risen from the dead. Men of that school who had not been seen at the polls for years & several whom we supposed dead for years were in the hottest of the fight."[2]

Many Democrats, after studying the returns, sincerely thought that there had been a stupendous outpouring of people in Jackson's behalf; they actually believed that popular democracy had been attained in the United States. By their propaganda, they had, of course, already conditioned themselves for such a heady result, as, for example, when General Edward P. Gaines told Jackson that "the approaching contest is, I think, more now than at any former period considered by the sound planters, farmers & mechanics of the country, as a great contest between the *aristocracy* and democracy of America." How easy it was for them, therefore, to read the returns from Pennsylvania, Virginia, North Carolina, Ohio, and elsewhere and conclude that the ordinary citizen had been jolted into political maturity, that he had "revolted" against the rule of the privileged few. Probably their misconception was due in part to the absence of an adequate frame of reference. All they had for purposes of comparison were the 1824 election results, in which the total vote throughout the United States hardly amounted to 355,000. Hence, Jackson's victory in 1828 appeared the more astounding, and newspaper editors and politicians engrafted upon it greater significance than the facts warranted.

It is natural for a political party to exaggerate the meaning of their victory or the dimensions of their popular appeal. What confounds understanding, however, is the extent to which the National Republicans agreed with the interpretation placed on the election by the Democrats. They confirmed, sanctioned, and propagated the claim that Jackson and the Democratic party represented the great mass of American people. "Well," sighed one of them, "a great revolution has taken place. . . . This is what I all along feared but to a much greater extent." "It was the howl of raving Democracy," sneered another, "that tiped [sic] Pennsylvania & New York & Ohio—and this will be kept up here after to promote the ends of the combination." "All our efforts," wrote one of Clay's party workers, "have not withstood the Torrent." Hezekiah Niles informed his readers that Old Hickory's "triumphant majority" was shaped by the "ardor of thousands" intent on acknowledging "his services to the country." And Edward Everett, one of the President's most quietly effective supporters in Congress, explained to his brother that the Hero won "by a majority of more than *two* to *one,* an event astounding to the friends of the Administration and unexpected by the General himself and his friends. . . . [They] are embarrassed with the vastness of their triumph and the numbers of their party."

This curious notion about the "vastness" of the victory and the extent of the 1828 Democracy was almost universal before the close of the year. Once accepted, the fiction of Jackson's unrivaled popularity as the sole reason for his election carried forward to succeeding generations. In 1827, after a series of defeats in congressional elections, the National Republicans blamed their losses on the absence of party. "Organization is the secret of victory," scolded the New York *American*. "By the want of it we have been overthrown." A year later they had a totally new excuse. Now it was the staggering numbers of frontiersmen, farmers, and workingmen who accepted Jackson as their own, dismissed his governmental inexperience as immaterial, and voted him into office in tribute to his military services to the nation. The mob now controlled the government.

While Jackson's victory was basically the triumph of an organized party and the new breed of politicians who structured it, at all levels of American society Old Hickory did in fact enjoy an enormous popularity that materially enhanced the Democratic campaign. By his military service he had contributed immeasurably to the glory and safety of the United States, and this naturally inspired admiration and gratitude. No doubt many voted for him in 1828 for this reason alone; yet they were not a "raving Democracy," nor was their number so large in the states as to constitute the margin of victory. Given a good organization to oppose him, Jackson could be beaten, as was proved by what happened in New Jersey. There, the vote rose from 20,000 in 1824 to 46,000 in 1828, and the majority turned the Hero down.

Still, it cannot be denied that Jackson's popularity was real and important to this campaign. His popularity had attracted professional politicians to him in the first place. Men like Van Buren, having been skinned in the factional brawl of 1824, now used the Hero's fame and reputation to seize political power in their states and in the national government. They capitalized on the appeal of a living, authentic legend. That appeal, backed by what the Little Magician called the "concentrated effort of a political party," produced the triumph of 1828.[3]

III

Although the election of 1828 did not trigger the "Rise of the Common Man," many glib-tongued Jacksonians during the campaign spoke convincingly of the contest as a struggle for "free principles and unbiased sufferage," between the few and the many, the rich and the poor. "The Aristocracy and the Democracy of the country," intoned the Albany Regency, "are arrayed against each other." This was superheated partisan rhetoric, almost totally devoid of truth, yet invariably appealing and persuasive. Quite a few Americans regarded Adams as an Eastern aristocrat, completely indifferent to their needs or hopes. Since the issue guaranteed a strong emotional response from the unsophisticated, the state committees shamelessly exploited it. They learned in 1828 that presidential elections are most effectively and successfully waged as democratic crusades. By linking organization and the ballyhoo of entertainment behind an appealing candidate who supposedly represented the common man, politicians were able to provide sufficient stimulation to stir the people from their lethargy to a fleeting interest in national politics.

Issues can also fire the electorate with political excitement whenever they are important and whenever they immediately touch the lives of the people. In future campaigns depressions, wars, and other national calamities would bring a truly vast upsurge of voter participation at the polls. Since so many of the issues raised in 1828 were deliberately fuzzed, the success of the Democrats and National Republicans in enticing over a million white males to exercise their suffrage was in itself an extraordinary achievement of party organization.

The two most prominent issues discussed in conversations and in the newspapers were Jackson's inadequate qualifications and Adams' alleged bargain. It does seem probable, however, that these arguments had their strongest appeal among voters previously committed to one or the other candidate. New Englanders were especially resentful of the "bucher's" pretensions, while Westerners found it difficult to disbelieve the bargain story.

Perhaps the most interesting issue in the campaign was the one least understood or explained. Democrats everywhere assured the people that Jackson's election meant the inauguration of governmental reform. Precisely what this meant in terms of legislative or executive action, politicians were not obliged to state; apparently, it was self-explanatory to anyone convinced that Adams' victory in 1825 was engineered by corrupt men of anti-republican leanings.

Those "conservatives" who opposed a strong central government or the "liberal" notions of the National Republicans naturally gravitated to Jackson. So, too, those who objected to any restraints applied by the government or such agents as the Second National Bank upon their speculative operations or their schemes for cheap money. (The Anti-Masons may be an exception to this generalization.) The tariff might have rescued the Administration in some Northern states, but Wright, Van Buren, and company effectively spiked that possibility. The result was an increase of votes for Jackson in the Northwest and Middle Atlantic areas without an equivalent loss in the South. For the first few months after the passage of the Tariff of 1828, some Southern hotheads talked of dismembering the Union but soon cooled off in the certain knowledge that Jackson as President would redeem his pledge and repeal the abomination.

Slavery, as such, was not an important national issue in this election, at least not openly. When it rose to the surface it was more plainly visible in the voting performance of particular religious and abolitionist groups in the North than among planters in the South. As a hidden issue it was not sufficiently influential to alter the voting majorities in either section of the country. Said Duff Green, rather optimistically: "The anti slave party in the North is dying away."

Anti-Masonry, while rapidly spreading into Pennsylvania and New England, had its greatest impact on New York. Jackson suffered severe losses because of it, but Adams also suffered by virtue of its divisive effect upon his party within the state. There were some compensations for Jackson, however, in the number of Freemasons who switched to him in self-defense. "There are many Masons," wrote one man, "who are active & many like myself seldom attend the Lodges [who] will be roused into active exertion sooner than endure the proscription which seems to be in preparation."

The Workingmen's movement, because of its recent origin, had only a slight influence upon the presidential question in 1828. Even in Philadelphia, Adams' defeat was fashioned in large measure by his failure to attract votes from among the German, Irish, and Scotch-Irish population. The President's personality, reputed haughtiness, extravagance, and desire for higher taxes to implement an improvements program, plus his father's connection with the Alien and Sedition Acts, were some of the reasons for his lack of popularity among these nationalities. His loss of New York City, by little more than 5,000, was due primarily to the Irish vote.

During the campaign most of the old Federalists disappeared into the two major parties. In some places, like Boston, they caused the Democrats considerable grief. Former Radicals wryly observed that wherever Federalists led the Democratic party, as in Delaware, Maryland, and New Jersey, the General faced certain defeat. Yet Buchanan, a former Federalist, provided Jackson with substantial assistance in Pennsylvania, however much he distressed the national party by his failure to verify Old Hickory's account of the bargain. Naturally, everyone wanted the Federalist vote, but not their name or reputation. "Although many Federalists attend and join in the deliberations," wrote Jacob Hill, describing the National Republican convention in Maine, "still they are not appointed to any of the committees. This is as it should be here. It will create no distrust or want of action on their part and it will throughout the state effectively silence the clamour that it was a federal convention." By the time the election ended, the Federalists were safely tucked inside their new political homes. In New England, an overwhelming majority of them joined Adams, just as in the South a preponderant majority joined Jackson. In the Middle Atlantic states, it is not as easy to follow their trail. In New Jersey, most likely, a slight majority of them went over to Jackson; in New York, they crowded into the Adams camp almost *en masse;* while in Maryland and Pennsylvania (except for the city of Philadelphia) they divided equally between the two parties. So ended what little remained of the once proud and powerful Federalist party. It almost seemed fitting that it should disappear with the defeat of a man called John Adams.

The extent to which any of these issues were injected by politicians into the canvass—if at all—depended on individual need. In many areas, local questions predominated over national issues. Because state committees oriented their campaigns to create popular majorities, only those questions that served this purpose were introduced and discussed; otherwise they were disregarded. The magnificent confusion over national issues may have distressed intelligent voters, but it did not markedly impede party growth. And the intensity of the growth was one of the most distinguishing features of the election of 1828.[4]

IV

Within a day after news of the "glorious" victory was flashed in Washington the high-powered Democratic organization again wheeled into action. The Washington Central Committee called a hurried meeting to consider ways and means of so conducting Jackson's inauguration as to make it a giant spectacle unrivaled in American political history. The members quickly concurred that each state should send a deputation to Washington to assist in the preparation in order that the national character of the election might be projected through to the inauguration. Still bursting with schemes and ideas to manipulate the public mind, despite the passage of election day, they debated various plans for the General's trip from the Hermitage to Washington, his re-entry into the capital, and, of course, his inauguration. One such plan called for the Hero's swift transferral to Philadelphia (to avoid the worsening road conditions of late winter), where he would take up residence until an appointed day, at which time he would begin a triumphant journey to the seat of government. Advance arrangements, as only the Democrats could provide, would ensure a line of cheering partisans along the route. Then, as he arrived in Washington every cannon in the District would sound the welcome. Finally, on March 4, 1829, the Democracy would be turned loose in a stupendous demonstration of their abiding affection for the Hero of New Orleans.

But not all Democrats liked the sound of such involved and complicated planning. Several Congressmen proposed instead that the date for counting the electoral ballots be advanced, after which a committee of Senators and Representatives would be sent to Tennessee to notify Jackson officially of his election and then, as a guard of honor, escort him to Washington in time for the March 4 inauguration. But this scheme, too, brought objections. A larger and more important group of Congressmen balked at tampering with the electoral procedure just to gratify the ingenuity of party planners. Instead, they proposed that the General arrive in the capital approximately three weeks before the first of March with as little "ceremony and parade" as possible. Then, on the day of the inauguration, the swearing-in might be embellished with an outdoor affair; but anything more elaborate, they contended, would be undignified and inappropriate.

While these various proposals were being discussed by Congressmen, state leaders, and the District's Central Committeemen, Jackson was flooded with invitations from scores of cities and towns to stop off in their communities on his way to Washington and receive some token of the population's respect and esteem. One small village, "9 miles west of Zanesville, Ohio," had a volunteer company called the *"Jackson Guards,"* and the members requested "the honor of parading in your presence."

Meanwhile, the Washington Central Committee dispatched Duff Green to New York to meet with party chiefs in that state and "induce" them to join "other deputers from other States at Washington that they might there determine as to the manner of conducting [Jackson's] inauguration in the most splendid manner." In addition, the New Yorkers were asked to appoint "a deputation to go to Nashville or Pittsburg [sic] to meet & escort [the President-elect] to Baltimore there to receive the Committee of Congress."

Van Buren, the dapper, ever-charming architect of the Democratic party, listened respectfully as Green outlined the tentative plans devised by the Washington Committee. When the editor finished his long monologue the Magician softly raised his voice in dissent. "Discreet men," he counseled, could never approve such "eclat." Not only would it offend Jackson, he ventured, but it would run counter to "the practices & principles of the Party. Ostentatious display neither added strength nor dignity to our Chief Magistrate," he said, "and is irreconcilable with the simplicity & truth of our Republican system." Yet a certain amount of "ostentatious display" could not be denied these overwrought Jacksonians. While they would never go so far as "to offer Incense at the altar of human greatness," nevertheless, they wished in some appropriate manner (preferably spectacular) to "mingle" their voices with the "enthusiastic cheers of surrounding millions."

These extravagant schemes to honor the Old Hero were without parallel in the nation's history. George Washington's trip from Virginia to New York to begin the operation of government under the Constitution touched off an unrestrained demonstration of public affection, but that occasion at least had the merit of spontaneity. Jackson's triumphal march to Washington and his inauguration on March 4 would be bigger and better because they would be organized and directed by experienced practitioners in the art of politics. "We regret . . . to see it intimated," exclaimed one reporter, "that much ceremony will attend his induction to office, and that a committee at Washington has charge of the subject." Political parties nowadays, he continued, have all but abandoned the traditions of the past in their preoccupation with "pomp and show" to tickle the popular fancy. He hoped that "republican plainness" would again prevail on March 4, because a circus atmosphere, such as the Washington Committee proposed, "cannot add anything to the popularity of gen. Jackson . . . but it may establish a precedent of a very unhappy, and, perhaps, dangerous tendancy."

Then, suddenly, all these grandiose plans were rudely brushed aside by the tragic death of Rachel Jackson on December 22, 1828. It was the very day that the Central Committee was closeted with several state "deputers" at City Hall in Washington to discuss the offer of the Pennsylvania legislature to provide a steamboat to carry the President-elect and his lady to Pittsburgh.

For years Rachel had suffered mild attacks "about the region of the heart," and during the campaign these attacks increased in frequency and severity. The cruel stabs at her moral character, stabs at a woman known for her pious and charitable works, her deep religious faith, and her "sweet" disposition, "wounded deeply her feelings and her pride." On Wednesday morning, December 17, as she went about her household chores, she felt a sharp pain exploding in her chest. She clutched at her heart, "uttered a horrible shriek," and collapsed. Five days later she was dead.

The Nashville Central Committee had been preparing a reception in Jackson's honor when the terrible news reached the city. The reception was promptly canceled, out of "respect for the memory of the deceased, and a sincere condolence [was expressed] with him on whom this providential affliction has fallen." The people of Nashville were asked instead "to refrain on to-morrow from the ordinary pursuits of life." Other committees in other cities also abandoned their scheduled celebrations when they heard the report, although a few staged small demonstrations on January 8. The Washington Committee, now in full consultation with congressional leaders, set aside their preinaugural plans and devoted themselves exclusively to the arrangements that would turn the nation's capital into a shouting mass of partisan Democrats on March 4, 1829.

After Jackson buried his wife he lingered at the Hermitage, shut off from the cares and problems of state, sealed against the new responsibilities that awaited him. Not until January 18 did he finally board a steamboat and begin the long journey to Washington. As he stepped aboard someone placed two "hickory brooms" in the bow of the boat; but the Hero paid them no heed. Ascending the river, other ships, packed with people, circled close by, the crowd saluting the brave warrior and shouting their huzzas. Each time he heard a salute Jackson came out on deck and returned the greeting. Although his heart was "nearly broke," he acknowledged each huzza with a tip of his hat. Such a gracious man, many agreed; such a true democrat. Could anyone imagine John Quincy Adams tipping his hat like that? No wonder Jackson had won the love of the American people.

The Hero arrived in Washington early in February 1829 but his appearance set off no demonstration, for, at his own request, none had been planned. Some uninstructed partisan fired a solitary cannon several hours after the General had retired to his rooms at Gadsby's Hotel, so at least there was one signal to herald the arrival of the people's choice.

In the interim, the Washington Committee completed its arrangements for the inauguration. The chairman, John P. Van Ness, along with editor Green and the other members, added the final touches to the prepared schedule of ceremonies. They did so in total disregard of the City Council. In the past, the marshal of the District of Columbia and the city officials had conducted the proceedings in keeping with "republican plainness." But times had changed and the Democratic party was not interested in simple little gestures to accompany the President's swearing-in. The Jackson election marked the "triumph of the great principle of self government over the intrigues of the aristocracy"—so said the Democrats—and it was necessary to have the people stand witness to the victory.[5]

Anyone who was present on March 4, 1829, was not "likely to forget that period to the day of his death." Somehow it seemed that half the nation had converged upon the capital at once, "like the inundation of the northern barbarians into Rome, save that the tumultuous tide came in from a different point of the compass." Strange faces peered into public buildings, inspecting what they owned, defying anyone who ordered them to move off. "I never saw such a crowd here before," said the startled Daniel Webster. "Persons have come five hundred miles to see General Jackson, *and they really seem to think that the country is rescued from some dreadful danger!*"

Most in evidence were the newspaper editors, who descended in a body on Washington to claim their reward for a contest well fought. From New Hampshire came the brilliant Isaac Hill; from Massachusetts, the scholarly Nathaniel Greene; from Connecticut, the quiet Gideon Welles; from New York, the jovial Mordecai M. Noah; from Maryland, the energetic Dabney S. Carr; from Kentucky, the talented Amos Kendall; and "from everywhere else," said Daniel Webster, "somebody else." Soon they were meeting daily at the house of the Reverend Obadiah B. Brown, an affable man who doubled as clerk in the Post Office Department during the week and as minister in a Baptist church on Sundays. Together, they prepared their ideas and projects and then hopefully took them to Jackson.

The morning of the inauguration was mild and balmy, and mobs began to form very early in all the streets and avenues leading to the Capitol. This was the first time in presidential history that the swearing-in ceremony was to take place out of doors, thereby giving many more people an opportunity to see and cheer the start of a new administration. According to the estimate of one man, between 15,000 and 20,000 people had arrived to witness Jackson's glory. The crowd was so great that the procession of dignitaries, arranged by the Committee, could scarcely make its way to the east portico where Jackson was to recite his oath and read his inaugural address. The "vicinity of the Capitol was like a great agitated sea" of humanity, pushing, shoving, clapping, jumping up and down, yelling for the ceremonies to commence. Finally a ship's cable had to be stretched about two-thirds of the way up the flight of stairs leading to the portico to hold the people back. "Never can I forget the spectacle which presented itself on every side," wrote one observer, "nor the electrifying moment when the eager, expectant eyes of that vast and motley multitude caught sight of the tall and imposing form of their adored leader, as he came forth between the columns of the portico."

The screaming and applauding "seemed to shake the very ground." Huzza! Huzza! Huzza! they cried. There the Hero stood, the personification of the American success story, a man who had climbed from log cabin to White House, all on his own. Then, "as if by magic," the "color of the whole mass changed . . . all hats were off at once, and the dark tint which usually pervades a mixed map of men was turned . . . into the bright hue of ten thousand upturned and exultant human faces, radiant with sudden joy." Like the great man that he was, Andrew Jackson bowed low before the majesty of the people.

When Chief Justice John Marshall moved forward to begin the brief ceremonies the shouting abated somewhat, though not enough to permit more than a few dozen men close at hand to hear the oath-taking. The people may not have heard what he said, but they saw Jackson bend forward and kiss the Bible. Again they cheered, loud bursts that stabbed the air. As Jackson turned to read his address, the crowd grew silent so they could hear, but he spoke so softly that only those within a brief space immediately around could distinguish his words; the rest just waited out the ten minutes or so that it took for him to finish his message.

In almost every particular the inaugural address was a model of political "in-betweenity." Short, turgid, suitably vague, it contained nothing that would anger or frighten his partisans. Among other things, he said that he would safeguard the rights of the states, "taking care not to confound the powers they have reserved to themselves with those they have granted to the Confederacy." He also wanted to "facilitate the extinguishment of the national debt, the unnecessary duration of which is incompatible with real independence." As for public works, Jackson uttered a classic sentence, one that would do credit to the most expert noncommittalist in his ranks. "Internal improvements and the diffusion of knowledge," he said, "so far as they can be promoted by the constitutional acts of the federal government, are of high importance." Finally, he said that the "recent demonstration of public sentiment inscribes on the list of Executive duties . . . the task of *reform,* which will require particularly the correction of those abuses that have brought the patronage of the Federal Government into conflict with the freedom of elections, and the counteractions of those causes which have disturbed the rightful course of appointment and have placed or continued power in unfaithful or incompetent hands." Every editor and politician in the crowd who could hear that last remark must have vibrated with joy and anticipation.

As Jackson finished, a thunder of cannons sounded close by, echoed moments later by the proud guns of the Navy Yard and the Arsenal. The people charged forward to grip the President's hand, and it was only with the greatest difficulty that he was rescued from the well-wishers and escorted to his carriage for the journey down Pennsylvania Avenue to the White House. A number of old Revolutionary officers stationed themselves around the President's carriage to serve as a guard of honor. And off they went down the unpaved avenue lined with a double row of poplar trees, the crowds applauding and Jackson gesturing his thanks. The former President did not accompany the Hero, for Adams, like his father before him, was a bad loser and could not face the inauguration of his successor. As quietly as possible he had moved out of the executive mansion into Commodore David Porter's house on Meridian Hill. Clay, too, seemed to have disappeared, which many thought was unlike the former Secretary and probably due to an overly long association with the Adamses.

Inside the White House, preparations had been made for Jackson to meet the people informally. But what took place was never planned by the Central Committee. A mob poured through the mansion to find the President and the refreshments they were promised—boys, men, children, women, "scrambling, fighting, romping." "The *Majesty of the People* had disappeared," wrote Mrs. Samuel H. Smith, and in its place roared the rabble herd. "No arrangements had been made, no police officers placed on duty," she complained. "The President, after having been *literally* nearly pressed to death & almost suffocated & torn to pieces by the people in their eagerness to shake hands with Old Hickory, had retreated through the back way or south front & had escaped to his lodgings at Gadsby's."

As rumored, a variety of refreshments were prepared for the reception, but each time the waiters opened the doors to bring them out, the mob rushed forward to assist the operation. An orange punch, laced with hard liquor, was spilled to the floor moments after it emerged through the pantry doors. Cut glass and china worth several thousand dollars were smashed in the struggle to get to the buckets of liquor. One Southern Congressman bemusedly watched "a stout black wench" sitting quietly by herself eating "a jelley with a gold spoon," totally unconcerned with the mayhem going on around her. The destruction reached such a pitch that tubs of punch, wine, and ice cream were finally carried outside to the garden to draw the crowd from the house. Men scrambled through the windows in hot pursuit, ladies fainted, and children screamed and cried at the incredible antics of their elders.

". . . We had a regular Saturnalia," laughed one Congressman who witnessed the spectacle. The mob, he said, was "one uninterrupted stream of mud and filth. . . . However notwithstanding the row Demos kicked up the whole matter went off very well thro the *wise neglect* of that great apostle 'of the fierce democracy,' the Chairman of the Central Committee, which body corporate so far from being defunct by the election of Old Hickory seems now to have gathered fresh vitality and has I believe even taken the old man under their parental guardianship."[6]

So the unhappy precedent had been established, just as the reporter feared, and the popular hero of the American people was inaugurated with all the "pomp and show" the Democratic party could discreetly organize—and then some.

v

The election of Andrew Jackson marked the beginning of those practices and procedures which have remained the distinguishing features of American politics; it marked the return of active competition between two national parties through which democracy works best in America. To be sure, the system had not evolved with equal success and balance in all sections of the country, nor were personal allegiances to one leader or another a thing of the past. Political habits of a people do not change quickly or easily, especially during a period of peace and relative prosperity.

The election did not initiate the rise of the common man, any more than it encouraged the people to hurtle the last suffrage barriers (wherever they existed) in an effort to overthrow an aristocracy. But it did provide the ordinary citizen—who had been "rising" for decades—with an elaborate party machine through which he could more effectively control the operation of government and shape public policy. The Democrats and National Republicans responsible for constructing this apparatus, from Jackson and Clay down to the lowest committee worker in the wards and captains' companies, may take credit for the "Revolution of 1828."

The restoration of the two-party system ended the political disorder of the Era of Good Feelings, a disorder that had continued for over twelve years. The revitalization of party practices and procedures resulted in the introduction of a variety of new forms of campaigning, including the worst horrors of American electioneering; yet many of these procedures encouraged the people to vote and thus stimulated the habit of democracy. Most significant of all, however, was the earnest endeavor of politicians in both parties to bid for mass support, to organize an effective popular majority. The revolution they began did not end in 1828. It still goes on.

NOTES

AN EFFORT has been made to keep the number of footnotes to an absolute minimum and wherever possible to work them into the text. To eliminate a clutter of individual citations, several of them have been combined into a single reference and placed at the end of each appropriate section.

The following abbreviations have been used in the footnotes:

CUL	Columbia University Library
DUL	Duke University Library
LC	Library of Congress
MHS	Massachusetts Historical Society
ML	Morgan Library, New York City
NYHS	New York Historical Society
NYPL	New York Public Library
NYSL	New York State Library (Albany)
PHS	Pennsylvania Historical Society
PUL	Princeton University Library
UNCL	University of North Carolina Library
URL	University of Rochester Library

CHAPTER 1

1. Benjamin F. Butler to his wife, Harriet, May 7, 1823, Benjamin F. Butler Papers, NYSL. George Dangerfield, *The Era of Good Feelings,* pp. 331-45. Martin Van Buren, *Autobiography,* pp. 142-56.

2. Clay to Francis Brooke, January 28, 1825, Clay to Francis P. Blair, January 8, 29, 1825, Henry Clay, *Correspondence,* pp. 109-12.

3. Butler to Harriet Butler, May 7, 1823, Butler Papers, NYSL. Gales and Seaton to Van Buren, September 15, 1824, John Forsyth to Van Buren, September 20, 1824, Van Buren Papers, LC. Romulus Saunders to Bartlett Yancey, December 31, 1823, "Letters of Romulus M. Saun-

ders to Bartlett Yancey," *North Carolina Historical Review*, VIII (October, 1931), 411. Adams' self-description is quoted in Marquis James, *Andrew Jackson*, p. 366.

4. Butler to Harriet Butler, May 7, 1823, Butler Papers, NYSL. Caleb Cushing Diary, entry for April 6, 1829, Cushing Papers, LC. Flagg to Van Buren, November 12, 1823, Van Buren Papers, LC.

5. Van Buren, *Autobiography*, p. 150. Edward Ingersoll to Clay, August 21, 1827, Henry Clay Papers, LC. William Plumer, Jr., to William Plumer, January 24, 1825, in Everett S. Brown, ed., *Missouri Compromises and Presidential Politics*, p. 134. Rufus King, "Notes," dated January 29, 1825, Rufus King, *Correspondence*, VI, 583. John Q. Adams, *Memoirs*, VI, 458, 462, 493, 501. Buchanan's letter to the editor of the Lancaster *Journal*, dated August 8, 1827, quoted in *Niles Weekly Register*, August 18, 1827.

6. Thomas Cooper to Gulian C. Verplanck, May 15, 1827, Verplanck Papers, NYHS. Robert V. Remini, *Martin Van Buren and the Making of the Democratic Party*, pp. 85-92. Clay to Brooke, February 10, 1825, Clay, *Correspondence*, p. 114.

7. Ben: Perley Poore, *Reminiscences*, p. 26. Clay to Brooke, February 10, 1825, Clay, *Correspondence*, p. 114. Jackson to William B. Lewis, February 16, 1825, Miscellaneous Jackson Papers, NYHS. Rufus King to John King, February 27, 1825, King Papers, NYHS. Adams, *Memoirs*, VI, 506-7. Clay to Crawford, February 18, 1828, Clay, *Correspondence*, p. 193. James D. Richardson, *Messages and Papers of Presidents*, II, 860-65. Wright to Minet Jenison, March 3, 1825, R. H. Gillet, *The Life and Times of Silas Wright*, I, 88. Thomas Hart Benton, *Thirty Years View*, I, 54.

8. Letters reprinted in *Niles Weekly Register*, July 5, 1828.

CHAPTER 2

1. Charles M. Wiltse, *John C. Calhoun, Nationalist*, pp. 313-17. Romulus Saunders to Bartlett Yancey, January 20, 1827, "Letters to Bartlett Yancey," *The James Sprunt Historical Publications*, X, No. 2 (1911), 61-62.

2. Claude Fuess, *Daniel Webster*, I, 297-99. George T. Curtis, *Life of Daniel Webster*, I, 249 note. Van Buren, *Autobiography*, pp. 157-58.

3. Samuel F. Bemis, *John Quincy Adams*, p. 73. Adams to Charles F. Adams, January 29, 1829, Adams Papers microfilm, MHS. Van Buren to Butler, December 25, 1825, Van Buren Papers, LC. Adams, *Memoirs*,

VI, 521; VII, 390. Leonard D. White, *The Jeffersonians*, pp. 389-90. Charles G. Sellers, Jr., *James K. Polk, Jacksonian*, p. 105.

4. Richardson, ed., *Messages and Papers*, II, 866-68, 872, 879, 882. Van Buren, *Autobiography*, p. 195. *Argus* (Albany), December 9, 1825. Tracy to Weed, December 3, 1825, Thurlow Weed Papers, URL. Jackson to Calhoun, July 26, 1826, Jackson, *Correspondence*, III, 307. Saunders to Yancey, January 10, 1826, *North Carolina Historical Review*, VIII (October, 1931), 454. Van Buren to P. N. Nicholas, November, 1826, Van Buren Papers, LC.

5. Van Buren, *Autobiography*, pp. 199-200. Richardson, *Messages and Papers*, II, 884-86, 893. Adams, *Memoirs*, VII, 112. *Register of Debates*, 19th Congress, 1st Session, pp. 142-43, 154-74, 234-62, 401. John H. Marable to Jackson, April 3, 1826, Jackson, *Correspondence*, III, 300. Eaton to Felix Grundy, April 2, 1826, Grundy Papers, Southern Historical Society, UNCL. Van Buren to Butler, April 12, 1826, Butler Papers, NYSL.

6. Benton, *Thirty Years View*, I, 65. *Register of Debates*, 19th Congress, 1st Session, pp. 1950, 2551. *United States Telegraph*, February 2, 1827. Wiltse, *Calhoun*, p. 331. Van Buren to Butler, May 14, 1826, Van Buren Papers, LC. *Register of Debates*, 19th Congress, 1st Session, pp. 442, 566-77; App., pp. 133-38. William N. Chambers, *Old Bullion Benton*, p. 134. Amos Kendall to Francis P. Blair, March 7, 1829, Blair-Lee Papers, PUL. *Register of Debates*, 19th Congress, 1st Session, pp. 717 ff.

7. Wiltse, *Calhoun*, pp. 333-34. Saunders to Yancey, January 10, 1826, *North Carolina Historical Review*, VIII, 454. Lewis Williams to Yancey (no date), Saunders to Yancey, January 20, 1827, "Letters to Bartlett Yancey," *The James Sprunt Historical Publications*, X, 55, 61. John W. Taylor to Clay, October 2, 1826, Charles King to Clay, March 21, 1826, Clay Papers, LC. Rudolph Bunner to Verplanck, April 28, 1827, Verplanck Papers, NYHS.

8. Van Buren, *Autobiography*, pp. 514-15. Van Buren to Jesse Hoyt, January 31, 1823, William Mackenzie, *Lives and Opinions of B. F. Butler and Jesse Hoyt*, p. 90. *Niles Weekly Register*, April 7, 1827. Statement, "Loans to Duff Green," May 20, 1826, Jackson, *Correspondence*, III, 301-2. Calhoun to Van Buren, July 7, 1826, quoted in Van Buren, *Autobiography*, pp. 514-15.

CHAPTER 3

1. Van Buren to Azariah C. Flagg, December 22, 1826, Flagg Papers, CUL. Ritchie to Van Buren, January 31, 1829, Van Buren Papers, LC. *Free Press* (Tarborough, North Carolina), March 27, 1827. *Raleigh Register and North Carolina Gazette*, May 12, 1827. *Southern Patriot* (Charleston), March 30, 1827. *Enquirer* (Richmond), quoted in the *U. S. Telegraph*, May 1, 1827, and in *National Journal*, May 3, 1828. Ritchie to William B. Lewis, September 16, 1828, Jackson Papers, LC. *Telegraph*, June 16, 1828. Supposedly, Jackson wrote Ritchie and told him that he agreed with "Governor Giles that Congress cannot make National Roads nor lay a tariff, except for purposes of revenue." *National Journal*, May 3, 1828. Bibb to Grundy, February 5, 1827, Grundy Papers, Southern Historical Collection, UNCL.

2. Van Buren, *Autobiography*, p. 514. Said Van Buren to Flagg, December 22, 1826: "If we are discrete [sic] & wise we can play a great part in the coming contest." Flagg Papers, CUL. Saunders to Yancey, January 20, 1827, *The James Sprunt Historical Publications*, X, No. 2 (1911), 61. Van Buren to Ritchie, January 13, 1827, Van Buren Papers, LC. James Parton, *Life of Andrew Jackson*, III, 147. Van Buren, *Autobiography*, p. 514.

3. Benjamin Estill to David Campbell, January 24, 1827, Campbell Papers, DUL. *Enquirer* (Richmond), March 28, 1827. Calhoun to Samuel L. Gouverneur, November 9, 1823, Gouverneur Papers, NYPL. James, *Andrew Jackson*, pp. 335-53. Parton, *Jackson*, III, 136, 141. Houston to Jackson, January 13, 1827, Jackson, *Correspondence*, VI, 490. Balch to Polk, February 5, 1834, Polk Papers, LC. Remini, *Van Buren*, pp. 155-61. James A. Hamilton, *Reminiscences*, p. 68.

4. David Campbell to James Campbell, November 11, 1827, John Campbell to David Campbell, November 3, 1827, December 7, 1827, Campbell Papers, DUL. *Enquirer* (Richmond), May, 1827. Ritchie to Lewis, September 16, 1828, Jackson Papers, LC. Macon to Yancey, November 3, 1827, Saunders to Yancey, January 20, 1827, Bartlett Yancey Papers, Southern Historical Collection, UNCL. Burton to Yancey, December 8, 1826, quoted in William Hoffmann, *Andrew Jackson and North Carolina Politics*, p. 6. Saunders to Yancey, February 26, 1827, *North Carolina Historical Review*, VIII (October, 1931), 461. Van Buren to Tazewell, April 30, 1827, Miscellaneous Van Buren Papers, DUL. *National Intelligencer*, April 7, 1827. *Register* (Raleigh), March 20, 1827. Saunders to Yancey, January 20, 1827, Bartlett Yancey Papers, UNCL. Mangum to Yancey, January 15, 1826, Edwin M. Wil-

son, "The Congressional Career of Nathaniel Macon," *The James Sprunt Historical Monographs* (1900), No. 2, p. 110. Rudolph Bunner to Verplanck, February 5, 1827, Verplanck Papers, NYHS.

5. Jackson to John Coffee, March 16, 1827, Jackson to Richard K. Call, May 3, 1827, Eaton to Jackson, January 21, 1828, Van Buren to Jackson, September 14, 1827, Jackson, *Correspondence*, III, 348, 354-55, 390, 382. John Campbell to James Campbell, August 23, 1827, Campbell Papers, DUL. Jackson to Coffee, May 12, 1828, Jackson to Lewis, July 28, 1828, Jackson, *Correspondence*, III, 403, 416. Jackson to Grundy, May 30, 1826, Grundy Papers, UNCL.

6. Jackson to Lewis, March 8, 1828, Jackson Papers, ML. Lewis to E. Haywood, March 28, 1827, Jackson-Lewis Papers, NYPL. The first notice concerning the Nashville Central Committee appeared in the *Telegraph* on April 9, 1827. The Committee included Overton, Lewis, Campbell, Claiborne, Balch, Catron, Foster, Brown, Whyte, Joseph Philips, Daniel Graham, Jesse Wharton, Edward Ward, Felix Robertson, John Shelby, Josiah Nichol, William White, and John McNairy. Jackson to Lewis, May 5, 1827, August 19, 1828, Jackson to Coffee, September 25, 1826, Jackson, *Correspondence*, III, 355, 314, 428. Parton, *Jackson*, III, 147. Clay to Hammond, December 23, 1826, Miscellaneous Clay Papers, DUL. *Telegraph*, May 27, 1828. Jackson to Houston, November 22, 1826, Jackson, *Correspondence*, III, 319. Eaton to Jackson, August 21, 1828, Lee to Jackson, August 12, 1828, Caleb Atwater to Jackson, September 4, 1827, February 28, 1828, Green to Jackson, October 22, 1827, Jackson Papers, LC. Will Hatcher, *Edward Livingston*, p. 319. Charles N. Hunt, *Life of Edward Livingston*, pp. 318-22. Livingston to Jackson, August 12, 1828, Jackson Papers, LC.

7. Buchanan to Ingham, August 16, 1827, Buchanan Papers, PHS. The letters of Beverley, Jackson, Clay, Buchanan, and Eaton in *Niles Weekly Register*, July 7, 21, August 11, 18, October 6, 1827. Jackson to Lewis, September 1, 1827, Jackson Papers, ML. Buchanan to Jackson, August 10, 1827, Jackson Papers, LC. *National Journal*, October 6, 1827. Major Allan Campbell to Jackson, February 4, 1827, Jackson, *Correspondence*, III, 333.

8. *Catawba Journal* (Charlotte, N.C.), May 1, 1827, quoting *National Intelligencer*. *National Journal*, July 24, 1827. Benton to Balch, February 22, 8, 1827, February 14, April 30, 1828, Jackson Papers, LC. Benton to Van Buren (no date), Levi Woodbury Papers, LC.

9. *Telegraph*, October 20, 1827. Kendall to Blair, February 3, 1829, Blair-Lee Papers, PUL. Houston to Jackson, January 5, 1827, Jackson, *Correspondence*, III, 331. *Whig* (Richmond), February 16, March 16,

1827. *National Journal,* March 1, April 10, 15, 1827. *National Intelligencer,* March 10, 13, 20, 22, 1827. Kendall to Blair, March 7, 1829, Blair-Lee Papers, PUL. *Telegraph,* January 24, February 9, June 23, 1828. *Statesman* (Boston), March 19, October 24, 1828. *National Journal,* June 9, 1828. Van Buren, *Autobiography,* pp. 240, 171. *Argus* (Albany), July 3, 10, 13, 1827.

10. William E. Dodd, "Andrew Jackson and His Enemies," *Century,* CXI (1926), 736. *Register* (Raleigh), April 28, 1827. *National Journal,* July 14, 1827. *Niles Weekly Register,* May 3, 1828. Kendall to Blair, March 7, 1829, Blair-Lee Papers, PUL. *National Journal,* July 14, 1827. Bemis, *Adams,* pp. 79-87. Jackson to Colonel John D. Terrill, July 29, 1826, Jackson, *Correspondence,* III, 308. *National Journal,* May 26, 1827. Saunders to Yancey, January 20, 1827, Bartlett Yancey Papers, UNCL.

11. *National Journal,* February 27, March 10, 22, 31, July 24, 1827. *National Intelligencer,* March 13, 20, 1827. *Free Press* (Tarborough, N.C.), July 14, 1827. *Catawba Journal* (Charlotte, N.C.), April 3, 1827. *Telegraph,* November 30, 1827, April 19, 1828. *Statesman* (Boston), March 17, 24, April 3, 9, July 21, October 17, 24, 1828. Homer J. Webster, "History of the Democratic Party Organization in the Northwest," *Ohio Historical Publications,* XXIV (1915), 31. *Niles Weekly Register,* July 28, October 6, 1827. Woodbury to Verplanck, August 29, 1828, Marcy to Verplanck, March 9, 1828, Verplanck Papers, NYHS.

12. *Telegraph,* March 13, April 19, 1828. *Patriot and Star Gazette* (Vermont), established in 1826; see reprints in *Patriot* (New Hampshire), July 7, August 4, 1828. Calhoun to Yancey, July 16, 1828, *The James Sprunt Historical Publications,* X, 75. Francis Baylies to Verplanck, August 4, October 26, 1828, Verplanck Papers, NYHS. W. H. Haywood, Jr., to Willie P. Mangum, June 7, 1828, Mangum, *The Papers of Willie P. Mangum,* I, 336. T. P. Moore to Verplanck, May 29, 1828, Verplanck Papers, NYHS.

13. Adams, *Memoirs,* VII, 431. *Telegraph,* September 1, 4, 1827. T. P. Moore to Verplanck, May 29, 1828, Verplanck Papers, NYHS. *Register of Debates,* 19th Congress, 2nd Session, pp. 498-99. David Morrill to Clay, September-October, 1826, Clay Papers, LC. *National Intelligencer,* March 10, 13, 20, 22, April 7, 19, 1827, June 25, July 9, 1828. *National Journal,* October 13, 1827. *Argus* (Albany), April 24, 1827. *Telegraph,* August 11, 1828.

14. Woodbury to Van Buren, July 1, 1828, Van Buren Papers, LC. Moore to Verplanck, May 29, 1828, June 13, 1833, May 16, 1834, Verplanck Papers, NYHS. *Telegraph,* April 19, 1828. *National Journal,*

March 22, 1827. "We were informed by an anti-administration man," wrote Peter Force, "that they [the Jacksonians] had a fund of $50,000 to establish presses in the several states." Arthur B. Darling, *Political Changes in Massachusetts, 1824-1848*, pp. 60-61. Johnson to Van Buren, September 22, 1827, Kendall to Van Buren, November 10, 1827, Van Buren Papers, LC. The Clay-Kendall relationship is narrated at great length by Clay in a letter published in the "Extra" *Telegraph*, July 26, 1828.

15. For the connection between the Regency and the Mechanics and Farmers Bank, see the Thomas W. Olcott Papers, CUL. Van Buren to Hamilton, August 25, 1828, in Hamilton, *Reminiscences*, pp. 78-79. Sidney Breese to Clay, July 21, 1827, Clay Papers, LC. *Niles Weekly Register*, October 4, 1828. *National Journal*, March 22, 1827. *National Republican and Ohio Register*, May 27, 1828. Parton, *Jackson*, III, 147. Hill to Woodbury, August 4, 1828, Woodbury Papers, LC.

16. Niles' figure of 2¼ millions actually referred to the privilege in England; he estimated, however, that the sum might be even higher in the United States, *Niles Weekly Register*, June 28, 1828. Marcy to Verplanck, March 9, 1828, Verplanck Papers, NYHS. Ritchie to Woodbury, September 3, 1828, Levi Woodbury Papers, LC. *National Journal*, May 24, 1828. *Argus* (Albany), March 23, 27, 1828. M. M. Noah to Van Buren, October 2, 1828, Van Buren Papers, LC. The cost estimate for a congressional election is given by Francis Johnson to James Barbour, August 31, 1827, James Barbour Papers, NYPL.

17. Saunders to Yancey, January 20, 1827, Yancey Papers, UNCL. Green to Bonsal, December 14, 1827, Duff Green Letter Book, LC. Barry to Balch, November 19, 1827, Atwater to Jackson, September 4, 1827, Jackson Papers, LC. Major Allan Campbell to Jackson, February 4, 1827, Jackson, *Correspondence*, III, 334. The incredible number of Democratic committees and meetings becomes evident on reading through the Adams and Jackson newspapers for 1827 and 1828. In New Hampshire—admittedly better organized than the other New England states—nine separate town meetings for Jackson were held in the space of six days. *Patriot* (New Hampshire), February 4, 1828. Adams, *Memoirs*, VIII, 76. Macon to Yancey, November 3, 1827, the *James Sprunt Historical Monographs*, p. 94. *Telegraph*, January 30, 1827. Buchanan to Samuel Ingham, August 16, 1827, Buchanan Papers, PHS. *National Journal*, September 4, 1827. David Campbell to James Campbell, March 19, 1827, Campbell Papers, DUL.

18. Henry Lee to Jackson, August 12, 1828, Jackson Papers, LC. Woodbury to Verplanck, August 29, 1828, Verplanck Papers, NYHS.

Edward Bates to Clay, October 8, 1828, Clay Papers, LC. Chambers, *Benton*, p. 149. "The Real State of Parties in Indiana," reprinted from the *Sun* (Ohio) in the *Statesman* (Boston), September 16, 1828. Major Allan Campbell to Jackson, February 4, 1827, Jackson, *Correspondence*, III, 334. John Campbell to David Campbell, November 3, 1827, David Campbell to James Campbell, November 11, 1827, Alexander Smyth to David Campbell, November 6, 1827, Campbell Papers, DUL. *National Republican and Ohio Register*, September 22, 29, 1826. Webster, "History of Democratic Party Organization," *Ohio Historical Publications*, pp. 16-18, 22.

19. *National Journal*, May 12, 1827. Major Allan Campbell to Jackson, February 4, 1827, Jackson, *Correspondence*, III, 334. Barry to Balch, November 19, 1827, Jackson Papers, LC. Hattie M. Anderson, "The Jackson Men in Missouri in 1828," *Missouri Historical Review*, XXXIV (1940), 317. *National Journal*, April 21, 1827. *Journal* (Indiana), January 9, 1828, quoted in R. C. Bailey, *The Old Northwest: Pioneer Period*, p. 162. R. M. Livingston to John W. Taylor, September 12, 1828, Taylor Papers, NYHS. *National Journal*, April 13, 1827. *Niles Weekly Register*, January 12, 19, 26, 1828.

20. Webster, "History of Democratic Party Organization," *Ohio Historical Publications*, pp. 20-22, 26. Jacob Hill to John A. Bailey, February 4, 1828, Bailey Papers, NYHS. Alexander Smyth to David Campbell, November 6, 1827, Campbell Papers, DUL. P. L. Tracy to John W. Taylor, July 10, 1828, Taylor Papers, NYHS. Henry Lee to Jackson, August 12, 1828, Jackson Papers, LC. For the influence of conventions on party discipline and organization, see Thomas Ford, *A History of Illinois*, sections of which are reprinted in Meyers, Kern, and Cawelti, *Sources of the American Republic*, I, 330-33. P. L. Tracy to John W. Taylor, July 10, 1828, Taylor Papers, NYHS. Henry Lee to Jackson, August 12, 1828, Jackson Papers, LC. Kendall to Blair, January 9, 1829, Blair-Lee Papers, PUL. *National Journal*, April 14, 1827. William H. Smith, *Charles Hammond and His Relations to Henry Clay and J. Q. Adams*, p. 47.

21. "Extra" *Telegraph*, March 21, 1828. Webster, "History of the Democratic Party Organization," *Ohio Historical Publications*, p. 32. Woodbury to Verplanck, August 29, 1828, William Bradley to Verplanck, November 13, 1828, Verplanck Papers, NYHS. "Extra" *Telegraph*, May 10, 1828. Lewis to E. Haywood, March 28, 1827, Jackson-Lewis Papers, NYPL. Duff Green to Jackson, October 22, 1827, Jackson Papers, LC. Marcy to Verplanck, March 9, 1828, Moore to Verplanck May 29, 1828, Verplanck Papers, NYHS. Green to William B. Lewis, September 2, 1827, Green Papers, LC. Ritchie to William C. Rives, Janu-

ary, 1828, Rives Papers, LC. John Campbell to James Campbell, October 27, 1827, John Campbell to David Campbell, November 3, 1827, Campbell Papers, DUL.

22. Lewis to Van Buren, August 8, 1828, Van Buren Papers, LC. Polk to Jackson, December 4, 1826, Jackson, *Correspondence*, III, 321. *Niles Weekly Register*, December 1, 1827, February 9, May 3, 1828. Parton, *Jackson*, III, 147. Duff Green to William B. Lewis, September 2, 1827, Green Papers, LC. *National Journal*, November 15, 1827. Atwater to Jackson, February 29, 1828, Jackson, *Correspondence*, III, 394. Flagg to Watson, July 1, 1828, Miscellaneous Flagg Papers, NYHS. Sidney Breese to Clay, July 21, 1827, Clay Papers, LC. Van Buren to Croswell, December 25, 1827, Van Buren Papers, LC. Bradley to Verplanck, November 13, 1827, Verplanck Papers, NYHS. Clark to Taylor, October 7, 1827, Taylor Papers, NYHS.

23. Atwater to Lewis, November 30, 1827, Jackson-Lewis Papers, NYPL. Baylies to Verplanck, October 12, 1827, Verplanck Papers, NYHS. John Morgan to Flagg, December 4, 1827, Flagg Papers, NYPL. Joseph McIlvaine to Samuel Southard, October 20, 1827, Southard Papers, PUL. Darling, *Political Changes in Massachusetts*, pp. 56, 68, 64. Baylies to Verplanck, February 24, October 26, 1828, Verplanck Papers, NYHS. Hattie Anderson, "The Jackson Men in Missouri in 1828," *The Missouri Historical Review*, p. 321. Ben Taylor to Jackson, August 29, 1827, Jackson Papers, LC.

24. Green to Bonsal, December 4, 1827, Green's Letter Book, LC. "Extra" *Telegraph*, March 21, 1828. *National Journal*, January 15, 1828. *Telegraph*, February 16, 1828. *National Journal*, July 17, 1827. John Campbell to David Campbell, November 3, 1827, Campbell Papers, DUL. Baylies to Verplanck, October 12, 1827, Verplanck Papers, NYHS. *National Journal*, April 22, 1828. *Niles Weekly Register*, January 19, 1828. *Telegraph*, July 2, 23, January 26, 1828. J. B. Derby, *Political Reminiscences*, p. 27. *American* (New York), November 12, 1828. R. C. Sands to Verplanck, 1828, Verplanck Papers, NYHS. *National Journal*, September 4, July 12, September 1, 22, May 15, December 8, 1827, June 3, 9, 1828. *Patriot* (New Hampshire), September 22, 1828.

25. William C. Bouck to Flagg, July 14, 1828, Flagg Papers, NYPL. Van Buren to Hamilton, September 16, 1828, Hamilton to M. Werner, September 15, 1828, Hamilton, *Reminiscences*, pp. 76, 79. *Patriot* (New Hampshire), July 28, 1828. Louis McLane to Van Buren, June 18, October 24, 1827, Van Buren Papers, LC. L. Stockton to Southard, October 20, 1827, Southard Papers, PUL. *Telegraph*, September 24, 1828. Parton, *Jackson*, III, 144.

26. Parton, *Jackson*, III, 144. *National Journal*, May 24, 1828. John

Robb to Jackson, August 28, 1827, Jackson Papers, LC. *Argus* (Albany), October 9, 1827. M. C. Jenkins to William C. Ruffin, September 11, 1827, Ruffin, *The Papers of Thomas Ruffin*, p. 103. *Argus of the West* (Kentucky), September 17, 1827. Leonard P. Curry, "Election Year— Kentucky, 1828," *Register of the Kentucky State Historical Society*, LV (1957), 197. *Patriot* (New Hampshire), July 14, 1828. George Bibb to Felix Grundy, February 5, 1827, Grundy Papers, UNCL. John Campbell to David Campbell, November 3, 1827, Campbell Papers, DUL. James Campbell to Verplanck, January 19, 1828, Verplanck Papers, NYHS. John Miller to Taylor, February 8, 1828, Taylor Papers, NYHS.

27. Jacob Lynch to William Campbell, November 5, 1828, Campbell Papers, DUL. *Republican* (Baltimore), September 22, 1827. Francis Baylies to Verplanck, 1828, Verplanck Papers, NYHS. Moore to Jackson, June 13, 1827, Jackson to Moore, June 16, 1827, Isaac Baker to Jackson, April 21, 1827, Jackson Papers, LC. Atwater to Jackson, November 30, 1827, Jackson-Lewis Papers, NYPL. *Free Press* (Tarborough, N.C.), April 14, 1827. W. S. Robeson to Balch, November 11, 1827, Jackson Papers, LC. Parton, *Jackson*, III, 137-38. Jackson to Lewis, December 25, 1827, Jackson Papers, ML. Lewis to Jackson, December 24, 1827, Jackson Papers, LC. Edwin A. Miles, *Jacksonian Democracy in Mississippi*, pp. 3-4.

28. Parton, *Jackson*, III, 138-40; *Niles Weekly Register*, February 9, 1828. It is extraordinary how the Administration papers attempted to denigrate the celebration. See the *National Journal* during February 1828, for example. Arthur P. Hayne to Jackson, March 12, 1828, Jackson Papers, LC. *Niles Weekly Register*, January 19, 1828. *Telegraph*, July 2, 23, January 26, 1828. *National Journal*, September 1, 4, July 12, December 8, 1827, June 9, 1828. F. Smith to Southard, January 27, 1827, Southard Papers, PUL.

29. John Campbell to James Campbell, August 23, 1827, Campbell Papers, DUL. "Extra" *Telegraph*, September 27, 1828. *Telegraph*, March 13, May 20, 1828. Adams, *Memoirs*, VII, 415-16. Bemis, *Adams*, p. 147. Buley, *The Old Northwest*, p. 164. Duff Green to Jackson, July 8, 1827, Jackson, *Correspondence*, III, 372. John Campbell to Elizabeth M. Campbell, November 3, 1828, David Campbell Papers, DUL.

30. Buley, *The Old Northwest*, p. 165. *Telegraph*, May 20, 1828. Darling, *Political Changes in Massachusetts*, pp. 56, 58, 68, 64. Hunt to Jackson, August 29, 1827, Jackson, *Correspondence*, III, 379. Atwater to Jackson, September 20, 1827, Jackson Papers, LC.

CHAPTER 4

1. Jabez D. Hammond to Henry S. Randall, June 28, 1849, Hammond Papers, NYHS. *Telegraph,* October 15, 17, 20, 22, 1828. Bemis, *Adams,* pp. 137-38. Adams, *Memoirs,* VII, 338. *Telegraph,* October 20, 26, 1827. William H. Smith, *Charles Hammond and His Relations to Henry Clay and J. Q. Adams,* pp. 45-46. Clay to Webster, April 14, 1827, Daniel Webster Papers, LC. John Binns to Clay, April 28, 1827, Clay Papers, LC. McLean to Jackson, September 22, 1827, Jackson Papers, LC.

2. *National Journal,* March 31, May 26, 1827. *Advocate* (New York), October 28, 1827. *Argus* (Albany), September 5, 1827. *National Journal,* September 11, 1827. Van Buren to Harmanus Bleeker, February 25, 1827, Miscellaneous Van Buren Papers, NYSL. Adams, *Memoirs,* VII, 431.

3. Clay to Webster, April 14, 1827, Webster Papers, LC. Darling, *Political Changes in Massachusetts,* p. 58. *Argus* (Albany), May 4, 29, 1827. Clay to Webster, October 25, 1827, Webster Papers, LC. Webster to Clay, October 29, 1827, Clay Papers, LC. Clay to Webster, November 8, 1827, August 19, 1827, Webster Papers, LC. Webster to Clay, September 8, 1827, Clay Papers, LC.

4. Robert E. Cummings to David Campbell, January 13, 1828, Campbell Papers, DUL. *National Journal,* March 24, 1827. Clay to Webster, October 25, 1827, Webster Papers, LC. Francis Baylies to Verplanck, April 6, 1828, Verplanck Papers, NYHS. *Free Press* (Tarborough, N.C.), July 14, 1827. *National Journal,* May 24, 17, November 8, 10, 15, 1827. Baylies to Verplanck, August 4, 1828, Verplanck Papers, NYHS.

5. *National Journal,* June 16, July 3, September 1, 1827. *Niles Weekly Register,* June 30, 1827, July 26, September 6, 1828. Clay to Webster, October 25, 1827, Webster Papers, LC. Leonard P. Curry, "Election Year—Kentucky 1828," *Register of the Kentucky State Historical Society,* LV (1957), 200-5. Porter to Clay, March 15, 26, 1828, John W. Taylor to Clay, May 7, 1827, Francis Johnson to Clay, April 29, 1827, Philip Markley to Clay, April 28, 1827, John Pleasants to Clay, May 4, 1827, Levi Lincoln to Clay, May 24, 1827, John Sergeant to Clay, August 23, 1827, Clay Papers, LC. Clay to Brooke, September 24, 1827, Clay, *Private Correspondence,* p. 179. William Smith to Clay, October 7, 1827, Clay Papers, LC. Clay to Webster, June 7, 1827, Webster Papers, LC.

6. Webster to J. E. Denisen, July 28, 1827, Webster Papers, LC. Webster to Clay, May 18, 1827, Clay Papers, LC. Rives to Verplanck,

October 16, 1827, Verplanck Papers, NYHS. Ritchie to Van Buren, March 11, 1828, Van Buren Papers, LC. Jackson to Houston, November 22, 1826, Jackson, *Correspondence*, III, 319.

7. Williamson to Southard, December 10, 1827, Southard Papers, PUL. Nathaniel Williams to John W. Taylor, September 24, 1828, Taylor Papers, NYHS. Crittenden to Clay, September 23, 1828, J. J. Crittenden Papers, DUL. Rives to Verplanck, October 16, 1827, Verplanck Papers, NYHS. *Niles Weekly Register*, January 19, 12, 1828. Clay to Francis Brooke, March 1, 1828, Clay, *Private Correspondence*, p. 197. Robert E. Cummings to David Campbell, January 13, 1828, Campbell Papers, DUL. C. Biddle to Southard, November 15, 1827, Southard Papers, PUL. R. Carlyle Buley, *The Old Northwest*, p. 162. William Smith to Clay, October 7, 1827, George Pendleton to Clay, December 1, 1826, Clay Papers, LC.

8. Clay to Francis Brooke, February 22, 1828, Clay, *Correspondence*, p. 195. Thurlow Weed, *Autobiography*, p. 297. *Niles Weekly Register*, November 10, 1827. Atwater to Jackson, November 30, 1827, Jackson-Lewis Papers, NYPL. A. B. Hasbrouck to John W. Taylor, March 10, 1828, Taylor Papers, NYHS. John Van Buren to Martin Van Buren, February 14, 1834, John Van Buren Papers, Private Collection. Henry Stanton, *Random Recollections*, p. 25. Marcy to Verplanck, March 9, 1828, and the postscript to it in Van Buren's handwriting, Baylies to Verplanck, April 6, 1828, Verplanck Papers, NYHS. *Niles Weekly Register*, August 30, 1828.

9. Van Buren to Jackson, September 14, 1827, Van Buren Papers, LC. Verplanck to Jesse Hoyt, January 22, 1828, Mackenzie, *Life and Times of Martin Van Buren*, p. 203. Granger to Weed, September 12, 28, 1828, Granger Papers, LC. Weed, *Autobiography*, p. 304. Van Buren to Cambreleng, July 4, 1827, Van Buren Papers, LC. John Willard to Flagg, August 5, 1828, Charles Butler to Flagg, September 5, 1828, Flagg Papers, NYPL.

10. *Niles Weekly Register*, June 14, October 18, November 1, 1828. Baylies to Verplanck, October 26, 1828, Verplanck Papers, NYHS. George Bibb to Felix Grundy, February 5, 1827, Grundy Papers, UNCL.

11. John H. Bryan to Bartlett Yancey, January 17, 1827, *The James Sprunt Historical Publications*, X, No. 2 (1911), 60. Joseph McIlvaine to Southard, October 20, 1827, Southard Papers, PUL. *National Journal*, October 30, 1827. William Richmond to John Bailey, April 16, 1827, Bailey Papers, NYHS. Marcy to Van Buren, January 29, 1828, Van Buren Papers, LC. Clay to Benjamin W. Crowinshield, March 18, 1827, *Quarterly Journal of Economics*, II (1888), 491. *Argus* (Albany),

July 24, August 11, 1827. Sergeant to Clay, August 23, 1827, Lawrence to Clay, November 8, 1830, Clay Papers, LC. *Niles Weekly Register,* October 13, 1827. *National Journal,* June 30, 1827. *Evening Post* (New York), June 27, 1827.

12. Earl G. Swen, ed., *Letters on Conditions in Kentucky 1825,* pp. 12-23. W. W. Worsley to Clay, November 3, 1826, Clay Papers, LC. Lewis to Van Buren, August 8, 1828, Van Buren Papers, LC. John R. Commons, *et al., History of Labour in the United States,* I, 216, 218, 195, 198, 202. *Mechanics Free Press,* October 18, 25, November 29, 1828. Edward Pessen, "Working Men's Movement in the Jackson Era," *Mississippi Valley Historical Review,* XLIII (December, 1956), 428-29.

13. *Register* (Raleigh, N.C.), May 15, 1827. *National Journal,* March 26, 1827. *Telegraph,* June 27, 1827. James, *Jackson,* p. 465. *Advertiser* (Boston), October 25, 1827, May 3, 1828. *Whig* (Richmond), March 16, 1827. *National Journal,* September 4, 1828.

14. The full text of the Coffin Hand Bill can be found in Jackson, *Correspondence,* III, App., 455-64. *National Journal,* May 26, 28, June 2, 16, 1827. "Extra" *Telegraph,* July 26, 1828. Parton, *Jackson,* III, 152-53.

15. Parton, *Jackson,* I, 265-306, 387-92. Chambers, *Benton,* pp. 50-53. *National Journal,* April 22, 1828. "Extra" *Telegraph,* April 12, 1828. Eaton to Jackson, March 4, 1828, Hugh L. White to Jackson, March 2, 1828, Jackson Papers, LC. *National Journal,* July 28, 1827. American State Papers, *Military Affairs,* I, 689. Monroe to Calhoun, December 28, 1827, March 16, 1828, Monroe Papers, LC. Jackson to White, March 30, 1828, Jackson Papers, LC.

16. Jackson to Nathaniel Williams, February 23, 1828, Jackson, *Correspondence,* III, 391. *National Journal,* July 15, 17, August 12, 1828. Jackson to Coffee, May 12, 1828, Jackson, *Correspondence,* III, 402. *Telegraph,* October 15, 1828.

17. R. C. Buley, "The Political Balance in the Old Northwest," *Studies in American History Inscribed to J. A. Woodburn,* p. 412. Sidney Breese to Clay, July 21, 1827, Clay Papers, LC. Crittenden to Clay, March 4, 1828, Crittenden Papers, DUL. Sargeant to Clay, August 23, 1827, Breese to Clay, July 21, 1827, John Pleasants to Clay, May 4, 1827, Webster to Clay, May 18, 1827, E. Whittlesey to Clay, September 4, 1829, Clay Papers, LC.

CHAPTER 5

1. Alexander Smyth to David Campbell, December 3, 1827, Campbell Papers, DUL. Smyth states that the meeting was dominated by the Pennsylvania, New York, Kentucky, and Tennessee delegations. He did not mention South Carolina. Francis Wayland, *Andrew Stevenson*, p. 75. Charles Ambler, *Thomas Ritchie*, p. 113. George Dangerfield, *The Era of Good Feelings*, p. 397. Jackson to Lewis, December 19, 1827, Jackson Papers, ML. Michael Hoffman to Flagg, December 15, 1827, Flagg Papers, NYPL. Henry Storrs to ?, December 11, 1827, Storrs Papers, NYHS. *National Journal*, April 22, 1828. John Tyler to J. Rutherford, December 8, 1827, Lyon G. Tyler, *Letters and Times of the Tylers*, I, 377.

2. Van Buren to Jackson, November 4, 1827, Jackson, *Correspondence*, III, 383. *National Journal*, September 1, October 13, 2, 1827.

3. *Telegraph*, March 28, 1828. *National Journal*, April 8, 1828. *Register of Debates*, 20th Congress, 1st Session, p. 379. *Niles Weekly Register*, May 31, 1828. Parton, *Jackson*, III, 148-49.

4. *National Journal*, July 24, 1827. Thomas Cooper to Verplanck, May 1, 1828, Verplanck Papers, NYHS. E. Sage to John W. Taylor, February 17, 1828, Taylor Papers, NYHS. Wright to Flagg, December 18, 1827, Flagg Papers, NYPL. Storrs to ?, December 17, 1827, Storrs Papers, NYHS. Flagg to Wright, January 16, 1828, Flagg Papers, NYPL. *Register of Debates*, 20th Congress, 1st Session, pp. 889-90. Clay to Crittenden, February 14, 1828, Mrs. Chapman Coleman, *Life of John J. Crittenden*, I, 67. Wright to Flagg, April 7, 1828, Flagg Papers, NYPL.

5. Calhoun, *Works*, III, 48-49. A. H. Shepperd to Yancey, April 17, 1828, Bartlett Yancey Papers, UNCL. John Tyler to Dr. H. Curtis, May 1, 1828, Tyler, *Letters and Times of the Tylers*, I, 387. Wright to Flagg, April 7, 1828, December 13, 1827, Flagg to Wright, March 13, April 13, 1828, Flagg Papers, NYPL.

6. *Register of Debates*, 20th Congress, 1st Session, pp. 1836-70. A. H. Shepperd to Yancey, April 17, 1828, Bartlett Yancey Papers, UNCL. Webster to Joseph E. Sprague, April 13, 1828, Webster, *Letters*, pp. 135-36. Webster, *Works*, I, 165. F. W. Taussig, *Tariff History of the United States*, p. 101. Van Buren, "Notes, August 4, 1840," Van Buren Papers, LC. Tyler, *Letters and Times of the Tylers*, III, 69 note. *Argus* (Albany), May 20, 1828. *Niles Weekly Register*, July 5, 1828.

7. Woodbury to Van Buren, July 1, 1828, Van Buren Papers, LC. Hayne to Woodbury, July 10, 1828, Woodbury Papers, LC. Green to Calhoun, August 10, 1828, Green's Letter Book, LC. J. de Graff to Flagg,

December 27, 1828, Flagg Papers, NYPL. Wright to Van Buren, December 9, 1828, Van Buren Papers, LC. *Niles Weekly Register,* August 16, 1828.

CHAPTER 6

1. *Telegraph,* October 20, 1828. Van Buren to Hamilton, August 25, 1828, Hamilton, *Reminiscences,* pp. 78-79. *National Journal,* September 1, 1827. David Trimble to Clay, October 22, 1828, Clay Papers, LC. Jacob Lynch to William B. Campbell, November 5, 1828, Campbell Papers, DUL. Chilton Williamson, *American Suffrage from Property to Democracy,* pp. 182-224.

2. Jeremiah Goodwin to Jackson, November 12, 1827, Jackson Papers, LC. *Telegraph,* October 17, 22, November 5, 1828. "Extra" *Telegraph,* December 15, 1828. Green to Jackson, November 12, 1828, Richard M. Johnson to Jackson, August 22, 1828, Jackson Papers, LC. Jackson to Lewis, October 19, 1828, James Hamilton to Lewis, October 3, 1828, Jackson-Lewis Papers, NYPL. Van Buren to Cambreleng, November 7, 1828, Van Buren Papers, LC.

3. Gaines to Jackson (no date), Jackson Papers, LC. Isaac Munroe to John Bailey, December 26, 1828, Bailey Papers, NYHS. Robert Wickliffe to Clay, October 7, 1828, H. Shaw to Clay, January 9, 1829, Clay Papers, LC. *Niles Weekly Register,* December 6, 1828. Everett to A. H. Everett, December 2, 1828, Everett Papers, MHS. *American* (New York), November 9, 1827. Van Buren to Ritchie, January 13, 1827, Van Buren Papers, LC.

4. Samuel Roberts to J. J. Donelson, November 15, 1828, Jackson Papers, LC. Michael Hoffman to Flagg, November 8, 1828, Flagg Papers, NYPL. Duff Green to Worden Pope, January 4, 1828, Green's Letter Book, LC. Baylies to Verplanck, April 6, 1828, Verplanck Papers, NYHS. Hill to John Bailey, February 4, 1828, Bailey Papers, NYHS. Walter Fee, *The Transition from Aristocracy to Democracy in New Jersey,* pp. 258-59.

5. *Niles Weekly Register,* December 6, 1828. *Telegraph,* December 23, 1828. Polk to Jackson, December 1, 5, 1828, James A. Hamilton to Jackson, November 24, 1828, John P. Van Ness to Jackson, November 29, 1828, Jackson Papers, LC. *Niles Weekly Register,* December 6, 1828. Parton, *Jackson,* III, 154-64. Thomas S. Hinde to Clay, February 3, 1829, Clay Papers, LC. Jackson to Coffee, January 17, 1829, Jackson, *Correspondence,* IV, 2. James, *Jackson,* p. 489. E. P. Gaines to Jackson, November 22, 1828, Jackson Papers, LC.

6. Parton, *Jackson*, III, 164-73. Daniel Webster to Mrs. E. Webster, February 19, 1829, Daniel Webster, *Private Correspondence*, I, 470. Ben: Perley Poore, *Reminiscences*, pp. 92-96. Richardson, *Messages and Papers*, II, 1000-1. Mrs. Margaret B. Smith, *The First Forty Years of Washington Society*, p. 283. James Hamilton, Jr., to Van Buren, March 5, 1829, Van Buren Papers, LC.

BIBLIOGRAPHY

IN THE PREPARATION of this work a variety of manuscripts, public documents, published correspondence, diaries, reminiscences, autobiographies, monographs, and scholarly articles have been used, the authors, titles, and (in the case of manuscripts) the location of which can be found in the footnotes. For the general reader there can be no better introduction to the history of this period than George Dangerfield, *The Era of Good Feelings* (London, 1953), a work notable for its readability, reliability, and intuitive insights into characters and events. A more recent study by Dangerfield is *The Awakening of American Nationalism, 1815-1828* (New York, 1965). Also brilliant are the opening chapters of Arthur M. Schlesinger, *The Age of Jackson* (Boston, 1946), which set the stage for the ensuing Jacksonian revolution and dazzle the reader with lifelike re-creations of the leading political figures. A fairly comprehensive, scholarly, though slightly anti-Jackson treatment of the period 1828-48 is Glyndon Van Deusen, *The Jacksonian Era* (New York, 1959). But for the 1828 campaign and election specifically, Florence Weston, *The Presidential Election of 1828* (Washington, D.C., 1938), is a well-organized and most helpful study.

By way of biographies there are several outstanding volumes. Samuel Flagg Bemis, *John Quincy Adams and the Foundations of American Foreign Policy* and *John Quincy Adams and the Union* (New York, 1949, 1956), do honor to both the subject and the author. William N. Chambers, *Old Bullion Benton: Senator from the New West* (Boston, 1956), is a model of biographical writing, and much of Professor Chambers' thinking is reflected in this study. Even those historians who disagree with Charles M. Wiltse's very friendly interpretation of *John C. Calhoun* (3 vols., Indianapolis and New York, 1944-51) will be forever in his debt for the wide, straight path he cut through the jungle of early nineteenth-century American political history. On Jackson himself, the best biography is Marquis James, *Andrew Jackson* (2 vols. in 1, Indianapolis, 1937), a highly readable and generally reliable, though partisan, narrative of the great General. More scholarly, if less lively, is John S. Bassett, *The Life of Andrew Jackson* (New York, 1931); while James Parton's *Life of Andrew Jackson* (3 vols., New York, 1861) is extremely valuable despite its age. A recent, short, one-volume study is Robert V. Remini, *Andrew Jackson* (New York, 1966).

Of the other major figures in this election, Clay, Webster, and Van Buren lack modern, full-scale biographies. Glyndon G. Van Deusen, *Life* of *Henry Clay* (Boston, 1939), is sound and judicious, but rather brief for its exalted subject. Both Clement Eaton, *Henry Clay and the Art of American Politics* (Boston, 1957), and Richard N. Current, *Daniel Webster and the Rise of National Conservatism* (Boston, 1955), are specialized books, yet extremely useful. The best Van Buren biography, though old and written without the benefit of extensive manuscript sources, is Edward M. Shepard, *Martin Van Buren* (Boston and New York, 1899). Denis T. Lynch, *An Epoch and a Man: Martin Van Buren* (New York, 1929), is breezy but not altogether reliable. For a discussion of Van Buren's career during the 1820's, see Robert V. Remini, *Martin Van Buren and the Making of the Democratic Party* (New York, 1959). There is an excellent chapter on the Magician in Marvin Meyers, *The Jacksonian Persuasion* (Stanford, 1957), a work otherwise noted for its most persuasive interpretation of Jacksonian democracy.

Other biographies of these leading figures include: Bennett C. Clark, *John Quincy Adams* (Boston, 1932); Margaret L. Coit, *John C. Calhoun, American Patriot* (Boston, 1950); Elbert B. Smith, *Magnificent Missourian: The Life of Thomas Benton* (New York, 1958); and Claude M. Fuess, *Daniel Webster* (2 vols., Boston, 1930).

Useful and in most cases excellent or competent biographies of lesser figures are: Philip S. Klein, *President James Buchanan: A Biography* (University Park, Pennsylvania, 1962); Charles G. Sellers, Jr., *James K. Polk, Jacksonian, 1795-1843* (Princeton, 1957); Marquis James, *The Raven: A Biography of Sam Houston* (Indianapolis, 1929); Llerena Friend, *Sam Houston* (Austin, 1954); John A. Garraty, *Silas Wright* (New York, 1949); Charles H. Ambler, *Thomas Ritchie* (Richmond, 1913); Joseph H. Parks, *Felix Grundy* (University, Louisiana, 1940); William C. Bruce, *John Randolph of Roanoke, 1773-1833* (2 vols., New York, 1922); Ivor D. Spencer, *The Victor and the Spoils: A Life of William L. Marcy* (Providence, Rhode Island, 1959); William E. Smith, *The Francis Preston Blair Family in Politics* (2 vols., New York, 1933); and William B. Hatcher, *Edward Livingston* (University, Louisiana, 1940).

The history of political parties in the United States is traced in a number of comprehensive and perceptive works. The best include: Wilfred E. Binkley, *American Political Parties, Their Natural History* (New York, 1943); M. Ostrogorski, *Democracy and the Organization of Political Parties* (2 vols., New York, 1902); and Eugene H. Roseboom, *A History of Presidential Elections* (New York, 1957). Of particular importance is Richard P. McCormick, *The Second American Party System: Party Formation in the Jacksonian Era* (Chapel Hill, 1966). A first-rate treatment of suffrage in the United States prior to the Civil War, is Chilton Williamson, *American Suffrage from Property to Democracy 1760-1860* (Princeton,

1960). All these works should be supplemented with state and regional histories for a more thorough analysis of party organization and development. A little known but excellent regional study is A. L. Kohlmeier, *The Old Northwest as the Keystone of the Arch of the Federal Union* (Indianapolis, 1938); while R. C. Buley, *The Old Northwest, Pioneer Period, 1815-1840* (Indianapolis, 1950) contains a great deal of useful and interesting material. Among the most valuable state studies are: Edwin A. Miles, *Jacksonian Democracy in Mississippi* (Chapel Hill, 1960); Lee Benson, *The Concept of Jacksonian Democracy: New York as a Test Case* (Princeton, 1961); Thomas P. Abernethy, *From Frontier to Plantation in Tennessee* (Chapel Hill, 1932), William S. Hoffman, *Andrew Jackson and North Carolina Politics* (Chapel Hill, 1958); Albert R. Newsome, *The Presidential Election of 1824 in North Carolina* (Chapel Hill, 1939); Walter R. Fee, *The Transition from Aristocracy to Democracy in New Jersey* (Somerville, New Jersey, 1933); and Dixon Ryan Fox, *The Decline of Aristocracy in the Politics of New York* (New York, 1919).

Richard Hofstadter, *The American Political Tradition and the Men Who Made It* (New York, 1948) contains two excellent interpretative chapters on Jackson and Calhoun. John William Ward, *Andrew Jackson: Symbol for an Age* (New York, 1955) is a brilliant analysis of how the Hero was cast in the image of his own age. Another important interpretative study is Edward Pessen, *Jacksonian America: Society, Personality and Politics* (Homewood, Illinois; 1969). On the American West as symbol and myth see Henry Nash Smith, *Virgin Land* (New York, 1950). An excellent study of the south is Charles S. Sydnor, *The Development of Southern Sectionalism, 1819-1848* (Batoh Rouge, 1948). Two fine studies of the impact of immigration on leading American cities are Oscar Handlin, *Boston's Immigrants* (Cambridge, 1941), and Robert Ernst, *Immigrant Life in New York City, 1825-1863* (New York, 1949). As for the Workingmen, the composition of their movement has set historians at odds for years. The disagreements can be traced in Edward Pessen, "The Workingmen's Movement in the Jackson Era," *Mississippi Valley Historical Review* (1958), Vol. LXIII and "The Working Men's Party Revisited, *Labor History*, Fall, 1963. See also Pessen's *Most Uncommon Jacksonians* (New York, 1968). In addition, an excellent study of the Workingmen is Walter Hugins, *Jacksonian Democracy and the Working Class* (Stanford, 1960). Joseph G. Rayback has written a very useful one volume *History of American Labor* (New York, 1959). On the basis of a statistical analysis and comparison of percentages of votes cast in presidential, gubernatorial, congressional, and local elections, Richard P. McCormick in "New Perspectives on Jacksonian Politics," *American Historical Review* (1960), Vol. LXV, finds the Jackson victory less than popular and questions the extent of the two party system in 1828.

There are a number of notable articles which have appeared in learned journals and have a direct bearing on the 1828 election. These include: Richard H. Brown, "The Missouri Crisis, Slavery and the Politics of Jacksonianism," *South Atlantic Quarterly*, Winter, 1966; James Staton Chase, "Jacksonian Democracy and the Rise of the Nominating Convention," *Mid-America*, October, 1963; Leonard P. Curry, "Election Year— Kentucky 1828," *Register of the Kentucky Historical Society*, LV, 1957; E. M. Eriksson, "Official Newspaper Organs and the Campaign of 1828," *Tennessee* Historical Magazine, VIII; Logan Esarey, "The Organization of the Jacksonian Party in Indiana," *Proceedings of the Mississippi Valley Historical Association*, 1913-14, VII; Mark H. Haller, "The Rise of the Jackson Party in Maryland, 1828-1829, *Journal of Southern History*, 1962, XXVIII; William G. Morgan, "John Quincy Adams versus Andrew Jackson: Their Biographers and the 'Corrupt Bargain' Charge," *Tennessee Historical Quarterly*, Spring, 1967; William G. Morgan, "Henry Clay's Biographers and the 'Corrupt Bargain' Charge, *Register of the Kentucky Historical Society*, July, 1968; Charles G. Sellers, "Jackson Men with Feet of Clay," *American Historical Review*, 1957, LXII; Michael Wallace, "Changing Concepts of Party in the United States: New York, 1815-1828," *American Historical Review*, 1968, LXXIV; and Major L. Wilson, "The Concept of Time and the Political Dialogue in the United States, 1828-1848," *American Quarterly*, Winter, 1967.

Two studies examine the minor parties in this period. Shaw Livermore, Jr. in *The Twilight of Federalism, 1815-1830* (Princeton, 1962) admirably traces. the Federalist party as it staggered, reeled, and finally fell into its political grave after the "knock in the head" it dealt itself .at the Hartford Convention. Charles McCarthy, "The Antimasonic Party: A Study of Political Antimasonry in the United States, 1827-1840," *Annual Report*, American Historical Association, (1902), Vol. I is the standard work on that subject. For background see also Whitney R. Cross, *The Burned-Over District* (New York, 1950). The Indian removal question is traced in Grant Foreman, *Indian Removal: The Emigration of the Five Civilized Tribes* (Norman, 1932). George R. Taylor, *The Transportation Revolution, 1815-1860* (New York, 1951), is a masterful work, as is Joseph Dorfman, *The Economic Mind in American Civilization* (3 vols., New York, 1946-49).

No bibliography for this period is complete without mention of Alexis de Tocqueville, *Democracy in America* (New York, 1954), a unique and penetrating insight into the period by a touring and wide-eyed Frenchman. Also important are Louis Hartz, *The Liberal Tradition in America* (New York, 1955); Alice F. Tyler, *Freedom's Ferment* (Minneapolis, 1944); and Frederick J. Turner, *Rise of the New West* (New York, 1935).

INDEX